Parables of the Kingdom

Parables of the Kingdom

Jesus and the Use of Parables
in the Synoptic Tradition

Mary Ann Getty-Sullivan

LITURGICAL PRESS
Collegeville, Minnesota

www.litpress.org

Nihil obstat: Rev. Robert C. Harren, J.C.L., *Censor deputatus*.

Imprimatur: ✠ Most Rev. John F. Kinney, J.C.D., D.D., Bishop of St. Cloud, Minnesota, July 6, 2007.

Cover design by Ann Blattner.

1   2   3   4   5   6   7   8   9

Library of Congress Cataloging-in-Publication Data

Getty-Sullivan, Mary Ann, 1943–
    Parables of the kingdom : Jesus and the use of parables in the synoptic tradition / Mary Ann Getty-Sullivan.
        p.   cm.
    Includes bibliographical references.
    ISBN 978-0-8146-2993-2
        1. Jesus Christ—Parables.   2. Bible. N.T. Gospels—Criticism, Form. 3. Synoptic problem.   I. Title.

BT375.3.G48 2007
226.8'06—dc22

                                                        2007024907

*For my husband, Dan Sullivan, who has shown me
and many others by example the power of parables.*

Contents

Chapter 1
Introduction to the Parables   1

Chapter 2
Parables in Mark   16

Chapter 3
Parables Matthew Shared with Mark   49

Chapter 4
Parables as Matthew Tells Them   77

Chapter 5
Parables According to Luke   113

Chapter 6
Parables of Luke's Travel Narrative   136

Conclusion   169
Appendix   Parables in the Synoptic Tradition   171
Notes   173

Glossary of Basic Terms for the Study of the Parables   183

Abbreviations   187

Bibliography   189

CHAPTER ONE

Introduction to the Parables

Parables are especially suited to religious language because they assert that God is both "like" and "unlike" persons, practices or events familiar to us. For example, God is like and unlike the woman who searched her whole house for the lost coin. God is also like the shepherd who leaves the ninety-nine sheep in order to search for the single sheep that has wandered away from the flock. Yet God does not "leave" anyone, not even the righteous who do not wander. With God, no single story or image tells it all; that would be idolatry. Rather, Jesus needed to use multiple parables that each illustrate different aspects of God's caring and faithful relationship with us and together help us appreciate various aspects of that love, justice, forgiveness, persistence, mercy, and kindness that is God.

There is a saying among storytellers: "The story begins when the teller stops talking." Jesus is a master teacher and a master storyteller. When we read the Synoptic Gospels, we see that much of Jesus' teaching comes in story form, as parables. By their nature, parables are meant to involve hearers and challenge them to change their perspective, their hearts, and their behavior. The parables invite us to live in a new way, in a way worthy of the Gospel.

Discovering Parables

Many very short "parabolic" sayings characterize both the Old and the New Testaments, which, as religious literature, is necessarily symbolic, poetic, imaginative, and nonliteral. By nature, parabolic language

1

is symbolic and that implies drawing images "outside the lines." In Matthew, Mark, and Luke, in particular, parables can mean proverbs, examples, similes, allegories, as well as the more familiar, expanded metaphors in narrative form, which are the object of our study. Once we understand that, we are impressed with the abundance of parabolic images we encounter in the Synoptic Gospels.

Many of the parables Jesus told were narratives. That is, they are stories that have a beginning, a middle, and a conclusion. There are characters and settings and sometimes dialogue. The story is short and conducive to easy recall. Its elements are usually vivid though not detailed. The parables are meant to involve the hearers who are drawn in by their familiarity with the situation that is described. But there is also in a parable an element of surprise, a hook, designed to present something new and different to the listeners. This has been called the "twist" or "gotcha" aspect of a parable. People might be either attracted to or put off by this element of surprise, but a good parable does not leave its listeners indifferent. They are meant to "get it." A parable challenges listeners to respond, although not necessarily in any single way. A good parable remains open-ended and contains a challenge to conversion, to change one's worldview and values.

What Is a Parable?

A well-known, much-used definition by C. H. Dodd tells us that a parable is a "metaphor or simile drawn from nature or common life, arresting the hearer by its strangeness, and leaving the mind in sufficient doubt about its precise application to tease it into active thought."[1] This useful description actually tells us four things about a parable:

(1) it is a comparison (a metaphor or simile),

(2) describing something new or unknown in terms of something very familiar (drawn from nature or common experience),

(3) with an unexpected twist (arresting in its strangeness),

(4) designed to engage its hearers and prompt some reaction from them (leaving the mind in sufficient doubt about its application to tease it into active thought).

This fourfold description will help us discuss, evaluate, and understand the importance of parables in the Bible, and especially in the Synoptic Gospels.

A Parable Is a Comparison

Parables are simple word pictures well suited to the oral culture of Jesus' original hearers. Jesus' parables compare one thing to another. A simile compares things using the terms "like" or "as." Some parables begin with the phrase, "The kingdom of God is like . . ." a mustard seed (Luke 13:19), or ten virgins who took their lamps and went out to meet the bridegroom (Matt 25:1). A metaphor is a little more subtle, comparing the disciples, for example, to light or salt, but without the terms "like" or "as": "You are the salt of the earth" (Matt 5:13) or "You are the light of the world" (5:14).

Thus, parable-like language is used to describe in familiar terms a world, a "kingdom," a "time" or a "place" that is unknown to us. Borrowing and building on the language of the prophets, Jesus speaks of the "day of the Lord" that will come as a "thief in the night" or "as the labor pangs" of an expectant woman. Disciples must act as the "children of day, not night." They are warned that the kingdom of God is not revealed to flesh and blood. The parables describe what is unknown in terms of what is known. Parables use the language of analogy and comparison.

A Parable Draws on Nature or Common Experience

Jesus' parables appeal to an audience familiar with the Galilean landscape. Fishing and farming were the main occupations of Galilean people in Jesus' time. Thus it is not surprising that Jesus used images from the fields and the sea that were typical of the environment in which he taught. Jesus speaks of fishing for people and of farmers who go out to plow the fields. Jesus describes the growing of seeds without human help and the amazing disproportion of an ample harvest to the tiny mustard seed that was sown.

A Parable Is Arresting in Its Strangeness

The real teaching value of Jesus' parables can be seen in the "twist" that changes the story's dynamic from a familiar one to a surprising one. The hearers are drawn into the story by Jesus' description of their common experience. Hearers expect to relate to Jesus' story and its characters and they are not disappointed.

But then there is a "gotcha" or shocking element that suddenly strikes the audience. Some are put on the defensive, realizing as the story unfolds that their own presuppositions or biases or practices are being undermined. What father expects to be treated disrespectfully and would eagerly embrace the practice of daily scanning the horizon to see if his wayward son will return? What laborers who have borne the heat of the sun doing backbreaking work expect to receive the same as those who have only shown up an hour before the payout? As a parable unfolds, hearers are likely to perceive the twist and, beginning to anticipate its implications, try to avoid them with protests, indignation, and rejection. The "kingdom of God," Jesus seems to be saying, is unlike our notions of patriarchy, of justice, and sometimes even of common sense.

A Parable Is Designed to Evoke Conversion

Parables are intended to get a commitment, or as Dodd says, to "tease the mind into active thought." Jesus is always searching for "understanding," often to no avail. But parables are not about intellectual assent. Moreover, parables are not meant simply to get someone to do something. The parable about the sower and the seed is not a commentary on sloppy farming practices versus a more effective and precise method of sowing. The parable intends to draw listeners, regardless of their profession, to envision a new way of being and doing that would include God's prolific generosity and an appropriate, proportionate human response. The intended response is a changed perspective that follows upon a changed heart. When Jesus praises the servant who alters the accounts of his master's debtors (see Luke 16:1-8), he is not advocating dishonesty. Rather, Jesus calls for his disciples to be as dedicated to the values of the coming reign of God as the "children of this world" (16:8) are to the concerns of their earthly masters. Obviously Jesus is not addressing only accountants nor is he thinking of worksheet balances. Rather, he is describing the single-mindedness that seems to characterize successful people and must be qualities of those participating in the promotion of God's reign.

Parables and Allegories

Many scholars have observed that parables (which they often distinguish from allegories) have only one point of comparison. This means that, generally speaking, Jesus' parables are best understood as extended metaphors rather than a series of metaphors in which many of the details represent different realities (which is how allegories may be described). But it is not necessary to exaggerate this distinction.[2] Some of Jesus' parables, such as the sower and the seed, for instance, are interpreted allegorically in the gospels themselves. That is to say, after speaking the parable, Jesus explains the meaning of several of the metaphors he used (Mark 4:15-17 and parallels in other gospels). For example, the seed sown on the pathways represents how the temptations of Satan rob people of the word that was sown in them. The seed sown on rocky ground has no root so that tribulation causes it to quickly wither and die.

A good parable often has more than one overall meaning or application. The purpose of the parables is to challenge hearers to change their hearts and minds and make themselves more open to the reign of God. Parables are not meant merely to compare gospel teachings to everyday realities either in the first century or today. Parables are meant to challenge and confront hearers and evoke a conversion. Parables are one of Jesus' preferred tools to involve hearers in the process of revelation so that they can better perceive the truths of the Gospel and participate more fully in the kingdom of God.

The Kingdom of God

Through parables Jesus taught about God and about the "kingdom of God." The first words of Jesus in Mark, the earliest of the gospels to be written, proclaim the arrival of the "kingdom of God." Mark pictures Jesus suddenly announcing, after being baptized and emerging from the desert where he was tempted, "This is the time of fulfillment. The kingdom of God is at hand. Repent, and believe in the gospel" (Mark 1:14-15). The kingdom of God appears as the heart and core of the message of Jesus.

This is but one example of many challenges that confronts us all as readers of the gospels. Any "kingdom" strikes us as an archaic and arcane reality, removed from our experience as regular people, as Americans, as people of a democracy. Certainly the "kingdoms' of the first century are foreign to our daily life. Those kingdoms include puppet kings of the Roman Empire and tax collectors who skim their share off the top of the arbitrary number they tax the poor. Kingdoms of the first century meant slaves and masters and stewards given responsibility for the land but accountable for its yield to shadowy and whimsical absentee landlords. If these are examples of values incorporated in the term "kingdom," how can that be an adequate term to use in relation to God? And how are we to understand the term today?

Not only is kingdom a concept foreign to us, it is a spatial term, a noun, that could suggest a place or state of being and that, too, is problematic. What Jesus describes seems much better conveyed by verbs or action words. That is one reason many commentators prefer the term "reign" or "rule" of God, which functions as both a noun and a verb. The "kingdom of God" is not a physical place but the event of God's triumph, God's reign. The *basileia* (the Greek term for kingdom) of God is the hope of God's people. Jesus taught his disciples to pray, "Thy kingdom come, thy will be done." These are parallel phrases meaning the same thing. God's reign happens where God's will is fulfilled.

God rules where and when people forgive unconditionally and without limit, where and when the boundaries of justice are broken and the disenfranchised, the excluded, the neglected, or the forgotten are heard, included, cared for, and remembered. Those known as "Samaritans," and "widows" and "lost sheep" challenge us to identify and eliminate our biases and opposition to our enemies so that God rules over aspects of our lives that have shut God out. The phrase "kingdom of God," like the term "parable" itself, ought not to be too narrowly defined.

Nonetheless, the phrase "kingdom (or reign) of God" has a long, revered history and significance in the Bible. It is mainly an eschatological[3] concept beginning to appear in the prophets. Later, during the Exile in the sixth century before Christ and afterward, apocalyptic passages of the Old Testament elaborated upon the phrase, "the kingdom of God." Eschatology refers to a future world conceived as a "time" and "place" when all human hopes will be fulfilled according to God's purposes. Micah describes it this way:

> [1]In days to come
>> the mount of the LORD's house
> Shall be established higher than the mountains . . .
> And peoples shall stream to it;
>> [2]Many nations shall come, and say,
> "Come let us climb the mount of the LORD . . .
> That he may instruct us in his ways,
>> that we walk in his paths." . . .
> [3]He shall judge between many peoples
>> and impose terms on strong and distant nations;
> They shall beat their swords into plowshares,
>> and their spears into pruning hooks . . .
> [6]On that day, says the LORD,
>> I will gather the lame,
> And I will assemble the outcasts,
>> and those whom I have afflicted.
> [7]I will make of the lame a remnant,
>> and of those driven far off a strong nation;
> And the LORD shall be king over them . . .
>> from now on forever.
>
> (Mic 4:1-7)

For Micah, then, God rules when there is peace among all nations. The crippled who were excluded from religious services because illness was seen as a judgment of God will represent the inclusive nature of God's reign. All will live together in peace and unity because all have one king, God.

Similarly, the Psalms picture an idyllic time and place where God rules over all. Psalm 102 promises a time when God will "attend to the groaning of the prisoners, / to release those doomed to die" (v. 21) and "all peoples and kingdoms gather / to worship the LORD" (v. 23). Psalm 145 likewise praises God, saying: "And your faithful bless you. They speak of the glory of your reign / and tell of your great works, / making known to all your power, / the glorious splendor of your rule" (vv. 10-13).

The apocalyptic writers promised a better day after the present suffering of oppression was ended by the coming triumph of God. In the book of Daniel, for example, the young men who were thrown into the fiery furnace by the wicked King Nebuchadnezzar sang out in praise to God, "Blessed are you on the throne of your kingdom, / praiseworthy and exalted above all forever" (Dan 3:54). It is the "one like a son of man" who receives "dominion, glory and kingship," which shall never "be taken away" according to Daniel 7:13-14. These images of God's rule depict a time and place where all know and worship God; when there is an end to suffering, and where there is peace.

In the Old as well as the New Testaments, the very phrase denoting the "kingdom of God" varied somewhat. The kingdom of God or kingdom of heaven appear as interchangeable. Rabbis taught that God's name ought not be pronounced, as a way of keeping the divine name holy. Matthew, drawing often on the Old Testament, prefers "kingdom of heaven," a phrase that emphasizes the heavenly origin and nature of the kingdom. Other New Testament phrases include the "kingdom of their Father" (Matt 13:43; 26:29) or "his (i.e., the son of Man) kingdom" (see Matt 13:41; Col 1:13).

The greatest blessings conceivable are found in the kingdom (see Matt 5:20; 7:21; 13:44-45; 18:3; 19:23; Mark 10:15; 10:23-25; Luke 12:32; 24:26). The mysteries of the kingdom are revealed to the disciples of Jesus (Mark 4:10-11), but those who reject the gospel will not understand these mysteries (4:12). A prerequisite for participation in the kingdom is conversion, the willingness to become as children. Indeed, participants in the kingdom are called its children (Matt 8:12; 13:38). Sometimes the kingdom is conceived as a banquet where all are welcome (see Matt 8:11; 26:29; Mark 14:25; Luke 13:28-29; 22:16, 18, 30).

Jesus' initial words reveal the gospel as the fulfillment of time and the arrival of the reign of God. Followers are expected to believe in this revelation of the reign of God and transform their lives in light of it. When Jesus says, "It is easier for a camel to pass through [the] eye of [a] needle than for one who is rich to enter the kingdom of God"(Mark 10:25), he is not talking so much about the wealthy going to heaven after death. This saying means rather that it is very difficult for God to reign in hearts where money is a distraction. At the very beginning of his public ministry according to Mark, Jesus announces that the time has come for God's will to be accomplished (1:15). What God wants to happen is about to take place. We learn that this nearness of God's reign is a secret not known to all (4:11). We learn it is only the beginning of something (4:30-32) that is quite big. What is going to happen will transpire in a way that is mysterious (4:26-29) but powerful (9:1). Because the reign of God has drawn near, it is both possible and imperative for people to "enter" it (9:47; 10:15, 23-24). People do this by believing the Good News that Jesus proclaims and by reflecting the power of the Gospel in the beauty of their lives.

Parables in the Old Testament

Speaking in parables was not a new way of teaching invented by Jesus. For hundreds of years before Jesus, the great teachers of Israel had employed this kind of short story. In fact, parables go back to the prophets who also used such stories to teach the meaning of the ways God works in history and how to worthily live as members of the people of God. The most famous example may be the prophet Nathan's confronting King David after his great sin, with this parable:

> [1]The LORD sent Nathan to David, and when he came to him, he said: "Judge this case for me! In a certain town there were two men, one rich, the other poor. [2]The rich man had flocks and herds in great numbers. [3]But the poor man had nothing at all except one little ewe lamb that he had bought. He nourished her, and she grew up with him and his children. She shared the little food he had and drank from his cup and slept in his bosom. She was like a daughter to him. [4]Now, the rich man received a visitor, but he would not take from his own flocks and herds to prepare a meal for the wayfarer who had come to him. Instead he took the poor man's ewe lamb and made a meal for his visitor." [5]David grew very angry with that man and said to Nathan: "As the LORD lives, the man who has done this merits death! [6]He shall restore the ewe lamb fourfold because he has done this and has had no pity." [7]Then Nathan said to David: "You are the man!" (2 Sam 12:1-7)

This wonderful little story has all the features of a narrative parable such as we find also in the New Testament. Nathan is sent to David to issue God's judgment, but he first invites David to act as judge. The story is one David the shepherd could well identify with. It draws a verbal picture of the harmony and care of a true shepherd for the one lamb he possesses and even treats as a member of the family! The outrage of David resonates with the reaction any of us would rightly share. But we are also wary, knowing that David is judging himself. In a sense, the chilling words of Nathan, "You are the man!" are not even necessary, at least for readers who have witnessed with what kindness and love God has treated David to this point. We read on to learn that David was immediately and deeply affected by the prophet's words, much more so than he might have been had Nathan prejudged him and condemned him from the beginning. David judged rightly that the rich man deserved harsh punishment and that a fourfold restitution ought to be made to the poor man. David recognized his own part in the story and his sin, and he repented sincerely. Such is the power of a good parable.

The use of parables, then, goes back at least to the prophets whose mission it was to speak on behalf of God. As times and circumstances changed, the people needed guidance to interpret God's will for them and the response that would be appropriate. The prophets often spelled out that interpretation for them.

The use of the word "parable" in the Greek translation of the Old Testament, called the Septuagint and signified as the LXX, shows that the term was not used in a narrow sense. The term "parable" in Semitic languages ranges from "proverb" to "story" to "riddle."[4] The Greek *parabole* usually translates the Hebrew word *mashal*, which embraces a variety of literary forms such as proverbs, riddles, taunts, metaphors, and allegories. There is a spectrum of meaning to the term that helps us to appreciate that, above all, parables use the language of symbols that appeal to the imagination. The fact that we are often puzzled by the meaning or meanings of a parable is one sign that it "works" as a teaching about God and the things of God. God cannot be reduced to an equation or formula or symbol. Even a really good parable does not capture the truth of God. No single story or image can communicate a truth that will effect a change in us. For that, we need to engage our own creativity and be open to recognize that this story is one that reveals something of God.

The whole book of Job is considered by many interpreters to be an extended parable that illustrates the meaning of disinterested piety in the face of intense though undeserved suffering. The Israelites believed that all people are sinners, yet Job is described as a completely just man who seeks to discover the cause of his suffering, but refuses to find it either in God or in his own sinfulness. The book of Job belongs to the "Wisdom literature" of the Israelites. Wisdom books discuss universal truths that transcend a particular time and place of human history. Clearly, for the Israelites reading this wisdom book, the lessons of Job are not historical. They do not much care when and where, or even whether, Job actually lived or what was the nature of his supposed offense. Rather, the story of Job is timeless, and even today readers relate to Job's situation whenever they are caught in a situation that challenges their belief in a just God. Job appears to be unwilling or unable either to accuse God of injustice or to admit that he deserves his suffering. Job is the story of a just person who believes in God even though his belief does not shield him from tragedy and illness and mental torment.

Jonah appears as yet another wisdom text in parable form. Readers or listeners can identify with the prophet who refuses to preach to the undeserving Ninevites for fear that they will be more responsive to the divine word than God's own people are. Jonah goes to great lengths to avoid obeying God's command. Often the prophets appear reluctant to speak the word of God, for, in the terms of Isaiah, "My thoughts are not your thoughts, / nor are your ways my way, says the LORD" (Isa 55:8). The strangeness of God's ways and commands are often met with skepticism, reluctance to believe, and outright rejection by human beings.

Parables in the New Testament

Jesus' use of parables was not unique or novel. The practice of telling stories as a teaching method was well known in Judaism, and grew even more popular especially in the 200-year period just before Jesus. It is particularly in this "Intertestamental period," the time between the end of the Old Testament and the beginning of the New, that the teachers in Israel, who came to be known as "rabbis," used parables and other stories to interpret the meaning of the Torah in ways that people of an oral society could readily understand. The rabbis, teacher-experts in the Law, used stories that were meant to resonate with the experience of their hearers, just as Jesus did.

Where Are Jesus' Parables Found?

It is remarkable that the parables Jesus taught are found almost exclusively in the Synoptic Gospels, that is, in Matthew, Mark, and Luke. Parables are one of the distinctive emblems common to these gospels that differentiate them from John, the last gospel to be written. John, though he is rich in imagery and symbolism, does not use the term *parabole*.[5] A similar word, *paroimia*, meaning "figure of speech," appears only in three places in John (10:6; 16:25, 29). In speaking of the shepherd who knows his own sheep, John comments, "Although Jesus used this figure of speech, they did not realize what he was trying to tell them" (10:6). In his Farewell Discourse to his disciples, Jesus says "I have told you this in figures of speech. The hour is coming when I will no longer speak to you in figures but I will tell you clearly about the Father" (16:25). A little later, his disciples respond, saying, "Now you are talking plainly, and not in any figure of speech" (16:29). In John, the term *paroimia* refers to an image Jesus' audience was supposed to understand but sometimes did not. Certainly some parable-like images occur in John. But Jesus is not pictured by John as teaching about the kingdom of God by use of the simple narrative stories called parables that are so characteristic of the Synoptic Gospels.

Outside the gospels, the term *parabole* in the New Testament appears only in Hebrews 9:9 and 11:19, meaning "symbol" or "prefigurement." The author of Hebrews refers to events of Scripture as a "parable" or symbol indicating things to come.

The Gospel of Thomas (*GTh*) provides another source outside the New Testament that contains many parables similar to the ones we find in the Synoptics. The Gospel of Thomas is a collection of 114 sayings supposedly dictated by Jesus to Thomas discovered in 1945 as part of the Nag Hammadi library.[6] It resembles the probable form of the sayings source known as "Q," a hypothetical collection of sayings that apparently was a source unknown to Mark, but used by both Matthew and Luke. It is difficult to date the Gospel of Thomas before A.D. 200, although some of the sayings and parables found there parallel ones also found in the Synoptic Gospels. Scholars are increasingly including parables from the Gospel of Thomas in their commentaries on the Synoptic parables.

Jesus' Use of Parables

The parables we know from the Synoptic Gospels are especially characteristic of Jesus' teaching. When we try to distinguish the actual teaching of Jesus himself from the words or events that may have been embellished by years of preaching about Jesus by the early church, we may employ some basic criteria.[7] For example, *the principle of multiple attestation* says that if a teaching or event appears in more than one source, it may be presumed authentic. Another criterion that a teaching actually came from Jesus himself is that it is sufficiently different from what we may find in contemporary teachers or writers or those who came before him. In other words, we could credit something as coming from Jesus if it is original and creative and not able to be attributed to someone Jesus might have been quoting. This is called *the criterion of dissimilarity*. A third principle for discerning material authentically from Jesus himself is *the criterion of coherence*, which says that the teaching must cohere or be consistent with and not inconsistent with other teachings known to come from Jesus. So, for example, if Jesus preached enemy-love, which we know from multiple attestation that he did, he would not have advocated murder. The criterion of coherence implies that his teaching on interpersonal nonviolence be consistent.

Parables are among the most authentic sayings of Jesus. Many of his parables are found in multiple sources. Further, the parables show originality and creativity on Jesus' part, while also being consistent with what we know about oral cultures. The parables are consistent with one another and with the rest of the gospel. In fact, parables offer an extraordinarily suitable vehicle for coming to know Jesus and for observing the characteristics peculiar to each gospel writer.

Care should be taken in comparing the gospels, to note the differences in the ways each of the Synoptic evangelists presents the parables. Sometimes even small differences in wording will give a parable a nuance peculiar to that evangelist's special concerns or emphases. Sometimes the context in which the evangelist places a parable suggests a unique role that parable might play in an evangelist's thinking. Mark and Matthew, for example, both present a discourse in parables at a key moment in the progress of Jesus' mission. While Luke's chapter 8 might also be considered a parable discourse, the parables there do not have the same force or purpose as they do in Mark and Matthew. But Luke is just as determined as the other evangelists to present parables as an effective teaching tool for Jesus. Furthermore, for the Synoptics, the parables occasion the unique emphases and themes specific to each writer.

The evangelists themselves probably composed some parables to illustrate aspects of Jesus' teaching as well as to reshape Jesus' own parables to fit new circumstances. Parables as we know them may show traces of a twofold, sometimes a threefold setting: the ministry of Jesus, the life of the early church, and an evangelist's editorial setting. It is sometimes impossible to work backward through the tradition, to a setting in the life of Jesus. But the ways in which the evangelists use Jesus' parables and add their own stories help us to see the great significance of this manner of teaching for the whole gospel.

The Synoptic Gospels' Use of Parables

According to the Synoptic Gospels, Jesus and his disciples undertook a single journey from Galilee to Jerusalem where Jesus was put to death. Jesus at first performed miracles and taught the people, often in parables. Many followed Jesus, but many did not. To some extent, the parables are a means by which the faithful are separated from the unfaithful. The Synoptics encourage the faith of believers and warn unbelievers of the consequences of rejecting the Messiah sent by God. The earliest believing communities consisted primarily of Jews familiar with the prophesies and promises of the Scriptures, especially through the prophets. Eventually, especially after the Temple in Jerusalem was destroyed by the Romans in A.D. 70, the community of believers was becoming more Gentile than Jewish. The Scriptures were used by the community to explain Jesus' identity as well as to describe what was required of Jesus' disciples. In fact, all four gospels may be said to have two central concerns: *christology* or how to explain and portray Jesus' Messiahship, especially in the light of the cross, and *discipleship* or what was necessary to be considered and ultimately judged a true follower of Jesus.

The Synoptics include many of the same parables. Mark, Matthew, and Luke will give each of them his own characteristic slant and trademark emphases. We will study the relationship and the differences of each of the Synoptic Gospels, using the parables as the lens to bring their unique qualities into focus. Most of the material Matthew and Luke have in common, which is not in Mark, are sayings of Jesus, including parables. Thus, we will find that Matthew and Luke use the parables found in Mark, although they may put their own spin on these parables, changing their emphases by changing where they are placed or how they are received, for example. In addition, Matthew and Luke have a number of parables not found in Mark. Some of these might be from a source scholars identify as Q, and others may be unique to either Matthew or Luke. Some commentators think Matthew used a source for the parables unique to his gospel and call this source "M"; the source for the parables in Luke that are unique to him is referred to as "L." These are hypothetical sources that may help to explain some of the differences between the gospels (see chart on p. 184).

Common Themes of the Synoptic Parables

There are a number of themes that are present in other parts of the gospels, but are accentuated in a special way through the parables. Some of these themes are:

- *great reversals*. Some parables exemplify proverbs such as "the last shall be first and the first last." Others, such as the Rich Man and Lazarus, show that the values of this world are not consistent with those of the kingdom of heaven, which reverses them.

- the progress and hope of *growth and transformation over time*. This is a theme found especially in nature parables. Small seeds become great trees; fig trees sprout leaves and indicate not only the present season, but help us anticipate the future. Such parables urge listeners to expect change, to be hopeful about limitless possibilities of transformation, to expect fulfillment of promises and a manifestation of God's power and grace.

- the surpassing *joy of finding what had been lost*, a joy that exceeds the original feeling of having something. Listeners easily identify with the woman who threw a party to celebrate finding the lost coin, or the overwhelming joy of the father whose son he thought dead returned home.

- the effect of *mixing ingredients*. One parable speaks of a woman mixing yeast with flour to make bread, another says salt flavors meat and preserves it like nothing else. Weeds are found among the wheat that was sown. A dragnet hauls in fish together with dregs and the two must be sorted out.

Sometimes parables are *combined* either to create tension or to produce an overall effect. For example, a series of parables express tension between certainty of the *parousia*[8] and a solemn warning that constant vigilance and preparedness are needed. Another series may illustrate not only the simple experience of finding something needed, but the inexpressible joy of finding what was really valuable after thinking it was lost for good. Searching for a treasure can cause people to sacrifice everything in order to procure it.

Naming the Parables

We are as familiar with many of the traditional "names" of the parables as we are with the stories themselves. And this presents another problem with reinterpreting them with new eyes. Often the names are an attempt to be descriptive, but their emphasis is misplaced. For example, a parable in Matthew is often called "Workers in the Vineyard" (Matt 20:1-16) but the outlook of the parable is the startling, unlimited goodness of the Vineyard Owner. The so-called parable of the "Prodigal

Son" really focuses on the overwhelming love and forgiveness of the "Prodigal" (the term means generous) Father (Luke 15:11-32). We have attempted in many cases to rename parables where the traditional title seems to be a misnomer. This is not simply a change for change's sake but to suggest with the title an aspect of the parable that deserves special attention. We want to identify the parable in an appropriate way that draws attention to the character or characters who ought to be observed, studied, imitated, or whose thinking or behavior invites a change of perspective or, more importantly, a transformed worldview.

CHAPTER TWO

Parables in Mark

Introduction

The Gospel of Mark probably got its name from the patristic identification of its author as John Mark, cousin of Barnabas and sometime companion of Paul (Acts 12:12, 25; 13:5-13; 15:37-39; Col 4:10; Phlm 24; 2 Tim 4:11). Mark is also associated with Peter (1 Pet 5:13). Actually we cannot know for certain Mark's identity. The gospel itself suggests that the author was a second-generation Christian who created a new form known to us as "a gospel." This is a narrative of Jesus' words and deeds, told by his original followers and handed down by them orally for three or four decades until these events were finally recorded in writing as a story.

Mark depicts Jesus' ministry as a journey that proceeds from the northern region of Israel, south to Jerusalem. Jesus begins by performing miracles (see Mark 1–10) and ultimately arrives in Jerusalem (11:1), only to be put to death on the cross a few days later (chs. 14–15). Mark's presentation of this narrative is governed by his understanding of Jesus' identity: Jesus is the hidden and suffering Messiah whose message is only grasped through faith.

Christology and Discipleship

Mark's Gospel is not a biography of Jesus nor is it merely a historical presentation of the facts of Jesus' life and ministry. As a theological narrative, Mark presents christology and discipleship. Mark's short gospel of only 661 verses portrays Jesus as the Christ, God's anointed one. He is the Messiah promised in the prophecies of the Old Testament. Jesus teaches his followers the meaning of discipleship as he proceeds to his death on the cross.

Mark's Gospel, probably the first to be written, circulated in the early Christian communities. It served to instruct and encourage believers, to warn unbelievers, and to reach out to those who never heard of Jesus. Mark's Gospel was written during times of persecution, either just before or during a Jewish uprising against Rome (66–72), when Rome was cracking down on the rebels. In addition, Nero (Emperor 54–68) had shown Rome's cruelty against any perceived threat to its sovereignty. The Christians Mark addressed were disappointed in the delay of the promised return of Jesus. In the face of persecution from Rome, Christians were wondering if they might be wrong to believe that Jesus is the Messiah. Peter and Paul had been put to death under Nero. With this leadership gap, Christians were confused and frightened. Mark's Christians no doubt longed to see some evidence that their own faith and suffering were not in vain.

Jesus the Teacher

Jesus is a teacher according to Mark. But surprisingly, Jesus' verbal teachings are quite short in the first part of Mark's Gospel. For example, Jesus' first words in Mark announce that the kingdom of God has come (Mark 1:14-15). Jesus speaks to dispel demons (1:25) and to respond to his opponents (2:8). Jesus makes pronouncements regarding family (3:34-35) or the legality of curing on the Sabbath (3:3-4). But all these teachings are very succinct, almost one-liners. When Jesus expels a demon, the crowd is amazed and says, "This is a new teaching with authority!" (1:27). According to Mark, the crowds are astounded at Jesus' teachings, but often the effectiveness of his teachings is more in the deeds he performs than in words he uses.

Mark's Portrait of the Disciples

One of the most intriguing aspects of Mark is his portrayal of the disciples of Jesus. The first thing Jesus does after proclaiming that the "kingdom of God is at hand," is to invite people to "follow" him (1:15). On the one hand Mark says that many in fact followed Jesus, immediately and generously abandoning all for the sake of becoming disciples of the kingdom. Mark recounts that Simon and his brother Andrew, as well as James and his brother John, immediately left their fishing boats and followed Jesus (Mark 1:16-19). Others are similarly described as ready and willing to become Jesus' eager disciples: Levi the toll collector (2:13-17), Bartimaeus (10:46-52), and Mary Magdalene and some other women who came from Galilee and followed Jesus to the cross, the tomb, and beyond (15:40-41, 47; 16:1, 9-10).

Yet the disciples of Jesus are amazingly slow to understand or to progress in comprehending either who Jesus really is or the true nature of his mission. In a variety of ways Mark conveys the "secret" or "mystery" of Jesus and what he came to do. For example, Jesus often forbids people to speak of his cures. Or sometimes, even after Jesus has performed a miracle, which Mark often calls a "mighty work," the disciples wonder aloud, "Who is this?" a question they never seem able to adequately answer (see 4:41). According to Mark, no one truly proclaims Jesus' identity as God's Son until the centurion at the cross, seeing that Jesus died, confesses, "Truly this is the son of God" (15:39).

In Mark's Gospel, Jesus himself seems to be ambivalent about getting out his identity and his message. Often when Jesus cures people, he tells them not to speak of what he has done for them. Jesus does not permit the demons to speak "because they knew him," Mark says (1:34). Jesus instructs the leper who had been healed, "See that you tell no one anything, but go show yourself to the priest" (1:44). But then the leper goes away and publicizes his cure to everyone he encountered, and Jesus' fame spreads far and wide (1:45). Even when Peter acknowledges, "You are the Messiah," Jesus warns him and the other disciples, "not to tell anyone about him" (8:29-30). For Mark, Jesus' identity is mysterious and can only be known by participating in the cross and resurrection. The journey to Jerusalem becomes an instruction on discipleship and faith. Part of the mystery is that the identity of Jesus and the nature of true discipleship is only discovered through fidelity in the midst of suffering that leads to the risen life. *Wisdom of liturgy – repeated, chance to discover & rediscover*

The Parables in Mark

When we consider the parables in Mark, we note immediately that there are not many of them. And yet Mark says that "without parables (Jesus) did not speak to them" (Mark 4:34). We find a cluster of parables in Mark 4. Then we must skip to chapter 12 to find another parable in a story about wicked tenants. Just after Jesus has arrived in Jerusalem, he tells this parable to a hostile audience of the Jewish leadership there who are conspiring to put him to death. The parable appears to give them all the impetus they need to turn their treacherous conspiracy to put Jesus to death into action. Finally, two small parables appear in Mark 13, the parable of the fig tree (13:28-29) and that of the doorkeeper (13:34-37).

In summary, Mark presents a discourse in parables near the beginning of Jesus' ministry, in Galilee. And then he has Jesus address his opponents in a powerful parable followed by two mini-parables near the end of the gospel narrative, when Jesus is in Jerusalem. The parable clusters of both chapter 4 and chapters 12–13 are meant to provoke Jesus' audience to hear and to act. Mark leaves open-ended the reaction to the first set of parables. The reaction to the last parables seals Jesus' fate and causes his opponents to carry out their plan to put Jesus to death. The parables have served their purpose in evoking a reaction among Jesus' listeners. The story, unless interpreted through faith, ends tragically, with Jesus' death on the cross. Mark 4 and 12-13 provide excellent examples of the role of parables in the teaching of Jesus. It is the parables of these chapters that we will examine.

A Sermon in Parables (Mark 4)

Jesus first speaks at length in Mark 4, delivering a sermon that is really a series of parables and metaphors. Mark presents parables as the chosen, typical way Jesus communicates. As he teaches, Jesus uses images to describe the effect of his message and to identify his true disciples. In chapter 4 the term "parable" has the meaning of "illustration" and also of "riddle." It means both a comparison that reveals but also could conceal Jesus' purpose and identity, as well as the meaning of "the kingdom of God." Strictly speaking there are only three parables in Mark's chapter 4, all having to do with seeds, providing images taken from agricultural practices that were familiar to both Jesus and his audience. All three of the parables compare the kingdom of God to an experience taken from the daily life of a first-century Galilean audience, but only the last two explicitly mention "the kingdom of God."

Introduction and Conclusion to Mark's Parable Chapter
(Mark 4:1-2, 33-34)

The relatively long parable about sowing seeds dominates Mark's chapter 4 (see 4:1-20). The parable itself appears in verses 3-9 following a short introduction chock full of Markan characteristics. Mark's introduction in 4:1-2 is parallel to the conclusion in verses 33-34:

> [1]On another occasion he began to teach by the sea. A very large crowd gathered around him so that he got into a boat on the sea and sat down.

And the whole crowd was beside the sea on land. ²And he taught them at length in parables, and in the course of his instruction he said to them . . .

³³With many such parables he spoke the word to them as they were able to understand it. ³⁴Without parables he did not speak to them, but to his own disciples he explained everything in private.

The parallels between the introduction and the conclusion of this parable section of Mark are one example of *inclusion*, the technique of beginning and ending a unit with a similar word or phrase. Mark thus brackets the whole series of parables, making them a unit to be considered together. Mark uses stories his audience can identify with in order to emphasize that Jesus is a teacher who uses unique methods.

The introduction itself in 4:1-2 displays a number of other features characteristic of Mark. For example, Mark uses *anticipation* and *repetition*.[1] The evangelist had already depicted Jesus teaching beside the sea and instructing his disciples to have a boat ready for his use in chapter 3, where he says, "Jesus withdrew toward the sea with his disciples. A large number of people [followed] from Galilee and from Judea" (3:7). And then Mark tells us, "He told his disciples to have a boat ready for him because of the crowd, so that they would not crush him" (3:9). Mark often will anticipate an event as he does here, suggesting the boat and the press of the crowds, so that when Jesus needs to embark on the sea, the boat is there. Such anticipation also helps to provide the thread of the narrative that will pick up the story of the calming of the storm following the parables sermon (see 4:35-41).

Sometimes Mark's style seems awkward and repetitious, as in 4:1-2 where he has a threefold emphasis on Jesus' teaching: "he began to teach," "he taught them," and "in the course of his instruction." Similarly, Mark three times mentions the "sea," all in verse 1. Even so, it is not easy to picture the scene. Mark's purpose is less for dramatic symmetry than to emphasize the role of Jesus as teacher, with the crowds and the disciples as those who are instructed. Therefore, Jesus is seated in a boat and the crowds appear to remain on the land. The posture of sitting is one taken by the rabbis; it is a posture of authority. The students gather around the teacher, standing and eager to learn.

Likewise, as the chapter unfolds, there is some confusion about the setting and whether there is really a change of scene as the sermon progresses. In the beginning, Mark suggests that Jesus embarks in the boat because of the size of the crowd. In 4:10, Mark says that Jesus is "alone," although he adds that "those present along with the Twelve" question him about the parables. There appears to be a rapid and unexplained change of scene, since Mark has nothing about the return of the boat to land or about the departure of the crowds. Yet in 4:35, after the discourse in parables, Jesus is on land, leaves the crowds, and again gets into a boat.

Private instruction to Jesus' disciples is typical of Mark. Jesus explains his message to his disciples specifically and answers their questions in 4:10, 34; 9:28, 35; 10:10, 32; 12:43; and 13:3. This pattern may be influenced by rabbinic practice of a public statement followed by private explanation to disciples. Readers of Mark understandably become confused by his juxtaposition of scenes where Jesus is pressed by crowds (4:1), alone, but together with his disciples (4:10), by the sea (4:1), in private (4:34), and then in a boat (4:35). The change of scene appears more for theological reasons than literary or dramatic ones. Mark will emphasize that Jesus focuses on his disciples, who receive special instruction and attention. Often this is done in private or in a "house" (e.g., 1:29, 32-34; 2:1, 15), a symbol for the church that moved away from the more public synagogues where Jesus also sometimes taught the people (e.g., 1:21, 39; 3:1). Yet the word is spoken, like the seed that is sown, for all to hear and receive. Responsibility for accepting the word and acting on it is with the hearers.

Parable of the Sowings (Mark 4:3-9)

Let us now turn to the first and dominant parable of chapter 4 and try to situate it in the context of Mark. The parable of the sowed seed, as Mark tells it, is this:

> [3]"Hear this! A sower went out to sow. [4]And as he sowed, some seed fell on the path, and the birds came and ate it up. [5]Other seed fell on rocky ground where it had little soil. It sprang up at once because the soil was not deep. [6]And when the sun rose, it was scorched and it withered for lack of roots. [7]Some seed fell among thorns, and the thorns grew up and choked it and it produced no grain. [8]And some seed fell on rich soil and produced fruit. It came up and grew and yielded thirty, sixty, and a hundredfold." [9]He added, "Whoever has ears to hear ought to hear."

This is sometimes called "The Parable of the Sower," which implies a particular emphasis in the interpretation. In fact, the parable admits several interpretations, depending on which "character" or element is chosen as the focus.[2] It might be called the parable of the Sower, the parable of the Seed, the parable of the Soil, or the parable of the Harvest. It might even more appropriately be named the parable of the Sowings.[3] The variety of possible interpretations makes this an excellent choice for Mark's (and our) first example of the open-endedness and multiple teaching functions of a parable. Considered as a parable of a sower, the seed, or the harvest, the focus appears to be centered on the activity of God. As a parable of the soil, the focus seems to be on how people receive the seed that God, the Sower, generously spreads. As a sowings parable, both God's activity and human reception provide focal points.

At first we might be struck at the reckless manner of sowing that seems to waste the majority of the seed. Modern methods of farming would include first plowing the fields to prepare the ground for planting. But some interpreters have noted that in ancient times farmers sowed seed rather carelessly, only to plow afterward. Commentators debate whether the sower's extravagance and generosity are emphasized or whether he seems to lack good sense in scattering the seed in such a haphazard manner. Rather than stand back and objectively critique the farmer's methods, we can better profit from hearing the parable as Jesus spoke it.

Introducing the parable, Jesus dramatically calls for attention to his words by inviting his audience to "Hear this!" With a single word in Greek (*akouete*) Jesus evokes the Scripture refrain from the Torah, the *Shema*, which is recited as a prayer by devout Jews daily, reminding them of their fundamental belief in the gift of the covenant by which they are God's chosen people:

> Hear, O Israel! The LORD is our God, the LORD alone! Therefore you shall love the LORD, your God, with all your heart, and with all your soul, and with all your strength. (Deut 6:4-5; [see Deut 6:4-9; 11:13-21; Num 15:37-41])

Such a reminder will recur in one of Mark's final scenes before the Passion when a Scribe approaches Jesus to ask, "Which is the first of all the commandments?" (12:29). Jesus replies in part with the *Shemaʾ Israel*, saying, "The first is this: 'Hear, O Israel! The Lord our God is Lord alone!'" The biblical link between hearing and doing or obeying is especially clear in the Greek where the word for "hear" (*akouein*) is also linked theologically to the word "obedience," (*hypakouein*). "To hear" means "to pay attention" and give heed to. Thus the *Shema* is both a prayer and also a confession of faith, one recited daily by the Jewish people.

At first it may appear that this parable is told rather clumsily or is in need of editing. For instance, there tends to be a repetition of terms that does not add to the impact of the story. Verse 5 can serve as an example: Mark says that there was "little soil" and "the soil was not deep." There is also repetition in the culminating verse 8 in the verbs, "came up," "grew," and "yielded." The phrases of this parable are strung together with the connective "and" that occurs fifteen times in the Greek telling of this short parable. But such "clumsiness" might be perfectly understandable if seen as typical of Markan editorial intervention.

Three times in this short parable Jesus uses repetition as a teaching tool. There are actually three series of three: three infertile sowings, three hearings, three yields at the end: thirty, sixty, one hundred. Further, close attention to the movement and images of the parable conveys a rhythm of time.[4] Each sowing mentions the seed and a negative situation the seed encounters, ending with the failure of the seed to produce. There would be no drama involved in simply listing three failures in contrast to the great harvest. The parable works because it vividly pictures small increments of the growth of the seed. The first seed, for example, cannot possibly survive; it is immediately consumed by birds. The second seed sown on rocky ground lasts a little longer before withering under the heat of the sun. The third almost buds, but is choked off by thorns before it can produce.

Jesus' audience would relate to the ascending hope that each successive sowing offered. They would expect the fourth effort to produce a good crop. But their expectations are surpassed. In describing the seeds that fell on good soil, Mark shows Jesus' unbridled enthusiasm. In Greek, there is a switch from the singular "seed" in verses 5-7 to the plural "seeds." There is also a shift in the tense of the verb, from aorist (a single action in the past) to imperfect (a past continuous action). These subtle changes suggest several sowings and continual growth. There are three actions involved in the growth: sprouting, increasing, producing fruit. These are in contrast to the three previous failures, further contrasting the ultimate triumph of the seed that fell on good soil.

We are also told that the seeds "fell" and brought forth and grew up and increased the yield thirtyfold, sixtyfold, and a hundredfold (see also Mark 10:30 where the "hundredfold" Jesus promises his disciples far surpasses anything they could have imagined or requested). In contrast to a 75 percent failure rate, the amazing harvest is extravagant. Jesus proclaims that the kingdom breaks into human life, changing everything.

The parable concludes by echoing the initial invitation in 4:9: *You who can hear, pay attention*. The Greek says *let the one who has ears to hear, let that person hear*. . . . This repetition forms an inclusion with verse 3, "Hear this!" and prepares for the statement on inadequate hearing in verses 10-12. They "hear and listen but [do] not understand" (4:12). In Mark, discipleship failures are linked to an inability to "hear" correctly. For example, in 7:14-17, the disciples "hear" the parable about the clean and the unclean but are without understanding (7:18; see 4:12). The disciples who do not understand Jesus' teaching about the bread are described as "having ears" but not hearing (8:18).

Summary (Mark 4:3-9)

The parable of 4:3-9 is a good example of Jesus' use of parables in Mark. It is especially appropriate to Jesus' Galilean audience. It is a word picture taken from ordinary life in an agricultural society. Commentators have sometimes discussed whether the method of sowing the seed indiscriminately, on rocky soil and among thorns, realistically portrays the way farming was done in first-century Galilee. To get waylaid by such discussions would be to risk missing the point of Jesus' repeated, "Hear! Listen!" The "twist" or the parable is that despite the sloppy manner of sowing and the thrice-repeated expectation that there would be little or no yield, the seed that does fall upon "good soil" produces thirty-, sixty-, even a hundredfold. It is astonishing! There is no proportion between the amount of work or preparation involved and the results.

This parable, like all parables, is intended to provoke a commitment, to be "heard" and acted upon. A parable by nature is open-ended, and Jesus' challenge at the beginning and end to "Listen" is so appropriate. The obvious sense of this fairly straightforward parable is that the three failed sowings are due to the obstacles and reversals in Jesus' ministry. Yet the most striking feature of the parable comes in the abundance of the harvest from the last type of soil. Even a tenfold yield would be considered good, so the thirty-, sixty-, hundredfold yield is extravagant. This represents the eschatological overflowing of divine blessings.

The lesson of the parable is that, despite what seem to be frustrations and failures in Jesus' ministry, it will certainly bear fruit, and in a manner exceeding all expectations. The same holds true for the success of the mission even of the flawed disciples. The parable was addressed to those who wondered whether the words and deeds of Jesus could be linked to the reign of God: it is an encouragement to those with little faith or hope.[5] The parable links Jesus' identity to his mission; if hearers fail to receive the word Jesus preaches, they will not produce fruit for the kingdom. If they really want to know what the reign of God is like, they must listen carefully and integrate Jesus' explanation of the parable that follows in Mark 4:10-23.[6]

Parables as Enigmatic (Mark 4:10-13)

Jesus tells his disciples: "The mystery of the kingdom of God has been granted to you. But to those outside everything comes in parables" (4:11). At first it seems that the audience will be left to ponder the meaning of the sowing parable with a dramatic pause. But Mark cuts to another setting, a behind-the-scenes conference, where "those around Jesus along with the Twelve" question him, apparently about this parable. That is surprising in itself when the meaning of the parable appears to be self-evident. Jesus gives them special instruction, but it only conspires to make his meaning all the more mysterious. He implies that the disciples are given more understanding than "those outside." Jesus also suggests that one of the purposes of his use of parables is to conceal the mystery of the kingdom from those who are not his disciples. Mark lets his readers eavesdrop on Jesus' conversation with his disciples as if to caution his readers to listen very intently. Mark says:

> [10]And when he was alone, those present along with the Twelve questioned him about the parables. [11]He answered them, "The mystery of the kingdom of God has been granted to you. But to those outside everything comes in parables, [12]so that
> 'they may look and see but not perceive,
>   and hear and listen but not understand,
>   in order that they may not be converted and be forgiven.'"
> [13]Jesus said to them, "Do you not understand this parable? Then how will you understand any of the parables?"

Jesus' reply to the disciples' question is so intriguing because Jesus gives here the key to *all* the parables. Jesus' disciples question him about the *parables* (plural) and Jesus takes the opportunity to explain why he speaks in parables in general before giving an interpretation of this particular parable not only to the disciples, but also by implication to the crowds. In this aside, Mark again uses inclusion, introducing the private conference between Jesus and his disciples with their question about the parables, and concluding with Jesus' challenge to understand this and all the parables. Jesus notes the double effect of revealing and concealing found in his parables: "to you is given . . . but to those outside . . . ." Mark seems to be emphasizing the enigmatic effect of parables, which reveal to some, but also conceal from others.

Jesus' comment on the purpose of his parables seems more confusing than enlightening. Indeed, these verses are among the most debated in the New Testament. Jesus would seem to be encouraging a sense of pride and superiority in his disciples because they have been given knowledge of the kingdom of God. Jesus also seems to be saying that a purpose of parables is to *prevent* "those outside" from understanding, repenting, and receiving forgiveness. This sounds as though Jesus himself teaches predestination, implying that some receive revelation and others "are consigned in advance to misunderstanding."[7] Jesus supports his teaching about the purpose of parables with an oblique reference to Isaiah, a reference Matthew will make more explicit in his version of this teaching (Matt 13:14-15). The Markan theme of misunderstanding, including the distinction between "you" and those "outside," and Mark's use of the Scripture to support Jesus' message are essential features of these verses.

The Distinction between "You" and "Those Outside"

Throughout his gospel, Mark says Jesus gives several insider explanations of the gospel when Jesus is "alone" with his disciples (4:34; 7:33; 9:2, 28; 13:3). Mark's reference here (4:10) is the first mention of the Twelve since their selection where they are named (3:14). Jesus' inner circle includes not only the Twelve but a larger group of disciples who accompany him on the journey to Jerusalem.

Mark says that the disciples question him about the parables, suggesting their question is about parables in general. The plural appears strange since Jesus had told only one parable so far, the parable of the sowings. Perhaps the questioners are asking about the other sayings of 3:23-27 where Jesus speaks about a kingdom being divided against itself. Or, this question may be an indication that this and the other seed parables of chapter 4 originally formed a unit. In that case Mark could have inserted into this unit the theory of why Jesus used parables for teaching (vv. 10-13) as well as his explanation for one of the parables, that of the sowings (vv. 14-20), as a paradigm for understanding all the rest.[8]

Mark presents this parable as exemplary of the way Jesus teaches and of Jesus himself. Before he explains this particular parable, Jesus tells why he speaks in parables in general.[9] There are implications for both insiders and outsiders.

Insiders

Jesus' response defines the "Twelve and those around" him as insiders. Jesus tells them, "to you has been granted the mystery of the kingdom of God." The passive form of "granted" suggests that God has bestowed this wisdom on Jesus' followers. Many forms of Greek religions were known as "mystery religions." Insiders are initiated into the mystery; the result is enlightenment about the gods and the quality of the divine-human relationship. But to outsiders, the rituals, beliefs, and ethical demands involved remained impenetrable. "Mystery" has a dual function in this context: to enlighten and to conceal. This Greek concept may have had some influence on Mark.

The term "mystery" in the singular appears only here in the Synoptics.[10] Its sense is the hidden purposes of God, which are only "known" through faith. The Greek term *mysterion*, like the English, has both the sense of revelation and of hiddenness, depending upon its reception. For insiders, a mystery is something intimate, unable to be objectified. We "enter into" a mystery and approach it with awe and reverence. *Participation* in the mystery is key. A mystery is different from a problem or a riddle that, once "solved," is eliminated. A mystery invites to greater involvement and commitment. The more significant a mystery becomes for us, the more we "understand" or "know" but the less able we are to extricate ourselves or separate ourselves from it. We identify with the mystery and keep exploring its levels and its meanings.

In the immediate context, the "mystery of the kingdom of God" seems to be related to the parable Jesus just told and also to the following parables of the kingdom (4:26-32) that refer explicitly to the kingdom of God. For Mark the kingdom of God has a strong christological focus (1:15; 9:1). It is not a reference to an objective time or place. It is the way inaugurated by Jesus and his ministry. Jesus invites his audience to accept him and the Gospel he preaches. When they do, they have been "granted the mystery of the kingdom of God."

Mark's Gospel is punctuated with the comment, "They did not understand," or some phrase meaning the same thing (see 3:21, 30; 4:13; 5:20, 40; 6:14, 51; 7:18; 8:21). "Amazement" is the usual response of the crowds who fail to understand. Especially in the first part of his gospel, Mark portrays the crowds and even the disciples as failing to perceive Jesus' meaning or even his identity. Jesus' miracles also meet with amazement and confusion. Most of the miracles of Mark occur in chapters 1–8. But Mark stresses that Jesus' deeds as well as his words baffle onlookers. Mark inserted the parable chapter in the midst of a series of miracles as if to demonstrate that Jesus was not quickly and clearly understood, despite his "mighty works." For Mark, Jesus is not merely or even primarily a miracle worker. Rather, Jesus' teachings and his identity belong to the "mystery" of the coming of God's reign.

Jesus does not have any delusions about his disciples' capabilities nor is he suggesting that they are superior to the outsiders. Mark is particularly insistent that the disciples, including the Twelve, despite their insider status, were slow to understand. Indeed, they *usually* misunderstood. Throughout the gospel, we hear that they were confused and dull and disappointing in their responses to Jesus. For example, after calming the storm at sea, the episode that follows the parable discourse, Jesus asks his companions, "Why are you terrified? Do you not yet have faith?" (4:40). Almost with an air of impatience, he asks his disciples in 8:21, "Do you still not understand?"

Even when Peter confesses, "You are the Messiah," Jesus tells him not to say this to others (8:29). Commentators refer to such statements as examples of the "messianic secret" characteristic of Mark and said to be one of the keys to Mark. That is, Mark presents Jesus' identity and mission as a mystery, even as the revelation of Jesus unfolds and he instructs his disciples about his mission. Despite the miracles, Mark says, even the disciples "do not understand." Mark tells us at the very beginning of his gospel that Jesus is the "Son of God" (1:1). Yet no human being confesses that Jesus is the Son of God until the centurion does so at the cross (15:39). Mark dispels all suspicion that it was easier for Peter and the rest of the Twelve who lived at the time of Jesus and witnessed his teaching and miracles than it was for subsequent generations of Christians to understand and accept Jesus and the Gospel he preaches. Rather, Jesus' earliest followers, like the readers of Mark's Gospel then and now, must accept Jesus and his message through faith. And that entails not only Jesus' initial invitation to follow him, but also his instruction all along the way to Jerusalem and the cross. The "knowledge" of the kingdom of God is more of a responsibility than a privilege.

Mark 4:10-13 could also be linked to the specific parable Jesus just told. Then the cautionary aspect becomes even clearer. Jesus is *warning* his followers that there is far more to true discipleship than merely receiving the word. Once the seed or word is received, it must be cultivated in "good soil" and produce a plentiful yield. In chapter 3 Mark told of the sending out of the apostles to preach and to cast out demons (3:13-15). Jesus instructs his disciples that the mystery of the kingdom of God is given as a responsibility of "those around Jesus and the Twelve" to share and spread the message of repentance and forgiveness.

As part of his answer to their question, Jesus challenges even his disciples with a question of his own, "Do you not understand this parable? Then how will you understand any of the parables?" (4:13). Jesus insinuates that this is an easy parable in comparison to other ones—especially perhaps for Mark—the "parable" of Jesus' own passion. Actually Jesus' challenge can be taken as a statement or a question "Don't you understand this parable?" Jesus seems to be referring to the parable of sowings. Yet Jesus may be challenging them to accept the "parable" or enigmatic saying of 4:10-12 where disciples are granted the mystery of God's kingdom that remains a riddle for outsiders.

All types of soil have received the seed. But the seed only survived and prospered in good soil that endured trials, rocks and thorns, and harsh weather. Followers of Jesus are cautioned in verses 10-13 that "knowing the mystery" is only the beginning. The mystery cannot make them complacent or lazy.

Outsiders

Outsiders, like the insiders, are self-defined, according to Mark. Although Jesus comes to proclaim the Good News of salvation accessible to all, reaction to him separates those willing to receive the kingdom of God from those for whom Jesus' message still remains a riddle and therefore inaccessible. Mark says that to those outside, "everything comes in parables" (4:11). Although the term "everything" is not specified, it appears to refer to the activity and words of Jesus, not simply to the parables themselves. The plural, "in parables," carries the sense of "parabolically," referring to Jesus' manner of speaking that is hidden as well as revealing, and not simply the content of his speech.

The description of the outsiders in Mark 4:10-13 seems to suggest predestination. God might be pictured as responsible for some not converting. Mark suggests that one purpose of parables is to prevent "those outside" from hearing and perceiving, seeing and understanding. In contrast, Matthew changes the wording to mean "effect" more than "purpose." Thus Matthew seems to soften the impression that parables are the means by which some are hardened to refuse the message of Jesus and especially of the parables.

Fulfillment of the Scriptures

Mark may have been thinking about the call of the prophets when he portrays Jesus referring to those who look but do not see, listen but do not understand in 4:12-13. Jeremiah had complained bitterly to God about the obstinacy of the people. God speaks through the prophet, saying:

> "Pay attention to this,
>> foolish and senseless people
> Who have eyes and see not,
>> who have ears and hear not." (Jer 5:21)

Certainly there is an echo of Isaiah as well:

> (And the Lord) replied: "Go and say to this people:
>> 'Listen carefully, but you shall not understand!
>> Look intently, but you shall know nothing!
>> You are to make the heart of this people sluggish,
>>> to dull their ears and close their eyes;
>> Else their eyes will see, their ears hear,
>>> their heart understand,
>>> and they will turn and be healed.'" (Isa 6:9-10)

While Mark does not explicitly cite these references, he does make a free translation, saying:

> But to those outside everything comes in parables, [12]so that
>> 'they may look and see but not perceive,
>>> and hear and listen but not understand,
>> in order that they may be not converted
>>> and be forgiven.' (Mark 4:11-12)

The Greek word *hina* (which is translated "in order that") means both purpose and result and may have been chosen to convey ambiguity. This small word makes verse 12 one of most difficult and debated verses in the New Testament. It comes down to whether misunderstanding and blindness were the *purpose* or *result* of Jesus' parabolic teaching. There are other examples in Mark where *hina* means "result," most often after verbs of ordering or desiring: 3:9; 5:18; 6:2, 8, 12; 9:9. Mark may be deliberately trying to echo the "hardening" idea from the Hebrew Scriptures that implies that God acts in the choice of those who will follow and those who will reject the divine will. Like Egypt and the Pharaoh, outsiders remain outside as long as they refuse to perceive and accept the meaning of the parables that will cause them to be converted and to believe.

A first-century Jewish audience would probably have immediately recognized the Scripture passage Mark refers to and the scriptural background of the "hardening" theme Mark echoes. With our contemporary bias for human liberty and free will, we may find the notion of God's overriding sovereignty harder to comprehend. According to the

Scriptures, however, God is the Lord of history. Humans cannot even resist or refuse to hear or to see except by God's will. Thus, for example, while God chose to liberate the Israelites from Egypt, the heart of the Pharaoh was "hardened." In a contest with God, whose attributes are so far beyond any power of ours, God will triumph. Readers are also aware that for Mark the kingdom of God is the overriding context in which the concept of "hardening" can be understood. God's reign is all important.

Summary (Mark 4:10-13)

Mark's composition of the parable and Jesus' explanation of why he speaks in parables emphasizes the enigmatic. The contrast between "those around him" and "those outside" frames the saying. The first group, the insiders, is granted knowledge of the mystery of the kingdom; for the outsiders all remains "in parables," that is, mysterious in the negative sense. These verses are not primarily concerned with the meaning of the parable of the sower. Instead they force the reader to confront the larger question: "What is the mystery of the reign of God?" Insight lies in the allusion to Isaiah. Those outside lack perception. Those around Jesus have repented and God has healed them. The mystery concerns the reign of God that Mark associates with the call for repentance (Mark 1:15) and forgiveness (2:1-12; 3:28-29). Only those around Jesus have caught on to what has been said and have received the forgiveness that belongs to the coming of the reign of God.

Mark 4:10-13 might appear at first as an interruption to the discourse.[11] But this "interruption" has all the characteristics of Mark's editorial style. It is really an explanation of the distinction between the crowds and the disciples. The crowds are left with a parable without explanation and the disciples receive the explanation and integrate it.

Like other parables, this one has a judgmental purpose. It challenges those who have been attracted to Jesus and have begun to accept his message. They must continue to be open, to hear and to learn and to respond. This and all the other parables also have an educational purpose. That is, parables are meant to explain why some do receive the message while others reject it. That is why Mark apparently is unconcerned to clarify Jesus' audience at any given point. The disciples ask for and receive an explanation while the crowds remain "outside." You must be "inside" to hear and accept the explanation. The others remain in obscurity and they are left with only a riddle. The parable itself distinguishes between the two as the quote from Isaiah implies. And the people's acceptance or rejection further identifies them either as disciples or as "outsiders."

Jesus registers amazement that even the disciples do not understand this parable and asks them, "Then how will you understand any of the parables?" The theme of the misunderstanding of the people and even of Jesus' closest associates is a familiar one in Mark. His disciples not only do not understand the parables, but they also do not understand the miracles or that the Messiah will suffer. In fact, their abandonment of Jesus in Jerusalem shows that they understand precious little of who Jesus is or what he is trying to teach them.

Explanation of the Parable of the Sowings (4:14-20)

After issuing a challenge to understand this and all the parables, Jesus goes on to explain the parable of the sowings, saying:

> [14]"The sower sows the word. [15]These are the ones on the path where the word is sown. As soon as they hear, Satan comes at once and takes away the word sown in them. [16]And these are the ones sown on rocky ground who, when they hear the word, receive it at once with joy. [17]But they have no root; they last only for a time. Then when tribulation or persecution comes because of the word, they quickly fall away. [18]Those sown among thorns are another sort. They are the people who hear the word, [19]but worldly anxiety, the lure of riches, and the craving for other things intrude and choke the word, and it bears no fruit. [20]But those sown on rich soil are the ones who hear the word and accept it and bear fruit thirty and sixty and a hundredfold."

The first verse sets the tone for the rest of the interpretation: "The sower sows the word" (v. 14).[12] The sower represents God, and the "word" represents Jesus and his preaching. Although it is clear that the seed is sown, it is not always effective. In fact, Jesus indicates that the word does not always bear fruit even among those willing to receive it. In Mark's version of the parable there are three enemies of the reign of God: Satan, "tribulation or persecution," and "worldly anxiety, the lure of riches" (4:17, 19).[13] These appear as obstacles to discipleship throughout Mark. Satan confronted Jesus in the desert in the beginning of the gospel (1:12-13). The other enemies appear in future episodes in Mark. For example, in the story of the rich man in 10:17-22, it is his wealth that turns the rich man away from following Jesus. In Mark 13 Jesus warns about coming persecutions and about tribulations (see 13:7-8, 17, 24; see also 10:30).

In apocalyptic thought, demons are sometimes portrayed as birds, a connection that might have influenced imagery in this parable. For instance, Mark 4:15 says that "Satan comes . . . among them and takes away the word sown." Perhaps the parable links opponents of Jesus with

Satan as they had previously been to Beelzebub (3:23-29). But it is Peter, one of the Twelve, who is actually addressed as Satan in 8:33. This chilling allusion may be suggested also by the phrase "sown in them." And 4:16 might also have the Twelve and specifically Peter in view. The "rocky ground" (which could be a word play on Peter's name) refers to those who first accept the word with joy but lack roots, so they fall away in trouble and persecution. The rest of the gospel narrative will illustrate that Peter began with initial enthusiasm but faltered in times of trouble. Mark will also record Jesus' prediction at the Last Supper: "All of you will have your faith shaken, for it is written: / 'I will strike the shepherd, / and the sheep will be dispersed'" (Mark 14:27). Perhaps Mark wants to counter any objection by members of his own generation who claimed that the original followers of Jesus had a better opportunity to witness miracles and identify Jesus as the Messiah than they did.[14]

It may be that the "thorns" in verse 18 are a subtle echo of the "thorns and thistles" in the Genesis story. They include the frustrations as well as the temptations that stifle the growth of the seed that first showed promise but was not strong because it lacked depth. Mark 4:19 envisions some of life's "blessings" such as wealth as choking the word that is sown. Cares of the world, love of riches, or desires for other things such as success, prestige, and comfort strangle the willingness to be a disciple, as the story of the rich young man shows. Throughout Mark there is an emphasis on the single-mindedness with which disciples must follow Jesus, despite hardships or the attraction of fleeting pleasures.

Finally, Mark has Jesus explain the single successful sowing that bears fruit far beyond anyone's wildest expectation. Mark also contrasts authentic and inauthentic "hearing." Mark 4:20 presents a succession of proper responses that counterbalances the triple failures: true disciples "hear the word, welcome it, and bear fruit." "Bearing fruit" is itself a metaphor for repentance, conversion, and good works. There is an astonishing abundance of the fruit that multiplies exponentially, thirty, sixty, a hundred times. This extravagant success is in contrast to predicted resistance and failure in verses 11-12. Mark's emphasis after all is on the triumph of God and of God's word. When it finds receptive hearts, the word of God can overcome all the possible obstacles, temptations, and opposition. God's word will flourish and grow and nothing can prevent it from doing so. This is the surprise and the point of Jesus' preaching.

Summary (Mark 4:14-20)

The explanation of the parable of the sowings is in fact the key to all the parables, as Jesus indicates in 4:13. Mark highlights the importance of Jesus' clarification of the parables and frames it by the repetition of an imperative of Jesus in 4:9 and 23: "Whoever has ears to hear ought to hear!" The different kinds of soil do not refer to different kinds of people (pure/impure, righteous/sinful, leaders/marginalized) who hear the word, but to their receptivity of the "seed." The "word" means the preaching of Jesus (as in 2:2; 4:33). Jesus points out that his preaching will not always appear to be effective, for there are powerful enemies of the kingdom such as Satan, tribulation or persecution and worldly anxiety, the lure of riches. Yet the triumph of God is certain. The harvest far exceeds any possible expectation. The abundant fruit in the end overwhelms the inauspicious, slow beginning. This disproportion is also a theme of other images and parables in this chapter.

Sayings about Light and Measures (Mark 4:21-25)

The relatively long parable of the sowings and Jesus' explanation are followed by an arrangement of several parabolic images. And so, Mark continues:

> [21](Jesus) said to them, "Is a lamp brought in to be placed under a bushel basket or under a bed, and not to be placed on a lampstand? [22]For there is nothing hidden except to be made visible; nothing is secret except to come to light. [23]Anyone who has ears to hear ought to hear." [24]He also told them, "Take care what you hear. The measure with which you measure will be measured out to you, and still more will be given to you. [25]To the one who has, more will be given; from the one who has not, even what he has will be taken away."

Sometimes the use of the commonplace shows how dissimilar this world is from the kingdom of God. So, for example, Jesus speaks of a lamp, a lampstand, a bushel basket, and a measure. He appears to be searching for a variety of images to show "that there is nothing hidden except to be made visible; nothing is secret except to come to light." Jesus uses these everyday images to illustrate aspects of revelation and wisdom. Just as there is no coexistence or proportion between dark and light, there is no worthy comparison for the indescribable and unimagined blessings of the kingdom.

The sayings in Mark 4:21-25 come from a collection of wisdom sayings and appear in Matthew and Luke in other contexts.[15] The presence of these sayings also in the Gospel of Thomas and in various contexts in the Synoptics strongly suggests, by the criterion of multiple attestation, that they were spoken by Jesus himself. Yet the various uses of them by the different evangelists shows how flexible the tradition was. Mark is the one who seems to have formed these sayings into a unified group and located them at this critical juncture in his parable chapter, adding insight about the qualities of a disciple as a wise person and the contrast between this world and the priorities of the kingdom of God.

The Seed Parables (Mark 4:26-32)

The two seed parables (4:26-29 and 4:30-32) that conclude the sermon are probably better categorized as similitudes, that is, concise comparisons based on daily realities. Jesus' audience would recognize as true the fact that seed grows while people sleep or that the mustard seed is really quite small if not actually the "smallest of all the seeds of the earth" (v. 31). That both of these similitudes have to do with seeds no doubt explains why they have been paired. They provide a fitting conclusion to the parable sermon:

> [26]He said, "This is how it is with the kingdom of God; it is as if a man were to scatter seed on the land [27]and would sleep and rise night and day and the seed would sprout and grow, he knows not how. [28]Of its own accord the land yields fruit, first the blade, then the ear, then the full grain in the ear. [29]And when the grain is ripe, he wields the sickle at once, for the harvest has come."
>
> [30]He said, "To what shall we compare the kingdom of God, or what parable can we use for it? [31]It is like a mustard seed that, when it is sown in the ground, is the smallest of all the seeds on the earth. [32]But once it is sown, it springs up and becomes the largest of plants and puts forth large branches, so that the birds of the sky can dwell in its shade" (Mark 4:26-32).

Each of these seed parables begins with a simple introduction, "And he said." These are the only two sayings that Mark explicitly identified as "kingdom" parables in their introductory formula (vv. 26 and 30). These two metaphors appear to be addressed to the same audience as the sowings parable of 4:3-9. That they are about "seeds" that are "sown" provides two further catchword links to the headline parable of this chapter. In all three, there is a contrast between small beginnings and extravagant results. The process is hidden and mysterious to humans, but inevitably growth is achieved. The images of the sowings and of the small seeds both stress that divine guidance and power, rather than human effort or potential, are key.

Indeed, the first similitude downplays any human participation. The man "scatters" the seeds, suggesting an even more casual effort than the farmer in 4:3 used. Jesus says this man "goes to sleep and gets up," the night-day sequence that reflects the order of Genesis and the process of creation. The man's role is passive, with no hint at the effort required of him for proper farming: the plowing and planting, weeding, cultivating, or nurturing. It is the growth that happens even while the man sleeps that is emphasized: the seed "sprouts" and "begins to grow," regardless of the man's activity. Finally, there are four stages of inevitable growth: "first the blade, then the ear, then the full grain," then ripeness. This growth shifts attention from reception of the seed signified by the different kinds of soil in the parable of the sowings, to the power by which the word of God produces a good result. No failure is mentioned or possible here.

The appearance in Mark 4:28 of the term "bear fruit" recalls verse 20 where the "good seed bears fruit." The growth happens as a result of an invisible power, automatically, without human involvement. In the next verse ("he wields the sickle at once"), Jesus draws on Joel 4:13 without indicating that he is doing so. Suddenly, as soon as the farmer wields the sickle, it's time for the harvest. The notion of harvest has overtones of eschatological urgency and this parable takes on a warning tone.

Mark introduces the next and final parable of the sermon in verses 30-32 with double rhetorical questions: "To what shall we compare the kingdom of God, or what parable can we use for it?" Perhaps the double question of Isaiah 40:18 provided inspiration: "To whom can you liken God, / with what equal can you confront him?" Such language is also characteristic of parables told by rabbis who might have been contemporaries of Jesus.

The mustard seed represents smallness, although it is not literally the absolute smallest seed, nor does it produce the largest plant in the world. Appealing to the imagination, Jesus uses this as a symbol of faith. The same image appears in Matthew 17:20 contrasting the small and apparently insignificant mustard seed with its potential for growth and strength. In Mark, Jesus goes on to describe the bush as large enough for "birds of the heavens" to make their dwellings in its shade. In Daniel 4:19-21 such a large bush is used as a symbol for Nebuchadnezzar.[16] Ezekiel 17:22-23 promises that God will produce a giant cedar with branches sufficient for every kind of bird to make a home in, an image that surely inspired Mark's allusion to the bush large enough to shelter the birds. For Mark, then, Jesus teaches that God's reign extends hope to all those suffering from discouragement at the apparent insignificance of faith in the face of great opposition such as Mark's church faced. The seed Jesus plants among his lowly disciples will spread and grow by the power of God and no resistance can stifle it.

Summary of the Parable Sermon in Mark 4

Although at first chapter 4 may appear to have been hastily thrown together, there is evidence that the chapter has undergone considerable editorial composition by Mark. The sermon in parables highlights central motifs of Mark's Gospel including Jesus' special instruction to his disciples, apart from the crowds, acceptance without understanding on the part of the disciples, separation of the insiders from outsiders, and an emphasis on "hearing" and accepting, including the possibility of suffering. A christology emerges that not only continues the portrait of Jesus as one who teaches with authority (1:27; see Mark 4:1-2) but also suggests that the death and resurrection of Jesus constitute the mystery of the kingdom.

Mark 4 combines the themes of christology and discipleship central to the whole gospel. In the parable of the sowings each unsuccessful sowing begins with a "hearing" (4:15, 16, 18) and the outsiders of 4:12 "hear but do not understand." Throughout Mark failure in discipleship is equated with improper hearing. Even the opponents "hear" the teaching of Jesus but do not let his teaching take root. Jesus preaches the kingdom opening and welcome to all, but it takes more than a simple hearing to accept and receive it. The enigma about the kingdom and its mystery is that one must become a member of it to understand it and any parable about it. This means adopting the way of life Jesus will describe in the rest of the gospel.

The Parable of the Tenants (Mark 12:1-12)

We now turn to the only other fully developed parable in Mark, besides that of the sowings found in chapter 4. This one is known as the parable of the wicked tenants and it appears near the end of Jesus' ministry, just before the beginning of his passion. The setting is Jerusalem. Jesus has arrived only recently. Soon he will be arrested, tried, and put to death. He would be handed over to the Romans by the Jewish authorities. Finally, Mark tells us, they delivered him up "out of envy" (15:10). In Jerusalem, various Jewish leaders challenge Jesus. Part of his response to their challenge is the following parable:

> [1]He began to speak to them in parables. "A man planted a vineyard, put a hedge around it, dug a wine press, and built a tower. Then he leased it to tenant farmers and left on a journey. [2]At the proper time he sent a servant to the tenants to obtain from them some of the produce of the vineyard. [3]But they seized him, beat him, and sent him away empty-handed. [4]Again he sent them another servant. And that

one they beat over the head and treated shamefully. [5]He sent yet another whom they killed. So, too, many others; some they beat, others they killed. [6]He had one other to send, a beloved son. He sent him to them last of all, thinking, 'They will respect my son.' [7]But those tenants said to one another, 'This is the heir. Come, let us kill him, and the inheritance will be ours.' [8]So they seized him and killed him, and threw him out of the vineyard. [9]What [then] will the owner of the vineyard do? He will come, put the tenants to death, and give the vineyard to others. [10]Have you not read this scripture passage:

'The stone that the builders rejected
    has become the cornerstone;
[11]by the Lord has this been done,
    and it is wonderful in our eyes'?"

[12]They were seeking to arrest him, but they feared the crowd, for they realized that he had addressed the parable to them. So they left him and went away (Mark 12:1-12).

For a long time many commentators believed this parable was more a creation of Mark than the actual words of Jesus. Three main reasons have been given for this.[17] First, the situation appears to be unrealistic. Secondly, the parable refers to historical events and figures unlike the generalizing tendency of, for example, the parable of the sowings. Finally, the parable ends with a prediction of Jesus' death, which some doubt could have come from Jesus himself. Indeed, there are a number of features that suggest Mark's editorial imprint: among them inclusion, the series of three, and use of the Scriptures.

Markan Literary Features

Mark uses the *inclusion* technique evident in so many of the episodes of his gospel. Mark's introduction is brief: "He began to speak to them in parables" (12:1). The initial reference to Jesus' "speaking in parables" is echoed in the reaction of the listeners who realize that "he had addressed this parable to them" (12:12), an example of Mark's framing technique or inclusion. Thus Mark reminds the reader at the end of the unit of what he said at the beginning. Another Markan feature shows how Jesus often draws his audience in by the *use of questions* (see 4:13, 21, 30). In this parable, Jesus involves his hearers by inserting the rhetorical question, "What, [then] will the owner of the vineyard do?" (12:9). And again, "Have you not read this scripture passage?" (12:10).

As in the parable of the sowings, Mark makes use of *a series of three*, implying repetition and progression. This is a familiar technique of a good storyteller, especially in an oral culture. The owner sends a servant twice, and the third time he sends his "beloved" son. Three times the reaction is hostile, each time getting a little worse. The parable itself is based on several *Scripture passages*, especially Isaiah 5:1-7. In this case, the Scripture passage is not simply joined to the parable, but actually provided the story for the parable itself. The relationship between the Old Testament Scripture and the parable is quite clear. The concluding verses make the Scriptures' influence explicit.

A familiar Markan theme of *understanding* is also visible in this parable. In contrast to the parable of the sowings in chapter 4 when not even the disciples understood, this time the listeners clearly perceive both the meaning of the parable and that it is addressed to them. Whereas Mark notes throughout his gospel that Jesus' listeners were confused or dull or just don't get it, this time they do. And their hostile reaction is foreboding since soon their attempts to arrest Jesus will succeed. The crowds in Mark are often presented as part of the background and even as favorable to Jesus' teaching. In this parable the crowds act almost as a kind of shield, for Jesus' opponents "fear the crowd." Soon the crowds will follow their leaders and join their voice in calling for Jesus' execution.

Jesus' audience is simply referred to as "they," but we can assume it is the same people who challenged his authority in Mark 11:27, namely the "chief priests, the scribes, and the elders." We read on a little further to learn that "They sent some Pharisees and Herodians to him to ensnare him in his speech" (12:13). And finally, in 12:18, some Sadducees pile on to question him about the resurrection. The context of the parable is one of confrontation between Jesus and the various leaders of the Jewish people. These leaders were usually divided in their beliefs. On the issue of whether Jesus deserves to die, they are unanimous. This time they understand the parable and realize that it was meant for them. Their reaction is to reject its implications and also Jesus himself.

A closer look at this parable reveals several elements that strike us as odd and unrealistic in this little story about the wicked tenants. Why, for example, would the owner send a servant, one at a time, to the tenants and not make a show of force at least after the first one was abused? Why would the tenants think they could claim the vineyard as their own after they abused and then killed the son? Why would this story be told in the capital city of Jerusalem rather than in its more natural setting of rural Galilee? These questions suggest that the parable calls for an allegorical interpretation rather than a purely realistic one. Yet some awareness of the probable original setting and of some assumptions shared by

Jesus and his audience can help us understand this parable and its important role in Mark's Gospel.

The Setting

Although told in Jerusalem, the more likely setting for the parable is Galilee, a region notorious in the first century for fomenting revolution and unrest. In Galilee, farming was a main occupation. Often large estates were owned by foreigners who exacted rent in the form of a portion of the land's productivity from tenant farmers. Frequently the delegates of the landlords were heavy-handed. Sometimes the tenant farmers would withhold payment or renege on the terms of their contract. Violence and seizure of property by the tenants were not unknown. In cases of unclaimed property, when no heir was identified, it was even possible to acquire ownership of the land.

Add to this the uneasy "peace" that existed between those in Palestine and their Roman occupiers and we can understand better the background for this parable. Galilee was, in fact, a focus of the Romans' concern and an area long suspected of plotting sedition and undermining good order. During Roman occupation when the north was known as "Galilee of the Gentiles" (see Matt 4:15), many in Jesus' audience would have been prone to sympathize with the tenant farmers' standing up to their oppressors. An insidious connotation to the term "Galilean" might even have played a role in Peter's fear when confronted by a servant girl in the high priest's courtyard, who accused him, "Surely you are one of them; for you too are a Galilean" (Mark 14:70). Jesus' own Galilean roots could have been a factor in the success of the Jewish authorities converting their religious charges against him into political ones that would carry some weight with Pilate. Josephus, the first-century Jewish-turned-Roman historian, maintained that there were over two hundred villages in all of Galilee, and modern archaeology has shown that his figure is not improbable.[18] There among the hills and the many dialects of the local population, revolutionary thinking and training for the eventual rebellion against the Romans found sympathy and support. Jewish nationalism was becoming more popular among the people and more of a problem to the authorities. The parable, which reflects such a climate of hostility between a foreign, absentee landowner and the working poor, is not so unrealistic as it might first appear.

The landowner sent delegates more than three times. His repeated and escalating efforts, culminating in the mission of his own beloved son, convey his earnestness and also his initial trust of the tenants. Despite their bad behavior, he repeatedly endeavors to win their cooperation with the contract he had made with them. Perhaps he realized, when the first missions failed, that the tenants might have some legitimate grievances. He would show his sincerity and forgiveness by sending an even more important representative. The thoughtful listener would begin to suspect this is no ordinary, "realistic" landowner. His perseverance and implied confidence in the tenants draws Jesus' audience to sympathize with this special vineyard owner. His rhetorical question tightens the story's grip on them: "What more could he have done?" A reasonable person would have to admit he had already gone far beyond any expectations. Only God would act in such a generous way.

The Scriptures

As Mark recounts it, not only does the parable reflect the political climate of the day, but it is also a parable drawn straight from the pages of the Jewish Scriptures. It is all the more powerful since the Jewish religious leaders in Jerusalem would have listened with interest to a story that painted as "wicked tenants" the hard-to-control Galileans. But Mark makes the point that these same religious authorities recognized that this parable was about them. Their recognition was due in no small part to the scriptural references in the parable. This parable is based on a passage from Isaiah that says:

> [1]My friend had a vineyard / on a fertile hillside; / [2]He spaded it, cleared it of stones, / and planted the choicest vines; / Within it he built a watchtower, / and hewed out a wine press. / Then he looked for the crop of grapes, / but what it yielded was wild grapes. / [3]Now, inhabitants of Jerusalem and men of Judah, / judge between me and my vineyard: / [4]What more was there to do for my vineyard / that I had not done? / Why, when I looked for the crop of grapes, / did it bring forth wild grapes? / [5]Now, I will let you know / what I mean to do to my vineyard: / Take away its hedge, give it to grazing, / break through its wall, let it be trampled! / [6]Yes, I will make it a ruin: / it shall not be pruned or hoed, / but overgrown with thorns and briers; / I will command the clouds / not to send rain upon it. / [7]The vineyard of the LORD of hosts is the house of Israel, / and the men of Judah are his cherished plant; / He looked for judgment, but see, bloodshed! / For justice, but hark, the outcry! (Isaiah 5:1-7)

The vineyard is an ancient symbol for Israel. Isaiah explicitly says that it means Israel. Isaiah also says that the vineyard owner is the "LORD of hosts," a reference to God. God has nurtured the vineyard, spading and clearing it, installing a tower and a wine press in anticipation of its harvest. When, despite the owner's continued efforts, the vineyard fails to produce, the owner asks, "What more could I have done?" Not finding an answer, he decides to "make a ruin" of the vineyard, which will not be further pruned nor hoed nor even watered by rain.

Although Jesus draws on this Isaian passage for his parable, some differences are notable. For instance, Isaiah first speaks of a "friend" (v. 1) who has a vineyard, but later clearly states that the vineyard owner is God (v. 7). Isaiah poses the question, "What more was there to do for my vineyard that I had not done? Now I will let you know what I mean to do to my vineyard." Jesus is more subtle, engaging his hearers with the rhetorical question, "What will the owner of the vineyard do?" Asked to assess this situation from a divine perspective, Jesus' audience is challenged to judge themselves. Mark notes their inability or unwillingness to do this, concluding the parable with the observation, "So they left him and went away" (Mark 12:12).

Isaiah blames the vineyard for not producing whereas Jesus accuses the tenants or overseers who refuse to surrender the profits from the vineyard's fruit. As the vineyard symbolizes Israel, the tenants represent Israel's leaders who are accountable to its owner. Isaiah refers to several steps taken by the owner that could reasonably assure the vineyard's production. Jesus echoes these measures: he planted it, hedged it, built a winepress and tower on it. The tenants abuse and kill first the owner servants and finally his "beloved" son. Jesus realizes the intention of the leaders to execute him and lays responsibility for the "son's" death on them.

Isaiah has nothing about an absent landowner nor his tenant farmers. Jesus evokes an image of a landowner who goes on a journey, trusting his vineyard to others. Perhaps these tenants felt justified in their efforts to defraud the landowner. Their real guilt comes when they not only abuse the messengers sent by the owner, but even kill his son, hoping to claim his inheritance. Readers might object that the idea of the owner going on a trip means that the owner could not represent God. But not every element of a parable has some hidden meaning in the story. There are a number of parables that feature the going away and the return of a landowner or master. The owner's travel fits the essentials of this parable that calls for others to represent him. And Jesus' audience does understand the parable's critique regarding their leadership.

Although the influence of Isaiah 5:1-17 on the shape and impact of the parable is the greatest, other passages from the Old Testament also form part of its background. For example, the prophets are often called "servants," and are thought to speak for God, helping the people interpret the will of God as times change. Often the prophets were mistreated just like the servants of the parable were. The mission of the prophets, like the servants, is to collect the owner's share of the profit from the fruit of the vineyard. The parable tells us that the owner of the vineyard sent "many" servants. More generally we can think of other Old Testament figures such as Abraham, Moses, and David. The reference to the "beloved son" suggests the story of Abraham and Isaac in Genesis 22. The stated intention of the tenants regarding the owner's son, "Come, let us kill him," exposes the apparent naiveté of the owner who had hoped, "They will respect my son." The tenants' intention echoes the plan of Jacob's sons to kill Joseph (Gen 37:19). Further, in both the case of Joseph's brothers and of the wicked tenants, jealousy or envy appear to be the motive for their malicious behavior. Indeed, the tenants treat the son even worse than they treated the servants, "throwing him outside" the vineyard. The final degradation is that he was even denied a decent burial.

Yet another Scripture passage describes the foolish and the wicked as those who make a pact with death, considering it a "friend" (see Wis 1:16–2:24). Their motto is "eat, drink, and be merry." The wicked conspire to oppress and kill the righteous whose manner of life condemns their evil ways. Similarly, the leaders of the people realize that Jesus' righteousness reproaches them. Their response is a concerted determination to eliminate him from their midst rather than to listen to his message, repent, and change their ways.

The parable nears its conclusion as Jesus pictures the owner finally resolving to exercise his authority as *kyrios* (i.e., LORD) of the vineyard. He will have the tenants put to death. The listener might think of scriptural examples of God turning Israel over to pagan nations who looted their land and waged war against them (see Amos 5:16-18; Isa 5:18-26; 47:6; Jer 2:29-37; 5:14-17). Just like Jesus, the Old Testament prophets before him uttered many similar threats against Jewish leaders in Jerusalem.

It may be tempting to see these events as reflecting a climate after the destruction of the Temple by Rome in A.D. 70. But is this a prophecy before or after the fact? Mark pictures Jesus' warning, "He will give the vineyard to others." The vineyard (Israel) is not destroyed as in Isaiah 5:5-6. It is the tenant farmers, that is, the Jerusalem leadership, who are punished. Who the "others" are is not clear. We ought not think that Jesus or Mark meant to give the vineyard (Israel) to Gentiles (e.g.,

Romans) or to Gentile-Christians. Jesus intended this parable for the leaders who were seeking his death. They themselves knew he meant it for them. Jesus warns the religious leaders that the vineyard that had been entrusted to their care would be entrusted to others, namely his disciples.

The unit ends with a quotation from yet another Scripture passage, this time Psalm 118:22-23, saying: "The stone the builders rejected / has become the cornerstone." This quotation is not directly related to the previous parable, but it makes the same point. It is possible that the similarity between the Hebrew word for son (*ben*) and stone (*eben*) explains why the parable and quote are joined. Whether the reference is to the cornerstone or capstone, the foundation or the crown, the meaning is that the stone essential to the building is rejected by the builders.

The phrase "This was the Lord's doing" continues the citation from Psalm 118:23. Originally the psalm referred to a surprising victory or the king's sudden rise to power. The surprising work of God in Jesus, especially the mystery of the Cross, elicits wonder and admiration on the part of Jesus' disciples. As such, this scriptural citation functions as a Christian creed; it is a statement of belief that everything that happened to Jesus, especially his passion and death, were part of the plan of God.

Many interpreters think that ending the parable with this scriptural quotation was the work of the early church; the parable was applied to Christ and understood to refer not only to his crucifixion but also to his resurrection, which is "wonderful" in the eyes of the believer. The use of this psalm by other New Testament authors suggests that it was a favorite for the early Christian community (see Acts 4:11; 1 Pet 2:7; also Rom 9:33; 1 Pet 2:6-8). Thus Mark is not the only one to see Psalm 118 as a scriptural basis for Jesus as the son of God and his rejection by Jewish leaders. Possibly Psalm 118 was included in an early Christian anthology of scriptural quotations known as "testimony books," which were used to explain certain elements of Christian faith such as the rejection and ultimately the death of Jesus, or to encourage nonbelievers to explore the Scriptures and understand that Jesus is the promised Messiah. From the beginning Christians searched the Scriptures (the Law, the Prophets, and the Writings known to us as the Old Testament) for answers to their questions and problems, especially regarding Jesus' manner of death and the inclusion of Gentiles into the church.

Again we see Mark's editorial hand in the reaction of the listeners: understanding at last! But without realizing it, now the crowds act to shield Jesus a little longer. The leaders seek to arrest him. Mark also reinforces the negative effect of parables on those who are "outside" and refuse to become followers of Jesus. Here Mark tells us "they left him and went away" (12:12). But the Jewish leaders do not cease in their efforts at trapping Jesus and turning the crowds against him (see 12:13; 14:1-2, 10-11, 43, 53-65; 15:1-15).

Parables of the Fig Tree (Mark 13:28-29) and the Doorkeeper (13:33-37)

Two short "parables" appear at the end of Jesus' last discourse in Jerusalem, just before his passion and death (see 13:28-37). Both are about watchfulness. Indeed, according to Mark, Jesus' last word before the Passion is a warning to his disciples, "Watch!" (13:37). The gospels are unanimous in recording the disciples' appalling inability to remember and heed this warning throughout the ordeal of Jesus' suffering and death. They fall asleep through fear and grief when Jesus is arrested. They flee from the Garden and are notoriously absent from the cross and burial. These lapses only reinforce the urgency and necessity of recalling Jesus' reminder to remain alert and to keep faith. Here is Mark's version of Jesus' final parables:

> [28]"Learn a lesson from the fig tree. When its branch becomes tender and sprouts leaves, you know that summer is near. [29]In the same way, when you see these things happening, know that he is near, at the gates. . . ."
>
> [33]"Be watchful! Be alert! You do not know when the time will come. [34]It is like a man traveling abroad. He leaves home and places his servants in charge, each with his own work, and orders the gatekeeper to be on the watch. [35]Watch, therefore; you do not know when the lord of the house is coming, whether in the evening, or a midnight, or at cockcrow, or in the morning. [36]May he not come suddenly and find you sleeping. [37]What I say to you, I say to all: 'Watch!'" (Mark 13:28-37)

The two parables complete Jesus' concluding remarks and the whole discourse of chapter 13. This chapter contains the so-called "eschatological discourse" in which Jesus relates the destruction of the Temple in Jerusalem to events of the end times. The discourse was prompted by the disciples' enthusiastic comments on the magnificence of the Temple (13:1). In response, Jesus notes ominously, "There will not be one stone left upon another"(13:2). The disciples, apparently alone with Jesus, press him by asking, "Tell us, when will this happen, and what sign will there be when all these things are about to come to an end?" (13:4).

The first of the two parables has to do with seeing the budding fig tree as a lesson illustrating the certainty of "these things" Jesus has been talking about. The second and final parable demands watchfulness of Jesus' disciples. In order to be worthy of their role as servants of the Lord Jesus, disciples must remain alert, awaiting Jesus' sure return. These parables belong together and complement each other. Unlike some of the other parables, there is no particular mystery about their meaning. Nevertheless a few comments are in order.

The Lesson of the Fig Tree (Mark 13:28-29)

Jesus uses the fig tree as a "parable," simply meaning "lesson" in this context, rather than a more complicated narrative. The lesson is realistic. Simply stated, appearance of leaves on a fig tree in the spring is an indication that summer is near. We instinctively notice the leaves sprouting and make preparations for summer. But there is also a symbolic meaning. Believers ought to be alert to the "signs" of the arrival of the Son of Man. Jesus has just spoken about apocalyptic events that will happen in advance of the end times (i.e., parousia). The events he described are catastrophic. Believers must interpret these events with hope rather than despair. They will remember Jesus' prediction, anticipate and prepare for the return of the Son of Man.

There are several indications in his gospel, and especially in the eschatological discourse, that Mark believed the parousia was imminent. In 13:30 Jesus says, "Amen, I say to you, this generation will not pass away until all these things have taken place." This verse echoes the sentiment of 9:1 when Jesus says, "Amen, I say to you, there are some standing here who will not taste death until they see that the kingdom of God has come in power." With his conviction about the near coming of the Son of Man, Mark encourages those who have become doubtful through fear or because of persecution. Mark explains the present suffering of believers as predicted and expected. We follow a crucified Messiah. If disciples encounter persecution and obstacles because of Jesus, they must realize these as evidence that "he is near;" indeed, he is "at the gates" (13:29).

Mark balances this reassurance of the sure and imminent parousia with a reminder that no one knows the day or the hour, "neither the angels in heaven, nor the Son, but only the Father" (13:32). Those who use this discourse of Jesus to instill fear and panic totally misinterpret its purpose. Jesus dispels the disciples' efforts to ascertain the exact time and in so doing urges constant vigilance. Yet believers long for the time of Jesus' return. In fact, one the earliest prayers of the Christian communities was a simple statement of faith and longing: *Marana tha*, which means, "Come Lord Jesus" (1 Cor 16:22; Rev 22:20; see also 1 Cor 15:23).

The Doorkeeper as Model Servant

Several of Jesus' parables use the image of master (*kyrios*) and servant (*doulos*). This image provides a link between the parable of Mark 12 of the wicked servants and Mark's concluding parables in chapter 13. Although our culture is unfamiliar with both the inequality and intimacy of the master-servant relationship, it belonged to the fabric of the society Jesus knew and he found it especially appropriate for describing the desired relationship he wanted to have with his followers. The earliest Christian writings indicate that the Greek word *kyrios* (Master or Lord) was one of the most common christological terms for Jesus.

In Jesus' day, servants included slaves as well as hired help.[19] Both were quite common in an economy that was labor-intensive. Servants as well as slaves were considered part of a household and as such enjoyed certain protections and even "rights." Practically speaking, assigned responsibilities defined servants and their value to the master. Additionally, masters and slaves shared a mutually dependent relationship. The economy demanded it.

The doorkeeper or watchman of our parable had a very important role. In the absence of elaborate locks or alarms, he was, literally, the "key" to the household. Whereas other parables and sayings of Jesus advocate performing certain works, the duty of the watchman was to "wait" and remain alert. This might be very challenging in the quiet of the night when everyone else was asleep. The watchman was on the alert for intruders and other threats. But his responsibility was all the more significant when it might be necessary to watch for a returning master in need of a welcome refuge at the end of a tiring and perhaps dangerous trip. The watchman would recognize the signals of the master's return and put in motion all the preparations for a fitting homecoming.

This parable presupposes a period when the master would be absent. That absence would be trying and tempting to the servants. A too literal reading of the parable might balk at the idea of the master (read God or Jesus) "going away," as was also the case in the parable of the wicked tenants in chapter 12. Yet from the human viewpoint, it sometimes seems as if God is absent. It would even seem that way to Jesus himself on the cross when he utters the words of Psalm 22:1, "My God, my God, why have you forsaken me?" (Mark 15:34). The parable "works" when we focus on the watchman. He does his job and fulfills his worth as a servant when he is alert and awake and waiting, absolutely certain that the master will return, though he has no idea when. The time of his arrival is not his concern. But everything of importance to the master is in the house which is in the watchman's charge. Jesus' discourse has discouraged the disciples from asking "When?" Jesus advocates the faithful, active watchfulness that proceeds from confidence in the master and in his relationship with his servant.

On the eve of the passion, as Jesus prepares for his own suffering and death, his solemn last words to his disciples take on a new urgency: "What I say to you, I say to all, 'Watch!'" At his anointing by the unnamed woman, Jesus warns, "You will not always have me" (14:7). At the Last Supper Jesus will tell his disciples, "All of you will have your faith shaken" (14:27). Peter, James, and John will be repeatedly invited to "watch and pray" with Jesus in the Garden (14:32-42). But only the women will "watch" as Jesus is crucified and see where he is laid in burial (15:40, 47). Jesus' own passion and the attendant suffering of his disciples are temptations to their faith. Undoubtedly the suffering of Jesus' disciples after the resurrection when they were scattered in disarray tempted them toward despair that God was with them. Faith in Jesus crucified might not have seemed an appropriate response to the threat that the Roman Empire represented to the small, apparently insignificant Christian movement. But Mark's Gospel reminds every generation that we are to be above all watchful, with faith in the master and confidence in his word that he will surely return.

Conclusion

It is remarkable that Jesus' preaching ministry begins and ends with parables. Although Mark has the fewest parables of the Synoptic writers, the strategic placement of parables in chapter 4 and in chapters 12 and 13 support Mark's comment that Jesus taught "with many such parables" (Mark 4:33) and "without parables he did not speak to them" (4:34). Mark adds that Jesus' parables were directed to his disciples' understanding. With his concluding parables Jesus seems especially concerned that his disciples not only understand but act on the parables' meaning.

CHAPTER THREE

Parables Matthew Shared with Mark

Introduction to Matthew

Often called the First Gospel and appearing as it does at the beginning of the New Testament, Matthew has always had pride of place for Christians. Indeed, Matthew contains some of the best-known passages in the Bible, like the Sermon on the Mount, including the Beatitudes and the version of the Lord's Prayer so familiar to Christians everywhere. The evangelist is sometimes mistakenly identified as the tax collector of the same name whose call to follow Jesus is recorded in Matthew 9:9 (see 10:3). The gospel itself gives evidence that its author was not an eyewitness but must have known the Gospel of Mark, which he copied, modified, and supplemented. Most commentators today propose a late first-century dating for Matthew, sometime between 85 and 90, possibly in Antioch, a stronghold of early Christianity where Peter was revered.

Matthew's Gospel is not a biography of Jesus nor is it merely a historical presentation of the facts of Jesus' life and ministry. Following the outline of Jesus' ministry proposed by Mark's Gospel, Matthew takes Jesus on a journey from Galilee to Jerusalem where he is crucified. In the course of this journey, Jesus instructs his disciples on the cost of following him. Jesus promises them that they will share the same fate as he himself faces at the hands of people who refuse to accept him as the Messiah or the message he brings. In addition to Mark's material, Matthew used a sayings source also known to Luke, identified by scholars as *Quelle* or simply "Q." It is possible that the material proper to Matthew alone also came from a preexisting source scholars have called "M." This material, unique to Matthew, could have come from the evangelist's own pen, guided by his knowledge of the tradition of Jesus and his own concerns about the church he was addressing.

The Situation of Matthew's Church

The destruction of the Temple by the Romans in A.D. 70 had disastrous effects not only on the Jews, but on the relationship between the Jews and the emerging community of disciples of Jesus who were known as Christians, and who called themselves the "church." By the time Matthew was written, these disciples were struggling with their identity since many fellow Jews were rejecting Jesus as the Messiah, whereas more and more Gentiles were becoming his followers. Although he was Jewish, in Matthew Jesus speaks of "their synagogues" (4:23; 9:35; 10:17; 12:9; 13:54), suggesting a rift between Jesus and his disciples on the one hand, and their fellow Jews who were influenced especially by their Pharisaic leaders to reject Jesus and his followers. Matthew is also the only gospel to use the term "church" (see 16:18 and twice in 18:17), an indication that by the author's time Christians were developing an identity that differentiated them from their fellow Jews.

Tensions between Jews and Christians were confusing and painful to both. Bereft of a common temple where Jews and those who followed Jesus could meet together, the separation that began over such issues as fasting and proper observance of the Sabbath became more pronounced. Synagogues had grown in prominence ever since the end of the Exile in Babylon, in the sixth century before Jesus. Especially in the century before Jesus, the great rabbis and their teachings shaped Jewish piety, liturgy, and observance more strictly along the lines of interpretation of the Torah. Leaders of Jewish groups such as the Pharisees, the Sadducees, and the Essenes formed the pluralistic Judaism of Jesus' day and influenced people's thinking with their debates.

By the time Matthew wrote his gospel, the Pharisees were the dominant Jewish leaders and teaching authorities who had survived the struggles with Rome of the preceding fifteen to twenty years. In Matthew's own day, Judaism was more monolithic than it had been when Jesus was preaching and teaching. Around the eighties, while Matthew was writing his gospel, the rabbis were debating which books were to be recognized as part of the canon of their Scriptures and what constituted keeping the Torah.

Matthew presents Jesus as the teacher of Israel, often in contrast and even in conflict with the leading Pharisaic teachers of the day. Jewish leaders are often portrayed in a negative light, even as "hypocrites" because of some of their religious practices. According to Matthew, Jesus teaches his disciples a way of holiness and of fulfilling the Law that was opposed to and distinct from the ways of the Pharisees and other religious leaders.

Themes of Matthew

All the gospels deal with issues related to christology (who is Jesus?) and discipleship (what does it mean to follow Jesus?), yet each gospel presents a unique portrait of Jesus and each has its own way of describing the disciples. Some of the following themes are emphasized in Matthew:

Jesus is the Messiah in Word and Deed: For Matthew Jesus is the Christ proclaiming the coming of the kingdom of heaven. Matthew takes much of the "secrecy" out of Mark's portrait of Jesus and uses exalted christological titles for Jesus in comparison to Mark. Jesus is the obedient Son of God in Matthew. Jesus is Emmanuel, God-with-us. Jesus has authority as Son of Man over the kingdom of God. As the Son of Man, Jesus will come to judge the world. The whole of the Scriptures is fulfilled in Jesus.

The deeds of Jesus illustrate that he is the Son of God, acting in God's name and performing mighty works. Jesus heals, confronting and dispelling evil. Matthew uses Jesus' teaching as commentary on his actions, clustering Jesus' sayings and organizing them into long speeches or sermons. Although the details of the structure of Matthew are debatable, almost all commentators identify in Matthew five major discourses. Those five discourses are: The Sermon on the Mount (Matt 5–7), The Mission Discourse (ch. 10), The Parable Discourse (ch. 13), The Discourse on the Church (ch. 18), and The Eschatological Discourse (chs. 24–25).

Prophecy and Fulfillment: Matthew demonstrates special familiarity with the Jewish Scriptures, showing on every occasion possible that the Scriptures are "fulfilled" in Jesus of Nazareth. Matthew cites Scripture to show that Jesus' words and deeds fulfilled "the Law and the Prophets" as the Scriptures were often called. More than the other Synoptics, Matthew explicitly quotes Scripture passages to support his claims that Jesus is the Messiah.

Righteousness: The Law and the Prophets consistently show the demands of true righteousness or justice, which means living according to the will of God. God alone is righteous. All people are sinners. God's law has established an order by which we can seek and know what is right. The Torah is God's "instruction" on righteousness. God is bound by the same law that is given to humans. The Law then, for Matthew, is not an objective or static reality, but a relationship, a covenant between God and people. Trust, confidence, and fidelity are all characteristic of God's relationship with people.

Church and Synagogue: The distinction and even the animosity between church and synagogue are more pronounced in Matthew than in the other Synoptic Gospels. The tension probably affected Matthew's emphasis on certain issues related to both church and synagogue such as judgment, true righteousness, leadership, and wisdom. So comprehensive is Matthew's presentation of these great themes that his gospel is sometimes called a "catechism" of the early church.

Jesus is the Authoritative Teacher: Matthew presents Jesus as the true teacher of the true Israel. There are false teachers and there is a pseudo-Israel. Opponents criticize Jesus, contending that he did not practice the Law, at least not as interpreted by the Pharisees, the teachers. For example, Jesus ate with sinners and he and his disciples did not purify themselves according to Jewish custom. They did not fast and they did not observe the Sabbath as the rabbis taught. According to Matthew, Jesus set up a dichotomy between his interpretation of the Law and that of the Pharisees, teaching, "You have heard it said . . . but *I* say . . ." (Matt 5:21, 27, 31, 33, 38, 43, emphasis added). Many believed that the rabbis had authority to teach what it meant to follow Torah. Matthew challenges his readers to identify which was the way of righteousness, the way of the Pharisees or the way of Jesus. In Matthew, Jesus admonishes his disciples that their righteousness must exceed the righteousness of the Scribes and Pharisees (see Matt 5:20).

Leadership: For Matthew, the scribes and especially the Pharisees are false leaders. Peter and the other apostles and disciples are the true leaders of the new Israel. Whereas Mark paints a bleak picture of discipleship failure, Matthew presents a more positive one. Matthew focuses on the church and the leadership required of those Jesus has chosen. Jesus' sermons present guidelines for his disciples to be used for decision-making, conflict resolution, reconciliation, and forgiveness. Church leaders are to be especially concerned for the "little ones" entrusted to their care and for those who stray. Peter's role as spokesperson for the disciples and head of the church is clearer in Matthew (9:8; 10:2, 40; 14:28-29; 15:15; 16:16-19; 17:24; 18:21; 19:27; 26:33). Even though Peter may deny Jesus, he will repent, weeping (26:37, 40, 58, 69, 73, 75). The disciples will be commissioned to make disciples of all nations, teaching them all that Jesus has commanded (28:16-20).

Judgment: Matthew might be considered the most apocalyptic of all the gospels. As the Son of Man, Jesus is the arbiter and judge, and that judgment is based on doing the will of God. Final judgment means the separation of good from evil, accompanied by much apocalyptic imagery about heaven or hell, outer darkness, fire, weeping and wailing, and the gnashing of teeth (13:42-43, 50; 22:13; 24:51; 25:30). Matthew's parables, in particular, underscore necessary decisions and the required actions that must characterize followers of Jesus.

The Parables in Matthew

Known for his organizational skills and clarity, Matthew balances the extraordinary deeds that reveal Jesus as the Messiah with long passages of clustered sayings of Jesus presented as sermons. So, for example, Matthew builds on the discourse of Mark 4 by adding more parables in a sermon that characterizes a "day of parables" (see Matthew 13). The term "parable," which occurs fifteen times in Matthew,[1] appears for the first time in Matthew 13. Here we find Matthew's version of the parable discourse he adapted and supplemented from Mark. Matthew pictures Jesus giving a major speech that functions as a turning point in the gospel, both for the people who listen to Jesus and for Jesus himself. To this speech Matthew adds the parable of the leaven he had from Q. He also supplements the speech with some parables unique to him: the parable of the wheat and the weeds, the treasure buried in the field, the pearl, the dragnet, and the scribe of the kingdom.

Matthew's parables manifest many of the same traits we find in the rest of the gospel. In particular, Matthew's parables often include a combination of action and dialogue, imaginative and reverential language, apocalyptic scenarios and allegory.[2] Many are dramatic parables where human decisions invite listeners and readers to identify and judge themselves. "Are you a faithful servant?" "What do you do with your talents as you await the return of the Master?" At times Matthew shows a love of extravagance or exaggeration. Mark's shrub (Mark 4:32) becomes a tree (Matt 13:32), the treasure and the pearl exceed all value (Matt 13:44-46); the debt of the servant is excessive (Matt 18:24), and the talents given to the servants equal wages from thirty, sixty and one hundred fifty years (Matt 25:15). Matthew also exhibits dramatically sharp contrasts and reversals. His parables contain more apocalyptic, allegorical, and symbolic elements than are found in either Mark or Luke.

Matthew's theological perspective further helps to shape his parables. Whereas Mark emphasizes the mighty works of Jesus, Matthew stresses Jesus' authoritative teaching: Jesus is the Messiah in deed *and* word. Matthew enlarges the two major Markan discourses of Jesus (see Mark 4 and 13). Matthew also adds a considerable number of parables, especially in chapters 13, 18, and 24–25.

Matthew's parables not only reflect conflicts with outsiders—for example, tensions between the early church and Jewish leaders—they are also used as warnings to the community. For example, the parable of the lost sheep becomes an exhortation to care for the straying little ones in the community (18:10). The unmerciful servant serves as a paradigm of the unlimited forgiveness that is to characterize community members, especially leaders (e.g., Peter in 18:21-22). Those to whom the vineyard is entrusted must produce fruit (21:34, 41; see 7:16-20). An invitation to the banquet and even entrance must not lead to pride and complacency (22:11-14). In Matthew the parables of Jesus become a summons to discipleship that is to exemplify the coming kingdom of God in the time between Jesus' resurrection and his return (28:16-20).

In this chapter on Matthew, we shall focus on the parables Matthew has in common with Mark. That is, we will study Matthew's parable chapter (13), based on Mark 4. Then we will see how Matthew adapts the parables found in Mark 12–13, namely the parable of the wicked servants, the fig tree, and the doorkeeper. We will reserve study of the remaining parables found in Matthew for our next chapter (4).

Matthew 13: The Chapter of Decision

Chapter 13 represents a turning point in Jesus' ministry. Until this point in the gospel, Jesus had addressed the crowds and his disciples almost indiscriminately, although throughout he pays special attention to his disciples. Now Jesus picks up the pace, almost provoking the leaders who had begun plotting against him (Matt 12:14). The parables presented here serve as a commentary on the rejection of Jesus by the Pharisees recounted in the preceding chapter. With the parable discourse of Matthew 13, Jesus will begin to describe the true Israel and distinguish it from pseudo-Israel. In the following chapters he will focus more and more on those who are listening to him and turn from those who are attempting to thwart his every move. For Matthew, one of the parables' aims is to help explain a painful reality for Jewish Christians: that is, that the majority of Jews did not accept Jesus as the Messiah.

By the time Matthew was writing, the leaders of the Jews were making it very difficult if not impossible for Jesus' followers to continue to worship in the synagogues. But Matthew consistently stresses that Jesus' disciples are heirs to the promises made to Israel. They see in the Scriptures a fulfillment of the promises that included them. Matthew speaks like a Jewish scribe, making Jewish arguments to illustrate for his readers that Jesus is a fulfillment of all their hopes. Although Matthew seems to indicate that many Jews have rejected Jesus, his teachings, and his followers, Jesus is nevertheless the Messiah the Jews longed for. The conflict Matthew envisions is an inner-Jewish struggle. Matthew does not think of the church apart from Israel but as the true Israel.

Matthew 13 is a discourse of narratives, consisting of eight parables, some accompanied by an allegorical explanation. (An allegory attributes symbolic meaning to some or all of the elements of the parable.) The subject of the discourse is the "kingdom of heaven," Matthew's unique way of referring to the "kingdom of God." Out of respect for his own Jewish heritage, Matthew does not use the name of God, which ought not be pronounced according to Jewish custom. Every parable of chapter 13 except for the first one about the sowings begins with the phrase "The kingdom of heaven is like . . ." (see 13:24, 32, 33, 44, 45, 47; see also v. 52 that speaks of the scribe instructed in the "kingdom of heaven"). This chapter represents the apex of the gospel, both structurally and regarding the kingdom. Jesus demands that his audience "decide" whether they will "hear" or not. They are asked to choose not only to listen to the parables, but to the Scriptures as well. And if they truly hear, they will become disciples and follow Jesus. They will obey and act according to the Gospel. They will come to understand, accept, and participate in the kingdom of heaven.

The Parable of the Sowings and Commentary (Matt 13:1-23)

Chapter 13 begins with the parable of the sowings (13:1-9). This is followed by sayings on the purpose of parables (13:10-15) and on the privilege of discipleship (13:16-17). Then Matthew offers his version of Jesus' explanation of the parable of the Sowings.[3]

The Parable of the Sowings (Matt 13:1-9)

The first parable of the gospel, with Matthew's introduction, reads as follows:

> [1]On that day, Jesus went out of the house and sat down by the sea. [2]Such large crowds gathered around him that he got into a boat and sat down, and the whole crowd stood along the shore. [3]And he spoke to them at length in parables, saying, "A sower went out to sow. [4]And as he sowed, some seed fell on the path, and birds came and ate it up. [5]Some fell on rocky ground, where it had little soil. It sprang up at once because the soil was not deep, [6]and when the sun rose it was scorched, and it withered for lack of roots. [7]Some seed fell among thorns, and the thorns grew up and choked it. [8]But some seed fell on rich soil, and produced fruit, a hundred or sixty or thirtyfold. [9]Whoever has ears ought to hear."

The Setting

Matthew introduces this speech with the phrase "on that day." This "day" does not refer to a twenty-four-hour time period so much as a "moment" of decision. Perhaps Matthew, who is steeped in Old Testament imagery, is alluding to the "Day" of the Lord, a day of judgment. From this "day" on, rejection of Jesus' message is done at personal peril. In Matthew, Jesus goes "outside the house," and proceeds down by the sea to teach. Jesus reenters the "house," which may stand for the church, in 13:36. Matthew alternates between the disciples and a more general crowd as Jesus' audience. Having addressed the crowds in 12:46, they are again indicated in 13:2. But then Jesus turns to his disciples (13:10-23). Next he speaks to "them," and finally he explains, apparently to his disciples, why he spoke to the crowds in parables (13:34-35).

Jesus assumes the posture of the teacher in the ancient world, sitting (13:1), as he did for the Sermon on the Mount (5:1-2), while a large crowd gathers around to hear him. In Matthew, the crowds are generally positive, at least until the time of the Passion. The crowds are "great," indicating that Jesus, like the sower of his parable, scattered the seed of his teaching widely. It is there for the people to accept or reject. But never far from Matthew's mind is an implied warning that their response has consequences.

In a rather awkward repetition, Matthew adds in 13:2 that Jesus "got into a boat and sat down" to teach from there. The second notice that Jesus was "sitting" reinforces his authoritative role as a teacher. The "boat" is a symbol later used of the church from which Jesus is pictured as teaching. So Jesus delivers this speech in parables from the boat while the "great crowds" stand on the shore to listen. The scene is especially well suited to one of the last parables of this chapter, that of the net, which catches "fish of every kind" in 13:47-49.

A final note of Matthew's introduction will be echoed at the end of Jesus' speech. Matthew says that Jesus "spoke . . . at length in parables" (13:3a). When he is finally finished speaking, Matthew concludes with these words: "When Jesus finished these parables, he went away from there" (13:53).[4] After chapter 13, Jesus will "go away from" his own hometown where he was rejected (13:54-58), and concentrate the preaching in the rest of his gospel on those who choose to hear and accept his message. Matthew portrays the choice for or against Jesus as becoming more pressing and urgent. Matthew will shift his emphasis from Jesus' preaching to the "great crowds," to Jesus' focus on the disciples who, as members of Jesus' true family (see 12:46-50), are those who both listen to Jesus' words and do what he commands them.

The Sowings and the Amazing Yield

Jesus paints a parable-picture his Galilean listeners can easily envision. The first figure mentioned is that of the sower by which many identify this parable: "A sower went out to sow." Jesus describes a generous or careless farmer who randomly tosses out the seed and lets it fall on any kind of soil, some along the pathways, or among the rocks and even among the thorny weeds. There the seed never stands a chance. The cost and effort that the farmer expended appear to be ill-advised; three times out of four, there will be little return. There are three unyielding types of soil and only one kind of soil with potential to produce good results. The apparently strange and wasteful actions of the sower are part of the "unusual" or surprising dimensions of the story that make this a good parable. The sower is a figure who stands for God. God's ways are not our ways, as Isaiah 55:8 says. Yet it can also be observed, that "Once the seed is sown, it is on its own."[5]

The gist of Jesus' teaching appears at first to be the receptivity of the different soils. The reference to "good soil" implies there is no defect in the seeds. Yet Jesus dwells not so much on the four kinds of soil that receive the seed or word, but on the extravagant growth of the seed that falls on good soil in contrast to the failures of the seed that fell on the path, the rocky ground with its shallow soil, or among the thorny weeds where it was choked.

Matthew hardly deviates from Mark in the telling of the parable itself, although there are a few small changes (compare Matt 13:3-9 with Mark 4:3-9). Mark forms an inclusion by beginning with the command to "Hear this" (Mark 4:3) and ending with "Whoever has ears to hear ought to hear" (Mark 4:9). Matthew omits Mark's initial command to "Listen," instead putting more emphasis on what Jesus the teacher is *saying* (Matt 13:3). Although not reflected in the NAB translation, Matthew uses the plural, "seeds," whereas Mark had used the singular, "seed." In 13:7, Matthew omits Mark's assertion that the seeds choked by thorns "produced no grain" (Mark 4:7). And finally Matthew inverts Mark's ascending order of the yield to emphasize its amazing disproportion of the seeds to their growth. Even the last and least amount shows the extravagant nature of the harvest from the receptive soil.

Matthew follows Mark in concluding with a general invitation and warning, "Whoever has ears ought to hear!" This formula appeared also in Matthew 11:15, in reference to those willing to accept the Baptist as Elijah. With this phrase, Jesus calls attention to a significant but puzzling, somewhat obscure teaching. Matthew is keenly aware that the response to the word is mixed. But most importantly, the response of "hearing" and acting have amazing, utterly unpredictable results, abundant beyond all imagining.

The Purpose of Parables and Blessing on Those Who Hear (Matt 13:10-17)

Matthew's most extensive editorial work appears in the section about the reason for Jesus' speaking in parables (13:10-17). The disciples question Jesus and receive a blessing as part of his response. As in Mark, the disciples come to Jesus for an explanation. But in Matthew they ask why he speaks to the crowds in parables, whereas Mark suggests that the disciples themselves understand neither why he speaks in parables nor this parable in particular (see Mark 4:10 and 13). Here's what Matthew says following his first parable:

> [10]The disciples approached him and said, "Why do you speak to them in parables?" [11]He said to them in reply, "Because knowledge of the mysteries of the kingdom of heaven has been granted to you, but to them it has not been granted. [12]To anyone who has, more will be given and he will grow rich; from anyone who has not, even what he has will be taken away. [13]This is why I speak to them in parables, because 'they look but do not see and hear but do not listen or understand.'" [14]Isaiah's prophecy is fulfilled in them, which says:
>
> > 'You shall indeed hear but not understand,
> >   you shall indeed look but never see.

¹⁵Gross is the heart of this people,
    they shall hardly hear with their ears,
        they have closed their eyes,
        lest they see with their eyes
    and hear with their ears
and understand with their heart and be converted
    and I heal them.'

¹⁶But blessed are your eyes because they see, and your ears because they hear. ¹⁷Amen, I say to you, many prophets and righteous people longed to see what you see but did not see it, and to hear what you hear but did not hear it."

The Privilege of Discipleship

Jesus' explanation appears as a sidebar with the disciples who approach him and ask why he speaks "to *them*" in parables. The setting for this question is simplified in comparison with Mark who alternates between Jesus speaking to the crowds, his being alone, his being by the sea, and being inside.

Matthew is deliberate in using the term "approach," usually depicting the disciples or others who come to Jesus with their questions or requests. The word "approach" appears three times in this chapter: twice of the disciples asking a question of their teacher (13:10, 36) and once in the course of the parable of the Weeds and the Wheat, pertaining to the slaves who approach their master (13:27) wondering what to do about the weeds. Throughout Matthew's Gospel various people "approach" Jesus, usually with an attitude of respect and reverence as appropriate to his authority as a teacher. Oftentimes the verb "approach" is accompanied by a reverential gesture toward Jesus. Jesus only rarely "approaches" others. One notable exception occurs after his transfiguration when Jesus "approaches" his disciples, touches them as if to reassure them, and says, "Rise, and do not be afraid" (17:7).

Matthew's Use of a Saying from Mark

Matthew inserted a saying in 13:12 found in Mark 4:25 as a way to accentuate the contrast between hearing and not hearing. Mark was warning Christians not to be slack about witnessing to what they have seen and heard. Matthew turns Mark's warning into a blessing. In Matthew's version of the saying, "rich" is used in a spiritual sense: "To anyone who has, more will be given and he will grow rich; from anyone who has not, even what he has will be taken away." Inserted here, Matthew heightens the sense of privilege for those who hear and the sense of loss for those who do not. Matthew repeats this same saying again in a parable, in Matthew 25:29. There it serves as a warning to those who would hide their "talents," that they cannot take their gifts for granted or they will lose them. This is the general sense in which the saying appears in the parallels of Mark 4:25 and Luke 8:18.

Matthew's explanation in 13:13 of why Jesus speaks to the crowds in parables (that is, "*because* they look and do not see, hear but do not listen and understand") is a much easier and clearer reading than Mark's. Mark emphasized the *mystery* of the kingdom of God, saying that Jesus speaks in parables "*in order that*" people would not see or hear or understand. The parables in Mark remain a riddle, in this case seeming to suggest predestination. Matthew, however, stresses the hardening motif. He says that, for the crowds and those outside the circle of discipleship, the parables remain riddles they do not understand because they do not go beyond a superficial "seeing and hearing" to real insight, understanding, and most importantly for Matthew, obedience. Jesus emphasizes "doing the will of the heavenly Father." Then Jesus immediately blesses the disciples themselves for seeing and hearing, understanding and obeying. They are thus depicted as converted and healed, just like the Scriptures promised they would be.

Matthew Quotes the Scriptures

Matthew 13:14-15 actually quotes Isaiah 6:9-10, a reference only implied in Mark 4:12. This is but one example of how Matthew stresses, at every point possible, that Jesus is a fulfillment of Scripture in what he says and does. Matthew simplified the mystery of this opening parable by omitting the last part of Mark 4:12 that says, "that they may not be converted and be forgiven." The disciples have been given to know the secrets; the others have not. By using the plural "secrets" (instead of the singular, as Mark did), Matthew refers to the teaching of Jesus. Similarly, the connection Mark makes between the prophecy and those who do not repent and receive forgiveness is broken by Matthew.[6] Listeners are responsible for their reaction to Jesus, for accepting or rejecting him. Matthew attributes responsibility to those who do not "see" and "hear." At the same time, Matthew omits the puzzling idea that Jesus deliberately taught in a confusing way.

Matthew and Mark both divided Jesus' audience into two groups—insiders and outsiders. Yet it can be said that Matthew focuses more and more, from chapter 13 until the end of his gospel, on the insiders, the disciples. It is the disciples who approached Jesus with their question

(v. 10) and his reply said that not only had they been granted the secrets of the kingdom of heaven (v. 11), but that more would be given them and they would grow spiritually rich (13:10-12). The scriptural quotation implied that many would *not* see or hear or understand or be healed. But Matthew dwells on the positive, on those who do see and do hear, turning the wording of Mark 4:25 into a blessing.

Matthew Adds a Blessing from Q

Matthew further embellishes his explanation of why Jesus speaks in parables by adding a blessing available to him from Q.[7] The disciples who had approached Jesus with a question receive a blessing as their answer. Thus Matthew idealizes the image of the disciples as the insiders who hear the word and understand its meaning for transforming their lives (see 13:23).

This is not the only context in which the disciples are blessed according to Matthew. The Beatitudes enumerate the blessings on those who listen to Jesus and do the will of God (5:3-12). Matthew has Jesus bless Peter after his confession that Jesus is the Messiah, the Son of God, adding that this was revealed to Peter, not by flesh and blood, but by "my heavenly Father" (16:17). Receiving a revelation and acting in obedience to it are indeed the greatest "blessings" for Matthew; they sum up the meaning of discipleship. This blessing on the disciples' "eyes and ears" (13:16-17) is the reverse of the warning implied in the use of Isaiah 6:9-10 for those who refuse to see and to hear. The blessing further illustrates the fulfillment of the Scriptures not only through Jesus himself but through his disciples.

Explanation of the Parable of the Sowings (Matt 13:18-23)

The interpretation of the parable in Matthew 13:18-23 follows Mark very closely with one notable exception: Matthew postpones Jesus' question about whether his listeners understand these things until near the conclusion of the discourse (13:51). Matthew also stresses that "understanding" must include action. Matthew has Jesus explain the parable of the Sowings in the following way:

> [18]"Hear then the parable of the sower. [19]The seed sown on the path is the one who hears the word of the kingdom without understanding it, and the evil one comes and steals away what is sown in his heart. [20]The seed sown on rocky ground is the one who hears the word and receives it at once with joy. [21]But he has no root and lasts only for a

time. When some tribulation or persecution comes because of the word, he immediately falls away. ²²The seed sown among thorns is the one who hears the word, but then worldly anxiety and the lure of riches choke the word and it bears no fruit. ²³But the seed sown on rich soil is the one who hears the word and understands it, who indeed bears fruit and yields a hundred or sixty or thirtyfold."

Matthew's interpretation of the parable begins with a renewed challenge to "hear" the parable (see 13:9). The classic title of the parable, often called the "parable of the sower," may come from verse 18; yet the parable itself does not dwell on the sower but on the soil that receives the seed. Matthew emphasizes "understanding" (see vv. 19, 23) more than Mark, with the implication that this also means integrating the message and acting on it. Thus, in verse 19 Matthew distinguishes between hearing and understanding. Without the latter, the evil one will snatch away what was sown. And in the concluding verse 23, Matthew drives home the same point. The good soil "hears the word and understands it." Such a reception will yield an abundant harvest.

Like Mark, Matthew supplies some concrete reasons for the hardness of heart of the outsiders: the evil one's activity, personal shallowness and worldly concerns, and the desire for wealth. Finally Matthew inverts Mark's escalating order of the resulting harvest. It is not too much to expect a hundredfold, though even the lesser amounts of sixty or thirty-fold would still be extravagant.

Summary

Matthew follows Mark in giving a dramatic, deliberate beginning to Jesus' ministry in parables. This major speech is inaugurated with the example of the prodigious sowing of seed that falls on all kinds of soil. Only the receptive soil produces. But the yield is abundant and completely disproportionate to its inauspicious start. This way of speaking and this particular example of a parable is an attention-getter. Jesus will go on to add several other parables and parabolic examples, meant to entice his audience to come closer to him and to act on a positive understanding of his word.

Other Parables of Matthew 13

Jesus' parable of the sowings is followed by a series of short sayings in parables that stress other aspects of Jesus' teaching on the kingdom of heaven. These parables can be paired based on the lessons and values they impart. For example, the parables about the wheat and the weeds in 13:24-30 and the one about the dragnet in 13:47-50 have to do with how insiders are to respond given the mixed reception to the word of the kingdom. Two pair of parables complete the sermon. All four of these parables concern the kingdom of heaven, its nature, and how one should respond to it. The first pair in 13:31-33, the parable of the mustard seed and of the leaven, illustrates the amazing contrast between the small beginnings and the final result. The second pair in 13:44-46, the treasure in the field and the pearl of great price, focuses on the willingness of the disciples to sacrifice everything for the surpassing value of the kingdom.

Weeds and Wheat (Matt 13:24-30)

[24]He proposed another parable to them. "The kingdom of heaven may be likened to a man who sowed good seed in his field. [25]While everyone was asleep his enemy came and sowed weeds all through the wheat, and then went off. [26]When the crop grew and bore fruit, the weeds appeared as well. [27]The slaves of the householder came to him and said, 'Master, did you not sow good seed in your field? Where have the weeds come from?' [28]He answered, 'An enemy has done this.' His slaves said to him "Do you want us to go and pull them up?' [29]He replied, 'No, if you pull up the weeds you might uproot the wheat along with them. [30]Let them grow together until harvest; then at harvest time I will say to the harvesters, "First collect the weeds and tie them in bundles for burning; but gather the wheat into my barn."'"

This parable has no real parallel in the other gospels, although it is possibly a rewriting of Mark 4:26-29, the parable of the seed growing secretly. In this case, Matthew has not only updated Mark's parable to suit the needs of his community, but he has provided it with an elaborate, allegorical interpretation (vv. 36-43) probably inspired by what Mark did with the parable of the sowings. It may be called a "kingdom parable," the first one in Matthew that is identified explicitly so (see v. 19).

The parable is about the "good seed" that was sown in a field. Afterwards, while the landowner and his household slept, an "enemy" came and sowed weeds among the wheat. Later the slaves working in the fields are scandalized to find the weeds. The householder orders his slaves to let both grow together until the harvest. This is the crucial part of the answer, advocating patience and tolerance until the final sorting. The mention of "gathering" four times (vv. 28, 29, and twice in 30) suggests that the parable is concerned with the believing community that "gathers" around to hear and follow Jesus.

Explanation of the Parable of the Weeds and the Wheat (Matt 13:36-43)

> [36]Then, dismissing the crowds, he went into the house. His disciples approached him and said, "Explain to us the parable of the weeds in the field." [37]He said in reply, "He who sows good seed is the Son of Man, [38]the field is the world, the good seed the children of the kingdom. The weeds are the children of the evil one, [39]and the enemy who sows them is the devil. The harvest is the end of the age, and the harvesters are angels. [40]Just as weeds are collected and burned [up] with fire, so will it be at the end of the age. [41]The Son of Man will send his angels, and they will collect out of his kingdom all who cause others to sin and all evildoers. [42]They will throw them into the fiery furnace, where there will be wailing and grinding of teeth. [43]Then the righteous will shine like the sun in the kingdom of their Father. Whoever has ears ought to hear."

The allegorical explanation of the parable of the weeds and the wheat is given to the disciples who request it, after Jesus tells a few more parables and then "dismisses the crowds." Jesus goes into the "house," a symbol of the church. Inside, he gives an explanation of the parable to his disciples. This explanation serves as both encouragement to them and a warning against complacency.

With this explanation Matthew moves to a new level of concern. Those who accept the proclamation of the gospel (the seed that is sown) become "children of the kingdom." But they live among the "children of the evil one."[8] In an allegory, different elements of a parable are given specific meanings. Matthew, like Mark, assigned such an interpretation to the parable of the sowings. He follows suit in giving a similar interpretation to this parable found only here. In his allegorical interpretation (vv. 37-39), Matthew gives eschatological equivalents to the elements in the parable. The elements are simply listed and assigned a meaning: the sower is the Son of Man, the field is the world, the good seed children of the kingdom, the weeds the children of the evil one, who is personified (see 5:37; 6:13; 13:19) and named the "enemy" and "the devil" in the following verse. The harvest is the end of the age, when judgment comes. The harvesters are the angels.

In the second part of the explanation (vv. 40-43) Matthew dramatically portrays the Last Judgment, including the separation it entails of the "evildoers" (literally, "those performing lawlessness") from the "just" (or "righteous" in many translations). The kingdom belongs to the Son of Man who has authority over the angels. He will bring the kingdom to its fullness at the "close of the age" (see vv. 39-40). The primary sin of the evildoers is that they "cause others to sin" (13:41; see 18:6-7), a major concern for Matthew. For this they will be thrown into the "fiery furnace, where there will be wailing and grinding of teeth." Matthew applies the apocalyptic vision of hell described as extreme distress and unhappiness (see 25:41). The phrase "wailing and grinding of teeth" becomes almost a cliché in Matthew (8:12; 13:50; 24:51; 25:30; the phrase appears only once in Luke 13:28).

The concluding phrase describes what will happen to the just ones. Matthew's expression echoes Daniel 12:3 but with some important changes. It is the "just" rather than the wise who will shine; the place of their shining is the kingdom. The details should not obscure the main point of the parable: the kingdom is a mixed body of saints and sinners on earth, until the final sifting by God's agents. Therefore tolerance and forbearance are necessary. No one should usurp divine judgment. More-over, the just must manifest themselves as those who produce the harvest. They faithfully expect the coming of the Son of Man in judgment. They avoid causing scandals. They shine as a light before others, giving good example and leading others in the kingdom.

With this parable of the weeds and the wheat, Matthew urges preparation for judgment and protects the church from charges of hypocrisy. An apparent problem is that Jesus' demand for patience might be construed as passive indifference, since there is nothing that can be done about evil. But Jesus' listeners understood that weeds left unchecked can choke the wheat; certainly the weeds need to be controlled. But they cannot be eliminated. And we cannot presume to be the "wheat" without considering the time of the approaching harvest. Then whether we are wheat or weeds will be manifest.

The Parable of the Dragnet (Matt 13:47-50)

47"Again, the kingdom of heaven is like a net thrown into the sea, which collects fish of every kind. 48When it is full they haul it ashore and sit down to put what is good into buckets. What is bad they throw away. 49Thus it will be at the end of the age. The angels will go out and separate the wicked from the righteous 50and throw them into the fiery furnace, where there will be wailing and grinding of teeth."

The parable of the dragnet (vv. 47-50) is particularly suitable to the setting by the sea. It makes one of the same points as that of the weeds and wheat: the kingdom is a mixed body. Patience is necessary, and we must leave the sifting, the separation, and the judgment to God.

Parables of the Mustard Seed and the Leaven (Matt 13:31-33)

> [31]He proposed another parable to them. "The kingdom of heaven is like a mustard seed that a person took and sowed in a field. [32]It is the smallest of all the seeds, yet when full-grown it is the largest of plants. It becomes a large bush, and the 'birds of the sky come and dwell in its branches.'" [33]He spoke to them another parable. "The kingdom of heaven is like yeast that a woman took and mixed with three measures of wheat flour until the whole batch was leavened."

The parables of the mustard seed and the leaven form a pair in both Matthew (13:31-33) and Luke (13:18-21).[9] The pairing by two evangelists reflects the evenhandedness of Jesus in word as well as deed. These parables, one about an experience familiar to men and the other very familiar to women, both portray the extraordinary results that are produced from inauspicious beginnings. That is the way it is also with "the kingdom of heaven" (vv. 31, 33).

The mustard seed might not literally be the "smallest of seeds," nor become the "greatest of garden plants." Matthew has a tendency toward hyperbole and exaggeration. But the point is clear that the growth is mysterious and wonderful and due to God's power, not human power. Matthew concludes this short parable with an allusion to several Old Testament passages, as he is wont to do (compare v. 32 with Ps 104:12; Dan 4:9, 12, 18, 21, 22; Ezek 17:22-24; 31:2-9). The picture of the "birds of the air" nesting in the branches of the mustard "tree" suggests the universal, all-embracing hospitality of the kingdom. There also may be irony in this nesting image if Matthew was thinking of the inclusion of the Gentiles, since birds do not usually dwell in the mustard shrub.

Then Jesus "spoke to them another parable," saying that "the kingdom of heaven is like yeast that a woman took and mixed with three measures of wheat flour until the whole batch was leavened" (13:33). It was the privilege of the chief woman of the household to knead the bread for the entire family and staff. The dough rises as a result of the catalytic effect of a small amount of leaven. This is a familiar domestic experience. Three measures represent an extraordinarily large amount of flour. The image contrasts the small amount of yeast required to leaven such an enormous batch of dough.

The woman "hid" the leaven in the flour just as the farmer "plowed" the mustard seed into the soil. Both images speak of something mysterious yet deliberate. In every other instance where leaven appears in the Scriptures it has the sense of corruption. This imagery was loaded with meaning from the experience of the Exodus when the Israelites were instructed to be ready to leave Egypt. Their hurried departure meant there was no time to wait for their bread to rise. The tradition of eating unleavened bread is rooted in this instruction and celebrated in the Passover liturgy. Similarly, attributing a negative sense to "leaven," St. Paul warns against the influence great sin can have on the community, saying "a little yeast leavens all the dough" (1 Cor 5:6; see also Gal 5:9).

This pair of parables, the mustard seed and the yeast, shows the contrast between the small beginnings and great results. It also serves to make rejection of Jesus' message, including the idea that the kingdom is already present, all the more mysterious. Matthew's version tries to explain the rejection of Jesus and his teaching. Meanwhile, Matthew advocates Christian perseverance in faith and tolerance of others.

Jesus' Use of Parables (Matt 13:34-35; See Mark 4:33-34)

Matthew has fashioned a long speech, combining Jesus' parables and noting that Jesus addressed them to the crowds on this long "day" of parables (Matt 13:1, 53). Matthew inserts an editorial comment in the midst of Jesus' sermon in parables. In 13:34 he says, "All these things Jesus spoke to the crowds in parables. He spoke to them only in parables." This verse is almost poetic in its carefully balanced structure of antithetical parallelism. Matthew omits Jesus' need to explain everything to his disciples because they generally understand his teaching (contrast v. 36 with vv. 51, 52).

Matthew remarks that Jesus' mode of speaking in parables is in accord with and also a fulfillment of the Scriptures. In 13:35 Matthew uses his familiar prophecy-fulfillment formula: "(in order) to fulfill what had been said through the prophet." This time the fulfillment citation, from Psalm 78:2, explains why Jesus, the Son of David, spoke in parables. The first line follows the LXX exactly: "I will open my mouth in story (*mashal*)." But the second, "I will utter what has been hidden since the foundation," is an independent reworking or paraphrase that returns to the idea of the mysteriousness of the kingdom alluded to in Matthew 13:10-17. For Matthew, Jesus uses parables to speak to the crowds, and their miscomprehension is in accord with God's will as reflected in the Scriptures, Matthew asserts. The unit of 13:34-35 serves as a buffer to break the series of parables and invites the hearer to reflect on what has been heard so far. Listeners are faced with the choice to become Jesus' disciples, who will eventually "understand" and act on the parables, or remain among the crowds for whom Jesus' teaching continues to be perceived as riddles.

The "Children of Light" and "Children of the Darkness"

This group of parables (the mustard seed, the leaven, and the weeds and wheat) reflects the contrast found also in Jewish apocalyptic writings between the "children of light" and "children of darkness." Both groups act in divergent ways until the final end. The ancient Jewish community at Qumran provides an example of an apocalyptic group that advocated a kind of patience, but only until such time as God would wreak vengeance and punishment on evildoers and finally vindicate the just. Matthew shares the overall view with such Jewish apocalyptic thought that foresaw a time when God would punish the wicked so that there would be "weeping and gnashing of teeth" in darkness and torment for those "outside" the community of the righteous.

The Concluding Parables (Matt 13:44-49)

The sermon concludes with four short "parables" peculiar to Matthew: the treasure, the pearl, and the dragnet and the scribe.[10] As already noted, the dragnet parable holds a message similar to the weeds and the wheat. The parable that involves the scribe of the kingdom will help explain how the disciples understand the parables.

> [44]"The kingdom of heaven is like a treasure buried in a field, which a person finds and hides again, and out of joy goes and sells all that he has and buys that field. [45]Again, the kingdom of heaven is like a merchant searching for fine pearls. [46]When he finds a pearl of great price, he goes and sells all that he has and buys it. [47]Again, the kingdom of heaven is like a net thrown into the sea, which collects fish of every kind. [48]When it is full they haul it ashore and sit down to put what is good into buckets. What is bad they throw away. [49]Thus it will be at the end of the age. The angels will go out and separate the wicked from the righteous . . ."

The images of the treasure and the pearl, both representing priceless value, form a pair. Both images also symbolize the required priorities of those willing to exchange everything to acquire the treasure or a single jewel. The note of "joy" must not be overlooked: the kingdom is such a priceless treasure that a wise person would gladly give all for the opportunity to seize it. It is the chance of a lifetime, demanding courage and resolve, but it is clearly worth the sacrifice. Half measures will not do for the kingdom of God.

The dragnet is the aquatic equivalent to the agricultural image of the harvest; both represent the last judgment that will finally separate the bad from the good. The mixture of the two is temporary. Ultimately what is bad will be destroyed. This, like so many of Matthew's parables, serves as a warning that the time of tolerance is limited. Angels, stock characters of apocalyptic scenarios so important for Matthew, are ready to carry out God's judgment and, "at the end of the age" (see 13:40; 24:3; 28:20), "throw away" what is bad. Only the righteousness will remain.

Treasures Old and New (Matt 13:52)

Finally Jesus asks, "Do you understand?" and his listeners answer, "Yes." Jesus is still addressing his disciples, the crowds having been dismissed (13:36). Matthew consistently credits Jesus' disciples with at least some understanding, in contrast to Mark, who repeatedly comments that they have no comprehension and, implying also, no faith. Here's how Matthew concludes Jesus' sermon in parables:

> [51]"Do you understand all these things?" They answered, "Yes." [52]And he replied, "Then every scribe who has been instructed in the kingdom of heaven is like the head of a household who brings from his storeroom both the new and the old." [53]When Jesus finished these parables, he went away from there.

Matthew has postponed Jesus' question to his disciples about whether they understand until the end of the day of parables. Matthew's question is also open-ended, without the negative connotation Mark ascribes to it when Jesus says, "Do you not understand this parable?" (Mark 4:13). In Mark it is a rhetorical question that goes unanswered; in Matthew the disciples respond that indeed they do understand.

The final short "parable" in Matthew 13:52 conjures up the image of a scribe who has become learned in the kingdom of heaven. This verse is important from several points of view. First, in its immediate context it is a kind of parable that concludes the sermon of seven other parables. It is a parable about making parables, a "meta-parable"[11] that invites the reader/hearer/disciple to enter the parabolic process through creating new parables to add to the ones just given.

Scholars debate the meaning of the "new and old" in this saying. Many think the "old" is the Old Testament, the new is Jesus' teaching about the kingdom. It is also possible that the old includes both the Scriptures and Jesus' preaching, while the new is what lies ahead, the crucifixion, resurrection, and especially the spread of the church under the guidance of the Spirit. In any case, it is good to remember that for Matthew the "new" is not novel but a fulfillment of the "old" (Matt 5:17-19). He does not envision a change or innovation in moral law, but he does practice and encourage storytelling to make the law appealing and understandable. Matthew 13:52 also suggests the existence and activity of Christian scribes in Matthew's church (see also 23:34).[12] The evangelist might have even added this verse to lend his own authority as well as the authority of the works of Paul and Mark who preceded him. All these earliest Christian writers were bringing out "old and new" from the inventory of the Law, the Prophets, Jesus, and his disciples.

Jesus' Own Reject Him

The day of parables is followed by a stark and astounding comment by the evangelist: "When Jesus finished these parables, he went away from there" (13:53). Matthew adds: "He came to his native place and taught the people in their synagogue. They were astonished and said, 'Where did this man get such wisdom and mighty deeds?' . . . And they took offense at him . . . And he did not work many mighty deeds there because of their lack of faith" (Matt 13:54, 57, 58). Thus Matthew juxtaposes the rejection of Jesus by people of his native town with the positive response from his disciples who continue to follow him and express their willingness to hear and understand. As in Mark, the parables become vehicles for defining who continues with him and who will reject him. From now on Matthew will focus more and more on the disciples who listen and try to act on Jesus' words. His enemies and opponents will become increasingly resistant and militant in their rejection. The day of parables becomes the day of separation of disciples from the Jewish leaders who oppose Jesus and will conspire to destroy him.

Matthew's source, Mark, resumes Jesus' teaching in parables only when Jesus has finally arrived in Jerusalem, near the end of the gospel narrative, with the parable of the wicked tenants (see Mark 12:1-12). While Matthew presents Jesus' parables as a more continuous way of teaching, he does eventually take up the parables Mark places near the end of his gospel. For both Matthew and Mark, parables express Jesus' last confrontations with the leaders of the people before he is arrested and put to death. So Matthew, like Mark, pictures Jesus in Jerusalem speaking the parable of the tenants (Matt 21:33-46) and the "lesson" of the fig tree (24:32-35) as Jesus prepares to undergo his passion and death.

The Parable of the Tenants (Matt 21:33-46)

This parable appears in all three Synoptic Gospels. We will focus on the changes Matthew makes to his source, Mark. Matthew stresses the repeated nature of the rejection and persecution of the servants culminating in the execution of the landowner's son. Matthew also heightens the eschatological dimension of this rejection and the judgmental nature of the parable itself.[13] The owner of the vineyard will come. What does the hearer, as a reasonable person, expect he will do to the tenants? The religious leaders confronted in the gospel judge themselves. That is what the parable's hearers are supposed to do. The "kingdom of God" is at stake and it will be taken away from "you" and entrusted to others who will produce its fruits. Readers cannot miss the strong warning and the sense of urgency in Matthew's version of this parable.

The dangerous confrontational pace picks up in the parable of the wicked tenants. Again Jesus presents a case with a series of three examples of growing hostility between a powerful landowner and his intransigent tenants. Adapting Mark 12:1-12, here is how Matthew 21:33-46, presents this parable:

> [33]"Hear another parable. There was a landowner who planted a vineyard, put a hedge around it, dug a wine press in it, and built a tower. Then he leased it to tenants and went on a journey. [34]When vintage time drew near, he sent his servants to the tenants to obtain his produce. [35]But the tenants seized the servants and one they beat, another they killed, and a third they stoned. [36]Again he sent other servants, more numerous than the first ones, but they treated them in the same way. [37]Finally he sent his son to them, thinking, 'They will respect my son.' [38]But when the tenants saw the son, they said to one another, 'This is the heir. Come, let us kill him and acquire his inheritance.' [39]They seized him, threw him out of the vineyard, and killed him. [40]What will the owner of the vineyard do to those tenants when he comes? [41]They answered him, 'He will put those wretched men to a wretched death and lease his vineyard to other tenants who will give him the produce at the proper times.' [42]Jesus said to them, 'Did you never read the scriptures:
>
>> 'The stone that the builders rejected
>>   has become the cornerstone;
>> by the Lord has this been done
>>   and it is wonderful in our eyes?'
>
> [43]Therefore I say to you, the kingdom of God will be taken away from you and given to a people that will produce its fruit. [[44]The one who falls on this stone will be dashed to pieces; and it will crush anyone on whom it falls.]" [45]When the chief priests and the Pharisees heard his parables, they knew that he was speaking about them. [46]And

although they were attempting to arrest him, they feared the crowds,
for they regarded him as a prophet.

Matthew, following Mark, opens the parable by describing the vine-yard owner's meticulous care in the construction and maintenance of the property. The owner reflects God's care of Israel as described by Isaiah 5:1-7. Jewish hearers would have immediately recognized Isaiah as the inspiration for Jesus' words.

God is the vineyard owner. The story is allegorical, but this time Matthew does not supply the meaning of the elements. And so the sig-nificance of the vineyard and even of the tenants is left for hearers to decipher. It could appear that the vineyard represents Israel because of the many echoes of Isaiah 5:2. In this case, it also follows that the tenants are the religious leaders, such as the "chief priest and elders of the people" (see Matt 21:23) who had challenged Jesus' authority. Matthew also mentions "the Pharisees" who, with the "chief priests," perceive that this parable was meant for them (21:45).

But the vineyard, which according to verse 41 is "given to others," is in verse 43 identified with the "kingdom of God." Further, Matthew says not that God will remove Israel's leadership and provide it with more faithful leaders. Rather, "the kingdom of God" will be taken "from you" and given to a nation (*ethnos*) or people that will produce the fruits of the kingdom. The "you" addressed consists not only of the opponents mentioned in the context but all who follow their leadership and example in rejecting John and Jesus and their message. The "nation" to whom the kingdom will be transferred is the community formed by the disciples of Jesus who are faithful to his word and who continue to seek and do the will of the heavenly Father.

In the parable, the servants or agents represent the prophets of Israel. In Mark's version, the owner sent a single servant, three times, one after the other. Finally he sent his "beloved" son (see Mark 12:2-6). Matthew indicates that a series of servants were sent twice, perhaps referring to Moses and the prophets. They met with escalating violence. The third time the owner sent his son who was not only abused, but murdered. The prophets have been rejected and persecuted from the beginning. The tenants represent those leaders who are about to commit the worst crime of all in executing God's son, Jesus.

The parable ends with the murder of the son. This, along with the preceding parable of the two sons (21:28-32) and the following parable of the king's wedding feast (22:1-14), is a parable of judgment. In Matthew's language, "judgment" can be referred to as the "coming" of God. Matthew refers to the owner's "coming" to deal with the tenants. After sending so many servants and finally his own son, the owner's intention of dealing severely with the tenants is beyond doubt.

Matthew explicitly draws the audience into the story by asking them to judge themselves. Jesus asks, "What will the owner of the vineyard do to those tenants when he comes?" (21:40). Mark treated Jesus' question as rhetorical and Jesus answered it himself. In Matthew, the conversation is clearly centered on the leaders who answer Jesus correctly. Their reference to the "wretched death" the tenants can expect may very well reflect what Rome did to Jerusalem and the Temple some fifteen years before Matthew wrote. By putting this judgment into the mouths of the very ones who are opposing Jesus, Matthew has them observe that the destruction of Jerusalem and the Temple was an element of the judgment of God on their own actions and negative response to Jesus.

But there is more to an adequate interpretation than identifying this event in history as evidence of God's judgment against certain people. Matthew is not saying that God has rejected the vineyard, Israel. Rather, Jesus is warning of God's judgment against anyone who fails the vineyard, i.e., the kingdom of God. Matthew introduces the Isaian text with a question to those who are supposed to know the Scriptures: "Did you never read in the Scriptures?" This type of question appears elsewhere by Matthew in conflicts with opponents (12:3, 5; 19:4; 21:16; 22:31). The formula suggests that a correct reading of the Scriptures will render the very same interpretation that Jesus the prophet and teacher gives it.

After the leaders have passed their judgment, Jesus solemnly introduces a warning, "Therefore I say to you" (vv. 43-44). These verses have been added by Matthew. According to Matthew 21:41 and 43, the tenants are put to death and the vineyard entrusted to others. The future leaders of the people will produce the fruit expected of a well-tended, nurtured vineyard. While the Greek term *ethnos* is often translated nation or peoples, it can possibly mean the Gentiles. But it could also simply designate a group of people, such as the leaders Jesus was addressing. He is not saying that the vineyard will be entrusted to Gentiles, but that its care will be entrusted to those who accept him. Jesus' opponents understood this parable to be referring to them.

This parable calls us to become increasingly honest and vigilant in our care for the kingdom of God. It has been entrusted to us, but this trust must not be taken for granted. Matthew presents the leadership of the church, of Jesus' disciples, in contrast to the leadership that first challenged and then rejected Jesus' authority, did not accept his teaching, and finally put Jesus to death. But Matthew is also challenging the church to become a worthy tenant of the vineyard by copying and adapting to itself a prophetic critique of Israel and its leaders. Matthew's purpose is not to condemn Israel or the leaders, but to provoke repentance and conversion. Matthew also urges his audience to serve the gospel with greater integrity of both understanding and action. There is no room here for an interpretation of this parable to mean that the "others" to whom the vineyard is entrusted means that the church has replaced Israel. The "others" are also accountable to the owner and must conduct themselves as worthy and just tenants of the kingdom, producing the fruits of righteousness.

The phrase "kingdom of God" is unusual for Matthew who typically prefers to speak of "the kingdom of heaven."[14] Here the "kingdom of God" refers not to the age to come but to a special relationship with God as a result of divine election, including the privileges and responsibilities of being God's people. This is never an identity to be taken for granted, either by the people of Israel or by the disciples of Jesus. Those who belong to the vineyard, the kingdom, will be known through their fruits, their ethical behavior, and their missionary activity, continuing the preaching of the Gospel in word and deed.

A final consideration also supports an interpretation that takes this parable to heart rather than attribute to it a judgment and condemnation against Israel or even its leaders. The key feature of the allegory is not the cheating of the tenant farmers but their violent treatment of the owner's emissaries, including his son. This parable illustrates the reverse reaction to that of the "sheep" who are judged righteous and "happy" ("blessed") because of what they did to Jesus and to the "least of his brothers and sisters" who are identified with him (see Matt 25:31-40).

The function of the Scripture verse in Matthew 21:42 is to elicit the self-recriminating response from the audience, much as Nathan's parable to David did (2 Sam 12:1-7). Nathan says to David, "You are the man!" (12:7). And David responded by proclaiming his guilt and declaring a period of fast and repentance for himself. Jesus' hearers and Matthew's readers ought to listen to this parable of the vineyard and apply it to themselves. What reception do God's emissaries have among us or within our own hearts? That is the issue for Matthew.

The Parable of the Fig Tree (Matt 24:32-35)

Matthew follows Mark very closely in presenting the "lesson" (i.e., *parabolē*) of the fig tree.[15] The image is a common one. The fig tree sheds its leaves in winter. When it buds and produces leaves in the spring, everyone knows that summer will soon follow. So it is with the coming of the Son of Man (24:30-31, 37), one of the early Christians' favorite images for Jesus. Matthew is less interested in which signs will portent his coming than in the fact that his coming is certain. This short parable is one of several Matthew uses in this last major speech of his gospel, often called "the eschatological discourse." Matthew edits the context for this parable more than the parable itself. In doing so, Matthew adds several parables to Mark's version (Mark 13:28-31) and accentuates the connection between the coming Son of Man and the believers' need for vigilance.

The "Parousia" of Jesus

Early Christians spoke of the return of Jesus in glory as his *parousia* (a Greek word that literally meant "arrival or coming").[16] The term originally referred to the appearance of a Roman emperor or his delegate that was greeted with fanfare and honors. Paul adapted this term for Christian use and first referred to the appearance of "Our Lord Jesus in his parousia" in 1 Thessalonians 2:19. Paul encouraged the Thessalonians to remain faithful and vigilant as they awaited the arrival of Jesus who would be accompanied by a host of saints called "the holy ones" (3:13). Christians who were suffering persecution were in danger of losing heart and abandoning their faith. They had learned that Jesus, who had been put to death but whom God has raised from the dead, would come again in glory to vindicate their belief and to judge the world.

Paul refers to Jesus' parousia in glory, in the role of judge, "on the day of the Lord," a phrase used by the prophets to signify a day of judgment and potentially a time of horror. But Paul used the image to console and encourage his fellow Christians. They cannot know the "times and the seasons," Paul writes (1 Thess 5:1). The Lord will come like a "thief" at night (5:4). His coming is as sure as the labor pangs of the pregnant woman portend the birth of her child (5:3).

Christian teaching about Jesus' coming in glory was based on Jewish apocalypticism, which also was forged during times of great oppression and suffering. The fundamental belief of both Jewish and later Christian apocalyptic writings is that God is faithful and will ultimately prove victorious against all opponents. There will be a reversal of fortunes: those who are oppressing God's people will themselves be judged and punished. But those who remain steadfast and faithful to God will be vindicated and rewarded.

Christians borrowed some of the main ideas of Jewish apocalyptic and applied them to Jesus. A significant image to facilitate their thinking was that of the "son of man" described in the book of Daniel, a late Old

Testament writing. Daniel had a dream in which he saw one like a human being who stands before the throne of God and receives "dominion, glory, and kingship" (Dan 7:14). This son of man will be present when the powers of the world will be judged. In the thinking of the New Testament, Jesus himself is the Judge, the one to come, who will exercise judgment and destroy evil at last. Although this complex background was known to the writers of the New Testament, the image of the son of man appears only in the later Old Testament writings.

Only Matthew among the evangelists used the term parousia to speak of the final coming of Jesus and only in chapter 24. The disciples approach Jesus, asking, "Tell us when will this happen, and what sign will there be of your coming, and the end of the age?" (24:3). Here Jesus' parousia is linked with the "end of the age," also a phrase unique to Matthew. The reference to "your coming" prepares the reader to identify Jesus as the Son of Man who will return to judge the world (see 24:27, 37, 39). The "end of the age" alludes to the two ages or worlds, a pattern common in Jewish apocalyptic that distinguished this age or world from the age or world to come.

Conclusion

Matthew follows Mark by developing a dramatic "day of parables" during which Jesus delivers a major, decisive discourse consisting of a series of parables. Matthew likewise follows Mark by concluding Jesus' teaching ministry with parables challenging listeners to accept Jesus as God's Son who will come again to judge the world. These parables remain riddles to those who refuse to "hear" and conform their behavior to the priorities of the kingdom of heaven. Matthew makes explicit use of the Scriptures to warn those who reject what Jesus the prophet teaches.

CHAPTER FOUR

Parables as Matthew Tells Them

The themes of judgment and separation of the good from the bad become increasingly prominent in Matthew as Jesus proceeds to Jerusalem and to his death. Matthew exhibits a preference for symmetry in his arrangement of ten more parables after his chapter 13. He presents three sets of three parables, and concludes with a final judgment scene that incorporates elements from the preceding parables. In these ten parables, Matthew, with increasing urgency, portrays Jesus teaching his disciples to proclaim the kingdom of God, especially in their actions. These parables integrate the themes so significant in Matthew's Gospel, particularly care of the vulnerable "little ones," Jesus' authority as Son of God because he does the will of his Father, and the exemplary faithfulness required of true servants awaiting the return of the master. Such characteristics of discipleship will provide the basis for the final judgment when evil will be eliminated and the righteous will receive the rewards Jesus has promised them.

Three Parables on God and the Disciples' Imitation of God (Matthew 18-20)

In Matthew 18–20, there are three parables advocating that the disciples imitate God's action, especially with regard to the lost and the "little ones" who have a special claim on their care. Jesus instructs his disciples to act as the shepherd who goes to extremes to seek out and find sheep that have strayed from the rest (Matt 18:12-14). Later, in response to Peter's question about the limits of forgiveness, Jesus tells of the servant who, having been given a reprieve from payment of a huge debt, failed to show mercy to a fellow servant who owed him a much smaller amount (18:21-35). Finally, in a third parable, Jesus tells of a vineyard owner whose payment to the last hired is the same as to the first hired (20:1-16). All three parables in this series are concerned with the disciples as leaders of the believing community, responsible for showing the way of imitating God in the kingdom Jesus proclaims.

Parable of the Shepherd (Matt 18:12-14)

Jesus describes authentic Christian leadership, which not only avoids causing scandal, but seeks to reconcile those who have wandered, to "find" them and to assure that none of them is lost. While the parable itself is similar to Luke 15:4-7, the introduction is typical of Matthew and the last verse (14) is unique to him. Here is how the parable appears in Matthew:

> [12]"What is your opinion? If a man has a hundred sheep and one of them goes astray, will he not leave the ninety-nine in the hills and go in search of the stray? [13]And if he finds it, amen, I say to you, he rejoices more over it than over the ninety-nine that did not stray. [14]In just the same way, it is not the will of your heavenly Father that one of these little ones be lost."

Matthew has Jesus introduce the parable with a question for his listeners, "What is your opinion?" This question appears several times in Matthew (e.g., 17:25; 21:28; 22:17, 42; 24:44; 26:53, 66). It acts as a challenge to Jesus' hearers to really listen to his words and make a judgment, not only about the situation Jesus describes, but about themselves. Jesus' audience was familiar with the extreme care a shepherd would show even for sheep that have strayed. Jesus requires his disciples to identify with the shepherd who goes in search of the missing sheep.

This invitation for listeners to judge for themselves is coupled with a statement in verse 13, introduced with the phrase, "Amen, I say to you." This phrase indicates the solemnity of Jesus' teaching, another characteristic of Matthew's style found throughout the gospel, especially in Jesus' discourses (e.g., 5:18, 20, 22, 26, 28, 32, 34, 39, 40; 10:15, 23, 27, 42; 13:17; 18:3, 13, 18). Jesus reminds his audience of a very common experience. When a person loses something of worth and then finds it again, he will rejoice in a way that surpasses his original appreciation of the lost item. Jesus does not imply that the other ninety-nine who never strayed are unappreciated. But finding what had been lost is a joyous experience that inspires gratitude.

Matthew stresses time and again the importance of doing "the will of your heavenly Father" (v. 14). God's will is the point of the short parable. The disciples are being instructed about leadership in the kingdom in which God reigns. They are reminded to seek first this kingdom. As good shepherds the disciples must seek out those who have strayed. Again, typical of Matthew, the lost ones are identified with the "little ones" who are dependent upon the care of the shepherd.

The shepherd can identify with the little ones, for in Matthew, Jesus' disciples are referred to as those with "little faith." Yet Matthew presents a more positive view of the disciples than Mark does. Jesus tells his disciples that although they could not drive out demons because of their little faith, even if they have faith as small as a mustard seed, nothing will be impossible for them (17:20). Matthew uses a single Greek word for "little faith" (*oligopistos* is found in 6:30; 8:26; 14:31; 16:8; the term appears only once outside of Matthew, in Luke 12:28) that sums up his description of the followers of Jesus who are only beginning to understand through faith the demands of discipleship.

The Image of the Shepherd

Matthew focuses on the shepherd who seeks out the sheep rather than on the sheep that has strayed. In so doing, Matthew shows the influence of Ezekiel 34 where the leaders of Israel as described as "shepherds." In Ezekiel 34:6 the shepherds of Israel are criticized for not bringing back the stray sheep. In contrast, God promises to serve as shepherd: "The lost I will seek out, the strayed I will bring back" (34:16a). A further indication that Matthew is concerned with church leaders is that he uses the same term here translated, "stray," in the sense of "deceive," in the eschatological discourse (see Matt 24:4, 5, 11, 24). There Jesus warns believers not to be led astray by false teachers, prophets, messiahs who will "deceive" you. Straying not only means failure to follow. In Matthew it also implies a failure of leadership. And straying involves not mere intellectual dissent, but more importantly, failure to heed and follow Jesus' ethical teachings.

Matthew introduces a subtle qualification suggesting that the search for the lost is not always successful (18:13). Matthew says of the shepherd, "*if* he happens to find (the lost sheep)" whereas the parallel in Luke 15:5 reads, "*when* he finds it." Matthew reflects the experience of the community's dealing with errant members. Sometimes the shepherd's efforts fail to find and return the stray sheep. But the sheep bear some responsibility, too. Matthew distinguishes between "wandering off" (18:12-13) and "perishing" or "being lost" (18:14). The shepherd actively tracks down those who have strayed so that they will not perish. In Matthew the ideal shepherd is God. The disciples are to imitate God in searching out the most vulnerable and those who have wandered astray.

"Seeking Out" Those Who Have Strayed

No one should cause a fellow disciple to sin (vv. 6-10). Further, those who have strayed must be found and, if possible, brought back to and reconciled with the community. The joy of the shepherd in finding the sheep, though not entirely absent from Matthew (v. 13) is emphasized more in Luke. By his addition of verses 10 and 14, Matthew has applied the parable to the shepherd's relentless care of the "little ones."

There is already in the writings of St. Paul a concern similar to Matthew's about what to do when a member of the believing community violates the moral code of conduct appropriate to followers of Jesus. In one case, for example, Paul advises the community to expel a member guilty of incest (1 Cor 5:1-5). Paul would later take a different approach regarding the contrite person of the Corinthian community who appears to have shown sufficient remorse to be reconciled with the community (2 Cor 2:1-4). If the young Pauline communities of the fifties wrestled with the issue of sin among Christians, it is all the more likely that later Christian leaders such as those addressed by Matthew would have had even more of the same type of problems facing them.

It is reasonable to assume that another related problem faced by Matthew's community was ambition for authoritative positions such as Peter represents in his role as spokesman for the disciples.[1] In Jesus' set of values, the humble are more important than the powerful, for dependence on God is what makes one open to God's rule. The little child is held up as an example (18:3). Matthew is concerned about the impact of church scandals on the "little ones." His focus is on the straying sinner and on the role of the "greatest" (see 18:1) or the leaders in the church to "search out," find, and return them to the security of the church.

Parable of the King and the Unworthy Servant (Matt 18:21-35)

Jesus' instruction on the care of the "little ones," including the "lost sheep," prompts Peter to ask about the limits of forgiveness, especially with regard to "brothers and sisters" who have strayed. Peter's question not only encompasses forgiveness, but also the issue of authority. Jesus issues a mandate to Peter with his parable of the King and the Servant presented in this way in Matthew 18:21-35:

> [21]Then Peter approaching asked him, "Lord, if my brother sins against me, how often must I forgive him? As many as seven times?" [22]Jesus answered, "I say to you, not seven times but seventy-seven times. [23]That is why the kingdom of heaven may be likened to a king who decided to settle accounts with his servants. [24]When he began the accounting, a debtor was brought before him who owed him a huge amount. [25]Since he had no way of paying it back, his master ordered him to be sold, along with his wife, his children, and all his property, in payment of the debt. [26]At that, the servant fell down, did him homage, and said, 'Be patient with me, and I will pay you back in full.' [27]Moved with compassion the master of that servant let him go and forgave him the loan. [28]When that servant had left, he found one of his fellow servants who owed him a much smaller amount. He seized him and started to choke him, demanding, 'Pay back what you owe.' [29]Falling to his knees, his fellow servant begged him, 'Be patient with me, and I will pay you back.' [30]But he refused. Instead, he had him put in prison until he paid back the debt. [31]Now when his fellow servants saw what had happened, they were deeply disturbed, and went to their master and reported the whole affair. [32]His master summoned him and said to him, 'You wicked servant! I forgave you your entire debt because you begged me to. [33]Should you not have had pity on your fellow servant, as I had pity on you?' [34]Then in anger his master handed him over to the torturers until he should pay back the whole debt. [35]So will my heavenly Father do to you, unless each of you forgives his brother from his heart."

A first reading seems to render a clear enough lesson from this parable. In answer to Peter's question about forgiveness, Jesus appears to say, "Watch out! If you do not forgive generously, in the end, God will not forgive you either!" The listener is left with the impression that God imitates human conduct. Many understand that Jesus is comparing God to the king. This impression is reinforced by the conclusion to the parable in 18:35 when Jesus says, "So will my heavenly Father do to you, unless each of you forgives his brother from his heart."

The King and His Servants

There appear to be good reasons for identifying the king depicted here with God. Elsewhere in Matthew, God or Jesus are referred to in the language of kingship. In Matthew 5:35, Jerusalem is referred to as "the city of the great King." And in 2:2, the Magi's description of Jesus as the "newborn king of the Jews" is just the provocation the paranoid King Herod needs to search for and kill Jesus. In Matthew 22:1-14 we hear of a king who appears to overreact when invited guests do not show up at his feast: he became enraged, sent out his troops, destroyed the people, and burned down their city. The implied warning would be especially potent in view of the fact that Matthew was writing just about a decade or so after the destruction of the Temple and of Jerusalem in A.D. 70. In the last parable of Matthew's Gospel, a parable about God's final judgment, a "king" divides the nations just as a shepherd would separate the sheep from the goats (25:31-46).

Certain internal aspects of the parable in Matthew 18:23-35 also suggest that the king represents God. The story is about forgiveness. The parable refers to servants or slaves, an image used of the disciples. And finally there is Jesus' concluding remark suggesting that at the final judgment God will invoke our forgiveness of others as a criterion for deciding whether or not we will be forgiven.

However, there are even better reasons to be wary of an identification of the king with God. The cultural image of king is taken from the Roman Empire that, already repressive during Jesus' time, was all the more so by the time Matthew was writing. Although the images used in this and other parables are clothed in the culture of the times, Jesus stresses how very different is the kingdom of God from any and all features of the Roman Empire, as well as of any other earthly king of the first century. The king of this parable, in particular, hardly presents a suitable image for God.

The parable draws us into the political climate and mores of the Roman Empire where slavery is an acceptable practice, and servants are minions of the king used to carry out his will and agenda. Men, their wives, and families could be bought and sold. Yet slavery, a completely objectionable institution for us, was an integral part of the economy of the Roman Empire. Taxes and tribute were the king's way of amassing wealth and keeping the population in check. As representatives of the king, certain slaves or servants wielded a fair amount of honor as well as skill.

At the beginning of the parable, Matthew pictures the king calling his servants to account. The huge debt the first servant owes is "ten thousand talents," an amount so overwhelming that the listener cannot conceive of this as a personal debt.[2] The enormity of that sum suggests tax or tribute owed by the population of a region. That the frightened official begs for more time reinforces the idea that he meant to extend his efforts to raise it from others. That explains his actions when he encountered someone in debt to him. Having failed to collect the king's money, but finally granted more time, he became all the more frantic to succeed. He knows and understands the rules that have brought him prestige. He has dishonored the king and barely escaped with his life. The experience made him realize just how shaky is the basis of his continued authority and power and even his very life.

Before he was "forgiven," the official was threatened with disaster: prison and the sale of his wife and children. He was forced to grovel at the feet of the king and beg for time and another chance. The king's next response suggests that he had to consider his own potential loss of face and honor. The dictator would hardly want to back-peddle, but realized that he could achieve more by at least a show of compassion. In a reluctant gesture, the king "let him go," thus at least appearing to be benevolent. If he had carried out his threat, the king would have lost a skilled and experienced servant. The official thereby becomes even more indebted to the king. He now owes the king his life. The official is ostensibly spared, but what lessons has he learned from his "Lord"? Having begged for more "time," he leaves the king's presence resolved to make up for the time that was lost.

The cycle of debt and woe is compounded. The official seeks out a "fellow servant" and demands that he pay what he owed. He does violence to him, choking him and insisting that the debt be paid. Even though the second servant begs for pity, the same word used of the king, the official refuses and imprisons him. It only appears as if the official acts contrary to what the king had done. But both are actually asserting control and keeping others enslaved as we learn in the unfolding of the rest of the story. The imprisoned man will have to involve others to satisfy the debt. Other subjects of the king become concerned that they could be roped into the conflict and its implications at any moment. They go over the official's head and seek protection from the more powerful patron, the king.[3]

The king responds swiftly and more violently than ever. Previously he had threatened prison and the sale of the official's family. Now he orders that the man be tortured. There is no longer any pretext of mercy or forgiveness. The king will exact every penny of the tax or tribute or debt, regardless of how huge it was or how hopeless the proposition of raising it from prison. The king reacts like the tyrant he is and expects others to be on his behalf, punishing the official for not being more like him in the first place. This second change of heart actually betrays the king's true disposition and attitude.

People of the first century would recognize in the king's and in the official's behavior the survival mentality they needed under the tyranny of Rome. They were used to being bullied and intimidated. If the king represents God, the concluding verse that warns that "my heavenly father" will do to you as the king did to his official means that God is like the Romans and acts in the same vengeful, unforgiving way. In the end, God would imitate humans and the kingdom of God would mirror human kingdoms.

Living by a Different Standard

After a closer look at the whole parable, we can begin to understand Jesus' teaching that the "kingdom of heaven" is not at all like business as usual in the Roman Empire. Peter's initial question had to do with the limits of "forgiving a brother." Jesus' response advocates imitating God in extending unlimited forgiveness. God does not act as humans do. But Jesus empowers his disciples to act as God does. Similarly, in the Sermon on the Mount, Jesus had described his "heavenly Father" as letting the sun shine on the good and the bad and the rain fall on the just and the unjust (Matt 5:43-48). Then Jesus drew the conclusion that disciples show themselves to be "children of the heavenly Father" when they love their enemies, do good to those who persecute them, and when they imitate God. Love of enemy represents the challenge to unlimited love that seeks to reconcile members of the community, brothers and sisters who have strayed like the lost sheep, or even those who have hurt the community and who are in need of forgiveness.

God does not and will not at the end imitate the kings of Rome. Jesus offers Peter insight into an alternate way of thinking and acting, so different from the king and his subjects described in the parable. Peter's question was about how often to forgive his "brother." Jesus speaks not of the ways of earthly kings, but of "my heavenly Father." Disciples' forgiveness must not be conditional, whimsical, or self-serving like the king's and his official's. If the disciples love according to the principles and guidelines of the Roman Empire, they will set strict, irrevocable limits to forgiveness. And if they remain within the parameters of the example of the Empire, they can expect a future "judgment" that is consistent with those limits. If, on the other hand, they live according to the model Jesus offers, they will imitate the "heavenly Father." They will act with goodness and mercy.

Like the ancient prophets who warned that alliances with earthly kings would bring on catastrophes, Jesus warns that accepting the pagans' view of God ends in disaster. Jesus' disciples must practice a different way of thinking and acting. Accepting the gracious forgiveness of a truly merciful God, disciples are empowered to extend mercy and forgiveness to others. It is their mission. In this way they proclaim and spread the kingdom of God.

The Prodigal Landowner[4] (Matt 20:1-16)

As he approaches Jerusalem, Jesus speaks a third parable about God and the imitation of God demanded of his disciples. Jesus also reveals his eschatological perspective that will increasingly dominate the remainder of his instructions to his disciples, especially his parables. In trying to get his disciples to adjust their thinking to his own vision about justice, Jesus compares the kingdom of heaven to a vineyard owner who goes out at various times of the day to look for workers to bring in the harvest. This parable is unique to Matthew and is told like this:[5]

> [1]"The kingdom of heaven is like a landowner who went out at dawn to hire laborers for his vineyard. [2]After agreeing with them for the usual daily wage, he sent them into his vineyard. [3]Going out about nine o'clock, he saw others standing idle in the marketplace, [4]and he said to them, 'You too go into my vineyard, and I will give you what is just.' [5]So they went off. [And] he went out again around noon, and around three o'clock, and did likewise. [6]Going out about five o'clock, he found others standing around, and said to them, 'Why do you stand here idle all day?' [7]They answered, 'Because no one has hired us.' He said to them, 'You too go into my vineyard.' [8]When it was evening the owner of the vineyard said to his foreman, 'Summon the laborers and give them their pay, beginning with the last and ending with the first.' [9]When those who had started about five o'clock came, each received the usual daily wage. [10]So when the first came, they thought that they would receive more, but each of them also got the usual wage. [11]And on receiving it they grumbled against the landowner, [12]saying, 'These last ones worked only one hour, and you have made them equal to us, who bore the day's burden and the heat.' [13]He said to one of them in reply, 'My friend, I am not cheating you. Did you not agree with me for the usual daily wage? [14]Take what is yours and go. What if I wish to give this last one the same as you? [15][Or] am I not free to do as I wish with my own money? Are you envious because I am generous?' [16]Thus, the last will be first, and the first will be last."

The parable unfolds in three scenes: the hirings, the payments, and a dialogue between the vineyard owner and the first workers he hired. The owner of a vineyard, at various hours of the day,[6] employs workers to harvest the grapes. The harvesting metaphor hints of the end time that is fast approaching. At the end of the day the workers are paid, beginning with those who had been hired at the eleventh hour, having labored a mere sixty minutes, and concluding with those who had worked twelve hours. This device allows for all the workers—particularly those who had toiled since dawn, working a very long day in the heat of the sun, to view the distribution of wages. Readers are drawn into the story by imagining, as Jesus tells it, what the laborers must have felt as the owner gave a full day's wage to those who had only worked a very short time. It is not at all surprising that the first hired expected that when their turn came to receive their wages, they would be compensated in a proportionate manner, even twelvefold, commensurate with the number of hours they worked.

But that is not how it happens. Instead, each of the harvesters received the same compensation, a *denarius*, "the usual daily wage."[7] That's what the first workers agreed to. That's what was just, even if at the twelfth hour, in view of their hard work and what they witnessed as they waited for their wages, their expectations changed. It might not seem to be fair. But as the landowner categorically tells them, "I am not cheating you" (v. 13).

The vivid details make this story one that is easy to visualize. At the third hour the owner sends out workers with the promise, "I will give you what is just" (v. 4). There is no bargaining or agreement with the others he sends out. The authority of the vineyard owner is accentuated in a number of ways: his orders to "go out into my vineyard," his questions to those standing around idle, his command to the steward to pay the workers, and his unanswered questions to the grumbling workers at the end. It is the first-hired workers whose attitude needs to be adjusted, but whose complaint seems to readers to be the most reasonable.

Good Versus Evil

Matthew's apocalyptic perspective sharpens the opposition between good and evil,[8] sometimes personifying evil. For example, in the Sermon on the Mount, in forbidding the taking of oaths, Jesus says, "Let your 'Yes' mean 'Yes,' and your 'No' mean 'No.' Anything more is from the evil one" (Matt 5:37). Jesus' disciples are taught to pray for deliverance from the evil one (6:13). It is the evil one who steals the word sown in people's hearts (13:38). A single time Matthew personifies good, when Jesus, responding to the rich young man, says "there is only One who is good" (19:17). "Your heavenly Father" is associated with giving good in 5:45, and with giving good things to those who ask in 7:11.

The owner accuses the first hired of having an "evil eye" that sees things wrongly. The charge is a serious one. Ancient and modern cultures have believed that certain individuals, animals, demons, or gods have power to injure with a glance. In the Wisdom tradition, there is a connection between the "eye," the window to the soul, and envy or covetousness: wickedness and deceit beguile the soul, and desire perverts the "eye," causing humans to think and act with malice (Wis 4:11-12). Even more plainly, Sirach says that the miser's selfishness obscures his "eye" and prevents generosity in himself or others:

> [8]In the miser's opinion his share is too small;
> [9]he refuses his neighbor and brings ruin on himself.
> [10]The miser's eye is rapacious for bread,
> but on his own table he sets it stale. (Sir 14:8-10)

Clearly Jesus is not endorsing a superstition or literally teaching that the eye itself is evil. Rather, this figurative language implies that selfish anxiety can prevent us from acting generously. In the first-century world, all goods were limited. Any gain of one could be considered loss to another. Evil-eye envy is a major character flaw, destructive for the person and the community. According to Matthew, twice Jesus says, "If your eye causes you to sin, tear it out" (5:29; 18:9). The disgruntled workers have evil-eye envy because the goodness of the vineyard owner makes all equal to one another. Similarly, Matthew 6:23 says: "But if your eye is bad [*poneros*], your whole body will be in darkness. And if the light in you is darkness, how great will the darkness be." This idea may be based on Deuteronomy 15:9: "Be on your guard lest, entertaining the mean thought . . . you grudge help to your needy kinsman and give him nothing; else he will cry out to the Lord against you and you will be held guilty." An evil eye produces selfishness and stinginess and prevents generosity. Similarly, Matthew 20:15 connects envy, jealousy, and lack of generosity. The first workers not only begrudge the master's generosity to the others, they betray their own presumption that they are better than the others and that they alone merit what is just whereas the others do not.

Jesus challenges his listeners to conform what they "see" to the "eyes" of the vineyard owner, to adjust their "eyes" to the perspective of the kingdom. The time is fast approaching when the workers can, in fact, expect "payment." Whether the "surprise" of what they receive is pleasant or not depends on whether their vision conforms to the unassailable criteria of the kingdom of God, namely mercy and justice. These values are not in conflict in God's kingdom. Mercy comes first, whether it be perceived as God's mercy toward others, or acknowledgment of our own unworthiness and gratitude for the gifts we have been given. Beware of the view, Matthew warns, based in envy, that we deserve more or better than the rest.

By repeating the proverb of reversal (Matt 19:30; 20:16), Jesus challenges his disciples to enter Jerusalem with him armed with a new vision of justice and a renewed trust in God as Lord. Jesus will suffer condemnation and be treated as the "last" or lowest of human beings. He will be sentenced to a death reserved for slaves and the worst of Rome's enemies. His disciples will be scattered and threatened. As they experience the truth of the proverb of reversal, they can be consoled with its promise. By identifying with the "last" they will receive mercy.

Confrontation between Owner and Workers

Matthew seems intent on deliberately setting up tension between the vineyard owner and the first hired. Remember that this parable follows Jesus' promise of a hundredfold reward to Peter and the first disciples who had sacrificed so much to follow Jesus.[9] Peter appears to seek reassurance that their reward would be commensurate with their sacrifices. Jesus' response refocuses Peter's attention to his initial call to follow Jesus (see 4:18-19). Early hires like Peter will indeed be compensated as agreed. But all workers, early and late, are "repaid" according to the standards of the kingdom of heaven. Jesus corrects Peter's all too human notion that some are better than others or deserve more consideration than others. The first hired expected special compensation and resented the idea that the last workers receive grace and gift. Based on the owner's merciful treatment of others, they changed their expectations of what they themselves deserved. They demand more so that the others seem to receive less. Jesus' answer challenges their presumption of superiority and entitlement while they also despise the last who are treated with the same mercy as they are. Jesus' parable aims at the conversion of such attitudes. The first workers challenge the authority of the owner to do as he pleases. Soon Jesus will show that his authority cannot be challenged.

The Upside-Down Justice of the Kingdom of God

In the parable, the problem for the disgruntled workers is not whether God is good or acts in a good manner, but that God's equal distribution is perceived by them as unjust. That is the basis of their complaint. But God's justice is not about each getting what each deserves or even gaining what each has earned. This parable turns upside down the human notion of justice. Listeners may wonder how this parable is an illustration of the saying that the last will be first and the first last. The proverb that envelops the parable (Matt 19:30 and 20:16) seems to apply only to one aspect of Jesus' story, the order of payment, an aspect that is really coincidental to the parable and serves primarily to assure a confrontation between owner and workers. The proverb really does not seem to fit the parable—or does it?

Reversal is a prime idea of parables, and this is no exception. In this parable, everyone is caught unawares. The payment at the end is a surprise not only to the last hired, who receive more than they expected, but to the first hired as well. No one received his due, or what he thought he was due. The parable is meant to highlight God's sovereignty and a graciousness that is not based on what is owed or earned. The difference between the last hired and the first is that the last were not complaining. The last hired realized instinctively that they did not receive what they deserved but that the "wage" was actually "gift." And they went away happy and grateful. The first hired grumble and complain, accusing the master (*kyrios* or lord) of injustice. Worse, they protest that he has made the last hired "equal" to them, as if that is wrong. Therein lies the lesson. The last are equal to the first and neither can earn the right to challenge their master. The upside-down character of the kingdom of God means that all are extended mercy, forgiveness, and the opportunity to work in the vineyard although no one deserves any of these.

Three Parables Illustrating Jesus' Authority as Son of God (Matthew 21–22)

With the beginning of chapter 21, Matthew pictures Jesus' arrival in Jerusalem as a triumphant king recognized by the people. In Jerusalem, Jesus confronts the Jewish leaders who challenge his authority. Jesus counters their questions with one of his own, asking these leaders whether John's baptism was of human or heavenly origin (21:24). When they answer that they do not know, Jesus responds with a series of three parables in 21:28 through 22:14. In the first parable, Jesus describes two sons of a vineyard owner and asks the leaders which of the two did his father's will (see 21:28-32). The second parable, taken from Mark, describes the wicked tenants who kill the son of the vineyard owner (21:33-46, see chapter 3, pp. 70–74, for discussion of this parable). The third parable, a version of which is found in Luke, tells of a king who held a wedding feast for his son but the invited guests refused to come (22:1-14). All three parables depict an authority figure that represents God: a householder with two sons, a vineyard owner, and a king. All three parables forecast the eventual judgment that inevitably will come to those who reject Jesus and his teaching.

The Parable of the Two Sons (Matt 21:28-32)

Jesus' first parable in response to the leaders in Jerusalem who challenge his authority is this:

> [28]"What is your opinion? A man had two sons. He came to the first and said, 'Son, go out and work in the vineyard today.' [29]He said in reply, 'I will not,' but afterwards he changed his mind and went. [30]The man came to the other son and gave the same order. He said in reply, 'Yes, sir,' but did not go. [31]Which of the two did his father's will?" They answered, "The first." Jesus said to them, "Amen, I say to you, tax collectors and prostitutes are entering the kingdom of God before you. [32]When John came to you in the way of righteousness, you did not believe him; but tax collectors and prostitutes did. Yet even when you saw that, you did not later change your minds and believe him."

The "vineyard" takes up the symbolism from the parable in Matthew 20:1-16 and links this parable of the two sons to the following one about the wicked tenants in 21:33-46. This first parable, aimed at the leaders of the people, focuses on the father's request that his sons work in the vineyard. As a matter of fact, working in the vineyard is what servants and even more so sons are expected to do. A good son would not balk at working to maintain his inheritance or think that it is work only for servants. Both are expected to obey the vineyard owner. Jesus' opponents had just refused to answer Jesus' question about John's baptism (21:24-27). Jesus then introduces his parable with a counter question, inviting them to give their opinion about which son did his father's will, and thereby judge themselves.

The choice is evident, even though both sons say one thing and do another. But the first son, despite what he said, clearly is the one who "did" his father's will. After initially refusing to obey his father, he "changed his mind" and went to work in the vineyard. To drive his point home, Jesus applies the parable to the Baptist (v. 32) and to "tax collectors and prostitutes" who repented and accepted Jesus because of John's preaching. The very leaders who opposed both John and Jesus tacitly admitted as much in their refusal to answer Jesus' question and their acknowledgment of John's popularity with the crowds. Jesus then warns the leaders that they, like the obedient son, must "change their mind" and believe. The point of any parable is to evoke a change of heart. The leaders will not accept the parable, although clearly they do understand it. The parable forces Jesus' opponents to judge themselves. Jesus' warning and his meaning could hardly be clearer.

Jesus' rhetorical questions at the beginning and end of the parable demand answers: "What is your opinion?" (21:28) and "Which of the two did his father's will?" (21:31). The leaders know and respond correctly: the son who did his father's will is the obedient son, the one who went to work in the vineyard. By answering correctly, the leaders judge themselves. The invitation to self-judgment functions as a warning to change behavior and conform conduct to the standards of the kingdom of God. Three times the phrase "by what authority do [you] do these things" (see 21:23, 24, 27) appears as the leaders confront Jesus. His response in a parable means that Jesus does what he does because he is the son of his heavenly Father.

The Authority of God's Son Who Does the Will of His Heavenly Father

Matthew's stresses the authority of Jesus who speaks and acts in obedience to God. Matthew says in 7:29, at the conclusion of the Sermon on the Mount, that Jesus "taught them as one having authority." The Greek word is *exousia* (see also 8:9; 9:6,8; 10:1; 21:23, 24, 27; 28:18); it also means "power." Jesus' words are effective. He teaches not only with words, but also with miracles that show God's power working through him. For instance, the centurion testified that he recognized Jesus' *authority* and therefore believed that Jesus could heal his servant (8:8-9). Similarly in the story of the cure of Peter's mother-in-law, Jesus shows that he has *authority* over the fever that afflicted her (8:14-15). Jesus not only has the power to work miracles, but he also has the *authority* to forgive sins (9:6). And the crowd that witnessed his cure of the paralytic glorified God for giving him such *authority* (9:8). In his farewell discourse at the end of the gospel, Jesus tells his disciples that "all authority in heaven and on earth" has been given to him (28:18).

Jesus shared his power or authority to preach and to heal with his disciples (10:1). While his disciples "follow" Jesus, often not knowing where they are going or what really is happening, Jesus' opponents continuously stand in his way and try to impede Jesus' journey. They challenge his authority and question Jesus in an effort to entrap him. All the way to the end of the gospel, Jesus encounters those who refuse to accept him or his teaching. Even as he arrives in Jerusalem and makes preparations for his passion and death, Jesus is confronted with hostility, especially that of religious leaders. Thus, the question by the opponents of Jesus regarding the source of his *authority* or power (21:23-27) is an identity question for Matthew. By rejecting Jesus as God's Son, these leaders are rejecting God.

One of Matthew's favorite ways of referring to God is as "my Father" or "my heavenly Father." Matthew also uses the phrase "your Father" or "our Father in heaven" or "our Father," as in the Lord's Prayer. And one of Matthew's preferred ways of describing Jesus is as the obedient Son of God, the one who does his Father's will. Jesus is the example of obedience to God for his disciples. At his baptism, Jesus is identified as God's Son (3:17). When Jesus is transfigured before them, his disciples are told, "This is my beloved Son, with whom I am well pleased; listen to him" (17:5).

The phrase "doing the will" of "my" or "your" or "our" "heavenly Father" sums up true discipleship for Matthew. Throughout his teaching ministry, Jesus instructs his disciples that they must "do the will" of his heavenly Father. For example, in the course of the Sermon on the Mount, Jesus says, "Not everyone who says to me, 'Lord, Lord,' will enter the kingdom of heaven, but only the one who does the will of my Father in heaven" (7:21). Similarly in 12:50, Matthew pictures Jesus saying, "Whoever does the will of my heavenly Father is my brother, and sister, and mother." Jesus tells his disciples that "It is not the will of your heavenly Father that one of these little ones be lost" (18:14). In the Garden, just before he is arrested, Jesus prays, "My Father, . . . your will be done" (see 26:39, 42, 44). Jesus is the obedient Son of our heavenly Father because he does the will of the Father.

Who Are the Righteous?

Jesus' application of this parable contrasts the reaction of the Jewish leadership unfavorably with that of "tax collectors and prostitutes," both groups considered immoral. Tax collectors were suspect because they often cheated and prostitutes because of their sexual sins. Both were further hated for their alleged connections with Rome. Tax collectors were willing to do Rome's dirty work at the expense of fellow Jews and sometimes took more than their share for themselves. Prostitutes were willing to sell themselves to Roman soldiers for money. By lumping these two groups of notorious sinners together, Jesus gains leverage in his contrast with the Jewish leaders. Even the worst sinners such as tax collectors and prostitutes repented and had a change of heart when they heard John preaching the way of righteousness.

"But," Jesus said to them "you" did not repent (21:32). In addition to his initial and concluding questions to them, this is the third instance in this short parable when Jesus directly engaged the leaders. The implication is clear that if they do not soon match their understanding, indicated with their correct response to his questions, with a change of heart and belief, they will not enter the kingdom of God. They are like the wayward, disobedient son, who refused to do the will of the father.[10]

The surprise element of this parable of the two sons may be in this contrast of the Jewish leaders who are opposing Jesus to the tax collectors and prostitutes who were converted and repented. The odious combination of sinners shines in comparison to these leaders. Holding up tax collectors and prostitutes as praiseworthy is rather shocking, but the application of this parable is clear even to Jesus' opponents who suffer in the comparison. After confronting him about the source of his authority, his opponents seem to cede direction of the discussion to Jesus. He scored points with the example of the "two sons." The next two parables will escalate Jesus' criticism of his opponents. They are like the wicked tenants who refuse to produce fruit from the vineyard and also fail to bring it to the owner. Their opposition also escalates. The leaders recognize themselves in these parables, as Matthew makes clear (see 21:45-46). But they will not change their minds about arresting Jesus and putting him to death.

The Parable of the Wedding Feast (Matt 22:1-14)

This parable has two distinct parts. Verses 1-10 tell of invited guests who refused to attend the king's wedding feast for his son. Verses 11-14 appear to be tacked on to this parable, providing a loose-fitting conclusion. Perhaps this is part of another, originally independent parable. Here's how the parable appears in Matthew 22:1-14:

> [1]Jesus again in reply spoke to them in parables, saying, [2]"The kingdom of heaven may be likened to a king who gave a wedding feast for his

son. [3]He dispatched his servants to summon the invited guests to the feast, but they refused to come. [4]A second time he sent other servants, saying, 'Tell those invited: "Behold, I have prepared my banquet, my calves and fattened cattle are killed and everything is ready; come to the feast."' [5]Some ignored the invitation and went away, one to his farm, another to his business. [6]The rest laid hold of his servants, mistreated them, and killed them. [7]The king was enraged and sent his troops, destroyed those murderers, and burned their city. [8]Then he said to his servants, 'The feast is ready, but those who were invited were not worthy to come. [9]Go out, therefore, into the main roads and invite to the feast whoever you find.' [10]The servants went out into the streets and gathered all they found, bad and good alike, and the hall was filled with guests. [11]But when the king came in to meet the guests he saw a man there not dressed in a wedding garment. [12]He said to him, 'My friend, how is it that you came in here without a wedding garment?' But he was reduced to silence. [13]Then the king said to his attendants, 'Bind his hands and feet, and cast him into the darkness outside, where there will be wailing and grinding of teeth.' [14]Many are invited, but few are chosen."

There are several indications that Matthew has done some fairly extensive editing in the parable of the wedding feast he adapts from Q.[11] In Matthew, the "man" appears as a "king." The occasion is a "wedding feast" for his son. The king sends out servants twice, urging the people to come. Only Matthew adds the horrendous punishment of those who refuse to come (they are destroyed and their city is burned) and of the guest who attended without a wedding garment (he is thrown out into the darkness).

A wedding feast for the king's son should be a very joyous occasion, not only for the king but also for his subjects. Yet this kingdom parable appears to be designed to strike awe if not fear in the hearts of listeners. The king's impressive authority is illustrated by his "sending" and his "summons." Three times the king sends envoys meant to do his bidding. Twice he sent his servants to summon invited guests. The third time he sent his troops to kill the people and burn down their city. The king's servants do his will. His subjects, however, are not only insubordinate; they defy him. They twice refuse the summons. In fact, the second time they lay hold of the king's servants, abuse them, and kill them. Finally the king reacts as Jesus' listeners would have expected. Enraged, he sent his troops who destroyed the murderers and burned down their city. A third time the king proclaims that the feast is ready. Now he sends out his servants to invite any and all they find. The servants gather the good and the bad alike so that the reception hall is full. The original parable might have ended here as does the parallel in Luke. The conclusion would mean that none of the invited guests participate in the banquet. Rather, outsiders are welcomed and take the place of those who had been invited but who refused to come and or had abused the king's servants.

The Wedding Garment

Matthew added the detail that the banquet was for a wedding. Matthew typically adds elements inspired by the Scriptures and calls for an allegorical interpretation of Jesus' parables. Marriage is a biblical symbol for the covenant relationship between God and God's people (see Isa 54:5; Hos 2:1-9). The wedding banquet also symbolized the peace and harmony experienced by those who participate in the kingdom (see Isa 25:6). Jesus is the Bridegroom and his coming went unrecognized by many of Israel who represent the invited guests. Their rejection of Jesus resulted in God's punishment on the city of Jerusalem and portends even more serious punishment in the future.

Matthew is unique in adding another element, perhaps one from an originally separate parable. In Matthew 22:11-13, the king arrives, expecting to survey a roomful of happy guests. But then the king spotted someone who was not appropriately attired. At once the king is transformed from observer to despot. He confronted the man who could offer no valid excuse. He orders his servants to "bind" the man's hands and feet and throw him outside into darkness "where there will be wailing and grinding of teeth." This incident is somewhat puzzling. How could the man, taken from the highways and byways, have anticipated that he would be attending a wedding feast? The king's violent behavior now appears as strange as his former patience with the invited guests. This overreaction of the king reminds listeners of his all-encompassing power. He angrily orders his servants to expel the man into the darkness. The image of "wailing and grinding of teeth" appear in Matthew to express extreme distress and misery (see 8:12; 13:42, 50; 22:13; 24:51; 25:30; also Luke 13:28).

In adding the image of the wedding garment, Matthew guards against the idea that the invitations were issued indiscriminately and that all who entered from the "main roads . . . and the streets . . . the good and the bad alike" to fill up the wedding hall were automatically worthy, whereas the originally invited guests proved not to be. Matthew, who places so much importance on moral conduct, would hardly be likely to say at this late stage in the gospel that ethical behavior did not matter. Rather, the required "wedding garment" signified baptism for the early Christians. And baptism symbolized not only a ritual, but immersion into new life evidenced by a change of behavior and conformity to the standards of the kingdom of heaven.

Finally, Matthew makes a concluding observation that appears only to add to puzzlement about the parable's meaning. How does the proverb "Many are invited but few are chosen" apply to the predicament of the man without a wedding garment? Matthew says that those admitted to baptism were not excused from moral responsibility. Just as not all who were originally called were found worthy, so not all who were included when the invitation was extended beyond Israel will remain chosen unless they don the garments of justice and participate in spreading the kingdom inaugurated by the Son, Jesus. The proverb actually provides a fitting conclusion for the whole parable. Matthew refuses to allow complacency, whether based on belonging to Israel, who represents those originally called, or on the claim of those later included because they are members of the church.

Although the invitation to attend the banquet remains open to all, Matthew insists that those deemed worthy are still subject to the judgment of the king for which they must always be ready. In the preceding parables Matthew has indicated the criteria for this judgment: seeking out and reconciling those who have strayed, unlimited and unconditional forgiveness of others, doing the will of the Father. Jesus has also insisted that compensation for work in the vineyard will be "just," but it is justice based on God's standards, not ours. And the element of surprise signified by the "wedding garment" warns us against pride and self-righteousness.

The king of this parable represents God.[12] Jesus has arrived in Jerusalem. Soon he will be put to death. Before his passion, however, he gives one final summons to discipleship and issues one final warning to all that the Son of Man is coming soon as judge. Matthew has identified God as the king of Jerusalem (5:32). The power of the king is underscored in a number of ways in this parable. For example, the king summons and orders and judges. The wedding feast for his son is a momentous occasion the king's subjects cannot ignore. The gospels refer to Jesus as the bridegroom (see Mark 2:19-20; Matt 9:15; Luke 5:34-35; John 3:29; also Rev 18:23). In the parable of judgment in Matthew 25, the bridegroom who is awaited by the ten attendants functions as an image for God (cf. Matt 25:1, 5, 6, 10). Soon Jesus will be arrested and put to death.

Before these events, however, Jesus delivers a climactic eschatological discourse (Matthew 24–25), calling on his disciples to be watchful and prepared with a life of good works. It serves as a final summons to discipleship and issues a final warning that the Son of Man will come as judge of all.

Three Final Parables of Vigilance

Matthew shapes Jesus' fifth and final discourse in chapters 24–25, called the "eschatological" discourse since it deals with the "last things" (the *eschaton*) and the coming of the new age in its fullness. Jesus describes the coming of the Son of Man and events that must happen before this coming. Matthew pictures Jesus warning his disciples about how they are to act, and especially how they are to remain constantly vigilant and alert as they await the parousia (or Second Coming). Although the disciples are curious to learn *when* this will happen, Jesus replies that the exact time is known only to God (24:3, 36). Jesus reorients their attention to the need for readiness. What is certain is that the Son of Man will return. The disciples are servants whose whole existence is given meaning by this event and by their preparation for it.

Jesus' final discourse may be divided into two parts, 24:1-44 and 24:45–25:46.[13] Matthew once again shows his preference for three, clustering three parables to open the second part. The first and the third are taken from Q, while the second is unique to Matthew. All three parables have a common theme: Jesus' demand for constant watchfulness and readiness for his return. Subthemes for all three parables include the need for wisdom, the possibility of a long delay of the master, and contrasting reactions to that delay.

The Faithful or Unfaithful Servant (Matt 24:45-51)

Many of Jesus' parables present his hearers with choices, and this one in Matthew 24:45-51 is no exception. Matthew's audience might think back to the parable of the two sons and, as they listen, consider which of the two servants "does the will" of the absent master. Again Matthew pictures a patriarchal household and an absentee master, but this time it is the servants' conduct rather than the authority of the master that is accentuated. Matthew uses generic lord/master (*kyrios*) and servant/slave (*doulos*) language, whereas Luke uses the term "steward" or "manager" to convey a certain status and trustworthiness of the servant's role. But Matthew also envisions servants entrusted with a great deal of responsibility, those upon whom the master depends a great deal. Matthew's version of the story is this:[14]

> [45]"Who, then, is the faithful and prudent servant, whom the master has put in charge of the household to distribute to them their food at the proper time? [46]Blessed is that servant whom his master on his arrival finds doing so. [47]Amen, I say to you, he will put him in charge of all his property. [48]But if that wicked servant says to himself, 'My master is long delayed,' [49]and begins to beat his fellow servants, and eat and drink with drunkards, [50]the servant's master will come on an unexpected day and at an unknown hour [51]and will punish him severely and assign him a place with the hypocrites, where there will be wailing and grinding of teeth."

The focus of the parable is on the behavior of the servants confronted with the delay in the master's return. Immediately before this parable, Jesus used the image of a thief who would most certainly take advantage of an empty house to break in (24:43-44). Any prudent householder would take precautions to prevent the thief from gaining entry. Similarly, in the absence of the householder, the servants must be reliable. If not, they are worse than useless. They are wicked. There is a paradox here: although it is expected, the master's return is also a surprise. The servants, like the householder protecting himself from the thief, must be prepared for the master's return, whenever that would be.

Contrasting Reactions: The Wise Versus the Wicked

Matthew begins with a characteristic question, designed to engage listeners: "Who, then, is the faithful (*pistos*) and wise (*phronimos*) servant (*doulos*)?" That one is contrasted with the "wicked servant" (*kakos doulos*). The term *pistos* can mean "believing" as well as "faithful or reliable." The latter sense prevails here: trustworthiness is characteristic of the Christian who shares in the ministry of Jesus himself. The word *phronimos* is found mainly in Matthew among the evangelists.[15] This term can mean wise, sensible, or shrewd. So, for example, Jesus sent out his disciples to teach and heal and warns them to be as "shrewd (*phronimos*) as serpents" (10:16). At the conclusion of the Sermon on the Mount, Jesus explains that the one who listens to his words and acts on them as like the "wise" person who builds a house on rock (7:24).

Again, Matthew prefers stark contrasts that leave readers with a clear choice between good and evil, true and false righteousness. In this parable, opposition is between the conduct of the "wise" and the "wicked" servant, and between the master's praise and condemnation. The reliable servant is blessed and given charge over all the master's property, whereas the wicked servant is condemned for his drunkenness and abuse and cast out with the hypocrites. In this parable there is more stress on the denunciation of the wicked servant than on the reward of the faithful one.

Some servants are entrusted with the care of the other servants, a trust especially important in the master's absence. The distribution of food obviously involves reliability, prudence, fairness, and daily diligence. The disciples distributed the loaves and fishes after Jesus multiplied them for the crowds (see 14:19; 15:36), thus sharing in Jesus' authority and mission. Acts addresses the issue of the distribution of the community's goods to all, a need that arose in the early church and was a concern for its leaders since it was considered part of the mandate of Jesus. Like the parable of the shepherd (18:10-14), this parable calls for the care of others that is continuous, enduring, and without limit. Matthew stresses that church leaders will be found faithfully taking care of their fellow servants when Jesus returns as the Son of Man.

In contrast, the evil servant takes advantage of the master's absence to overindulge in food and drink and abuse his fellow servants. His self-indulging behavior is summed up in the proverbial, "eat, drink, and associate with drunkards," conduct that suggests complete nonchalance about duty and responsibility. "Drunkenness" and sleep are associated with laziness. The wicked servant is not mindful of his duties, but consumes the food and drink of the household for his own pleasure. Paul also opposed the careless attitude expressed in the phrase, "Let us eat and drink, / for tomorrow we die," to sober and sinless conduct secure in the knowledge of God (see 1 Cor 15:32-33). Self-indulgence, while neglecting others and without concern for the consequences, is characteristic of the evil servant.

In his description of both the wise and the wicked servant, Matthew seems to draw on the wisdom tradition of the Old Testament. Jesus is the wise teacher of wisdom. Jesus speaks the words of Sophia or Wisdom personified.[16] Jesus reveals the reign of God to his disciples who demonstrate that they are "wise" because they do the will of God and imitate God. The disciples act on their master's behalf and serve their master's interests. They are servants who take their very identity from the master's trust.

On the other hand, wisdom connects self-indulgence with the abuse of others. Self-indulgence leads to persecution of others, especially those whose more prudent and moral conduct appears as a reproach to the excesses of the wicked. Thus, sinners, Wisdom 1:16–2:24 tells us, making a pact with death, say to themselves:

> [6]"Come, therefore, let us enjoy the good things . . .
> [7]Let us have our fill of costly wine and perfumes . . .
> [9]Let no meadow be free from our wantonness; . . .
> [10]Let us oppress the needy just man . . .
> [12]. . . because he is obnoxious to us;
>   he sets himself against our doings,
> Reproaches us for transgressions of the law." (see Wis 2:6-12)

In Matthew, Jesus says that a servant who is not reliable and wise is a threat and a liability to the master as well as to the whole household. The "evil servant" who takes the master's absence as an opportunity to abuse others has betrayed his master and forfeited the right to remain a part of the household. He would have to be utterly destroyed. Indeed the servant's "dismemberment," however startling on the lips of Jesus, seems appropriate in the eschatological context for one who was trusted as a valued servant, but whose actions betrayed that trust. Part of his punishment is that he is denied membership in the community but counted among the "hypocrites," a favorite term for Matthew to describe Jesus' opponents.[17] Hypocrisy is one of the major charges Jesus brings against the "scribes and Pharisees" in the preceding chapter 23 (see 23:13, 15, 23, 25, 27, 29; also 15:7). They are denounced for the dichotomy between what they say and what they do, and for their abuse of authority in claiming to be experts in the Law while neglecting its most important demands for mercy, faith, and good example. In rebuking the Jewish leaders, Jesus accuses them of hypocrisy because of the differences between appearance and reality, between their claims and their intentions, between externals and their hidden motives. Jesus also warns his followers against hypocrisy, for example, in the Sermon on the Mount (6:2, 5, 16; 7:5). Such a lack of integrity is the opposite of the wisdom demanded of Jesus' disciples. In 24:45-51, Matthew warns Christians and more specifically Christian leaders that they will receive the same judgment and condemnation that the scribes and the Pharisees do if they are hypocrites.

The parable concludes with a contrast between the affirming action of the master who increases the responsibilities of the faithful servant and the dreadful punishment of the evil servant. Matthew 24:50 speaks of the master's return "on an unexpected day and at an unknown hour," echoing Jesus' warning in verse 44: "So too, you also must be prepared, for at an hour you do not expect, the Son of Man will come." Jesus predicts a really terrible punishment for the evil servant: after being dismembered and assigned a place with the hypocrites, "there will be wailing and grinding of teeth" (v. 51). Matthew uses this phrase to suggest the horror of final condemnation. Such images of violence and destruction are part of the apocalyptic scenario Matthew presents to stress the urgency of Jesus' instruction to his disciples as he approaches his death. Dire warnings about chaos and destruction reserved for the wicked offset the inexpressible rewards and fulfillment that await the faithful and wise servant-disciples.

The Delay of the Parousia

A major source of anxiety for early Christians and a challenge to faith was in having to account for the in-between time after the death and resurrection of Jesus and before his return in glory. Opponents of the new Christian movement mocked belief in a Messiah who suffered the humiliating death on the cross. Christians proclaimed that Jesus would return, this time in power, to judge the world. But almost from the beginning of Christian preaching, there was concern among opponents and believers as well about when this would take place. Explaining the delay of the return of Jesus is part of the Christian adaptation of Jewish apocalyptic literature. Christians insisted that the delay had been predicted and that nevertheless Jesus would come just as he promised. They maintained that, in the interim, they were responsible for the care of the church and for spreading the Gospel.

Earlier writers, in particular Paul and Mark, reflect the view that the judgment of the world would come very soon. In First Thessalonians Paul addresses the issue of Christians who relinquished their work and were idle and gossiping as they literally did nothing but await Jesus' return (1 Thess 5:14-15; cf. 2:9-10). There are several indications in his gospel that Mark also believed that his own "generation" would see the return in glory of the Son of Man (Mark 9:1; 13:30). Yet both Paul and Mark also attempt to quell speculation about when the Messiah will return. Mark says, "But of that day or hour, no one knows, neither the angels in heaven, nor the Son, but only the Father. Be watchful! Be alert! You do not know when the time will come" (Mark 13:32-33). The New Testament authors insist that the "day of the Lord," when Jesus will return as judge, is surely coming. It is therefore necessary for Jesus' servants to be alert and vigilant. This admonition was meant to encourage Christians not to waste time in speculation or to give up hope. For believers, the parousia is not a frightening prospect but a certain, positive expectation of salvation.

Matthew suggests that it may be some time before Jesus' return, but that Christians must use the time wisely and effectively as they spread the Gospel. Matthew stresses that the disciples were mandated by Jesus to preach the Gospel, just like Jesus himself did. Mission is an integral part of discipleship (see Matthew 10, often called the Mission Discourse). The "reliable and wise servant" is praised for providing food for his fellow servants, nourishing them and encouraging them to faithful service even in the master's absence. On the other hand, the "evil servant" is one who abuses other members of the community (his "fellow servants"), and fails to distribute the food of fellowship and support to them.

The Parable of the Ten Attendants (Matt 25:1-13)

The evil servant of the preceding parable used his master's delay as an opportunity to abuse his position as well as his fellow servants. Here we have the group of five "foolish" attendants[18] who do not take into account the possibility of delay nor do they use the extra time to prepare for the inevitable arrival of the bridegroom. This parable, which appears only in Matthew, says this:

> [1]"Then the kingdom of heaven will be like ten virgins who took their lamps and went out to meet the bridegroom. [2]Five of them were foolish and five were wise. [3]The foolish ones, when taking their lamps, brought no oil with them, [4]but the wise brought flasks of oil with their lamps. [5]Since the bridegroom was long delayed, they all became drowsy and fell asleep. [6]At midnight, there was a cry, 'Behold, the bridegroom! Come out to meet him!' [7]Then all those virgins got up and trimmed their lamps. [8]The foolish ones said to the wise, 'Give us some of your oil, for our lamps are going out.' [9]But the wise ones replied, 'No, for there may not be enough for us and you. Go instead to the merchants and buy some for yourselves.' [10]While they went off to buy it, the bridegroom came and those who were ready went into the wedding feast with him. Then the door was locked. [11]Afterwards the other virgins came and said, 'Lord, Lord, open the door for us!' [12]But he said in reply, 'Amen, I say to you, I do not know you.' [13]Therefore, stay awake, for you know neither the day nor the hour."

Matthew heightens the expectation of the kingdom with the simple introduction "then." It is not only the ten attendants but the whole situation that is likened to the coming of the kingdom. The dedicated purpose of the attendants is to await the arrival of the groom whose coming inaugurates the celebration of the wedding feast. The division of the attendants into groups of five "wise" and five "foolish" is unusual in the parables of Jesus, but links this parable to the previous one. The contrasting choice takes on a certain urgency in this section of Matthew's Gospel. In fact, neither group of attendants adequately illustrates the final command that is expressed as a conclusion: "Therefore, stay awake, for you know neither the day nor the hour" (v. 13). Both groups fail to "stay awake."

It also seems strange to commend the "wise" for failing to show compassion to the others who desperately beg them to share their oil. This is especially true since in the preceding parable the reliable and wise servant was responsible for the care of fellow servants. But in this parable, the "wise" attendants are described as "those who are ready" (v. 10). Sharing their oil would mean the failure of *all* the attendants to do what they were meant to do, namely, be prepared and ready for the bridegroom. The "foolish" indicate their folly in two ways. First, they failed to anticipate the possibility of the bridegroom's delay and brought no extra oil with them. Secondly, they did not use the delay as an opportunity to procure additional oil but went to sleep instead. Then, while they went out to buy more, the bridegroom returned, went inside, and locked the door. Ultimately the bridegroom refused to recognize them when they came knocking and asking to be admitted. The wise, meanwhile, had been able to answer the cry that went up announcing the bridegroom's return. They trimmed their lamps and had them burning. The wise fulfilled their purpose as servants while the foolish did not.

Significantly, the foolish attendants address the bridegroom as "Lord" (*kyrie*), acknowledging with these words what the wise attendants did with their actions, that they knew the bridegroom was their master. In the previous chapter, Matthew implies that the bridegroom is the Son of Man (see 24:39, 42). The double cry, "Lord, Lord" reminds readers of Jesus' warning near the end of the Sermon on the Mount: "Not everyone who says to me, 'Lord, Lord,' will enter the kingdom of heaven, but only the one who does the will of my Father in heaven" (7:21). In both instances Jesus declares his rejection of unfaithful disciples, saying "I do not know you"(25:12; see also 7:23).

The Parable as Allegory

The details of the story raise a number of issues among commentators, including bridal and wedding customs about which we know very little. The parable seems to be best interpreted as an allegory, that is, a narrative in which the details are more symbolic than realistic; its significance is best understood in the light of that symbolism. In the case of this parable, wisdom involves being awake, watchful, and prepared for the parousia. Disciples fulfill their mission as servants, anticipating the moment of their master's return, which they expect with eager confidence. This parable does not spell out the real content of "being prepared" just as it does not detail the foolishness of being unprepared. Matthew's audience has heard repeatedly what is expected of the disciples of Jesus: active obedience to the Father's will, faithful attentiveness to the duties of servants, participation in Jesus' own mission of teaching and healing.

The parallel of 7:21-22 shows the dichotomy between saying "Lord, Lord" while failing to do the will of the Father. The distinction between the wise and the foolish also reminds one of the distinction between the wise person who does the words of Jesus and the foolish one who does not do them (7:24-27). This interpretation is strengthened by the following parable and especially by the scene of final judgment in 25:31-46. There, too, the Son of Man divides humankind into two camps, the sheep and the goats, the saved and the lost, on the basis of their actions, that is, the works of mercy they have performed.

There is symbolism, too, in the imagery of the lamp, the oil, and the fire. The lamps would light the way for the return of the bridegroom to reunite with his bride. Oil represents the good deeds needed to keep the lamps burning. That flasks of oil are required suggests that the distance down the road was significant and therefore there could be no delay after hearing the cry that the bridegroom is approaching. Trimming the lamps meant removing the used one and inserting a new wick, replenishing the oil, and lighting the lamp. These would necessarily be done quickly so that the returning bridegroom could find his way back to the house.

The "light" shines in the darkness and shows the way. It is there for everyone to see. In his exhortations to discipleship in the Sermon on the Mount, Jesus says, "your light must shine before others, that they may see your good deeds and glorify your heavenly Father" (5:16). In Matthew, Jesus also says that the righteous will shine like the sun in the kingdom of their Father (13:43). Light is a symbol of good deeds or proper moral disposition (see Mark 4:21; Luke 11:33). The lamp and oil are symbols in Judaism of the Law and studying the Law. The combination also implies "doing" the Law.

The parable ends with a warning that combines the admonition to "stay awake" (24:42) with the statement that "no one knows . . . the day or the hour" of the parousia (24:36). It seems at first that the call to "watch" is inappropriate since all ten fell asleep. But the verb "to watch" appears so often in New Testament apocalyptic that its sense came to express the idea of readiness. Whereas the servant of the previous parable actively violated the master's trust, the foolish attendants of this parable fail by inactivity and laziness. Their purpose and their very identity are to expect and prepare for the arrival of the bridegroom. Their folly was not so much in sleeping but in not having oil or light when needed. For Matthew, failure to fulfill the duties of a servant is as bad as abuse of those duties. The next parable will present a similar lesson.

Wise and Foolish Use of Talents (Matt 25:14-30)

The long parable on the use of talents appears as the last of the series of three parables on vigilance in Matthew. Like the other two, this one deals with master-servant relationship. In this case, too, there is stress on the servants' responsibility in the face of an absent master, but one who will surely return, especially in view of the considerable wealth he left behind in the care of servants. The parable seems to be from Q, but is adapted and edited by Matthew to reflect his apocalyptic perspective. Whereas Luke speaks of "coins," Matthew refers to "talents," a term signifying a very large sum of money, since a single talent may have been equivalent to the wage of an ordinary worker for fifteen years. Such a description of events in grand scale is characteristic of Matthew.

The phrases "faithful servant" (Matt 24:45; 25:23, 25) and "his possessions" (24:47; 25:14) link this with the first in the triad of vigilance parables. The description of the proper conduct of the first two servants may be a Matthean play on words. They are described as being "faithful over a little," which is hardly accurate since a talent is no "little" amount. In Matthew, however, one of the interesting descriptions of disciples is those of "little faith" (see 6:30; 8:26; 14:31; 16:8; cf. 17:20). Other Matthean characteristics of the parable include the emphasis on the judgment and the severity of the sentence for the servant who hid his talent, the length of the master's absence, and contrasting reactions to his trust. Here's how the parable appears in Matthew:

> [14]"It will be as when a man who was going on a journey called in his servants and entrusted his possessions to them. [15]To one he gave five talents; to another, two; to a third, one—to each according to his ability. Then he went away. Immediately [16]the one who received five talents went and traded with them, and made another five. [17]Likewise, the one who received two made another two. [18]But the man who received one went off and dug a hole in the ground and buried his master's money. [19]After a long time the master of those servants came back and settled accounts with them. [20]The one who had received

five talents came forward bringing the additional five. He said,
'Master, you gave me five talents. See, I have made five more.' [21]His
master said to him, 'Well done, my good and faithful servant. Since
you were faithful in small matters, I will give you great responsibilities. Come, share your master's joy.' [22][Then] the one who had received two talents also came forward and said, 'Master, you gave me
two talents. See, I have made two more.' [23]His master said to him,
'Well done, my good and faithful servant. Since you were faithful in
small matters, I will give you great responsibilities. Come, share your
master's joy.' [24]Then the one who had received the one talent came
forward and said, 'Master, I knew you were a demanding person,
harvesting where you did not plant and gathering where you did not
scatter; [25]so out of fear I went off and buried your talent in the ground.
Here it is back.' [26]His master said to him in reply, 'You wicked, lazy
servant! So you knew that I harvest where I did not plant and gather
where I did not scatter? [27]Should you not then have put my money
in the bank so that I could have got it back with interest on my return?
[28]Now then! Take the talent from him and give it to the one with ten.
[29]For to everyone who has, more will be given and he will grow rich;
but from the one who has not, even what he has will be taken away.
[30]And throw this useless servant into the darkness outside, where
there will be wailing and grinding of teeth.'"

Dialogue and the interaction of the characters contribute to the dramatic
realism. Listeners anticipate the return of the wealthy man who will
surely want to "settle accounts" with the servants in whom he has invested so much. The distribution of property is unequal, but each servant
is entrusted with goods "according to his ability," a phrase that has
served as a kind of definition of "talent" since Matthew's writing.

Upon the man's return, the narrative proceeds quickly and smoothly,
with notable repetition, through to the accounting from each of the three
servants. The first two servants parlay their talents and double their
returns. In contrast, the servant with only one talent digs a hole to hide
it. The first two servants give an almost identical report and are rewarded
with an identical blessing: "Well done, my good and faithful servant.
Since you were faithful in small matters, I will give you great responsibilities. Come, share your master's joy" (25:21, 23).

The Encounter with the Third Servant

The confrontation with the third servant who has hidden his talent
changes the mood and meaning of the parable. The third servant is
treated quite harshly, although we have almost come to expect this kind

of conclusion to parables in this final part of Matthew's Gospel. The third servant, admitting his own fear, expressed his assessment that the master was a "hard" man. The servant hoped that this perception would excuse his inactivity and he tries to return the unused talent. But the master denounces him as not only lazy but "wicked." The master takes away his talent and orders that it be given to the first man. For Matthew, the parable illustrates the proverb that "to everyone who has, more will be given . . . but from the one who has not, even what he has will be taken away" (25:29). Finally the third man is thrown outside into darkness and misery.

The severity of the master's judgment seems shocking. In the earlier parables of infidelity, the fault of the servants was clear. One indulged himself and abused his fellow servants. Others utterly failed in the performance of duties. But this servant only appears indolent and fearful. Many listeners, then and now, could sympathize with the poor man. But this is a kingdom parable meant to judge and provoke conversion. We are pressed to consider another perspective, identify the surprises, and evaluate what changes in reaction they demand. As the main figure in this parable, the master holds the key. He expected a return for the great trust he had shown his servants. The third servant offered as an excuse his belief that his master was a "demanding" man, "harvesting where you did not plant and gathering where you did not scatter" (v. 24). Since the servant knew that his master was demanding, he should have done everything in his power to produce a benefit for him. That is justice. On this basis, the servant is pronounced guilty out of his own mouth (15:14). He judges himself. Since he knew the master demands results, he should have invested the money and turned a profit.

The servant calls the master "hard," suggesting that he is also unjust. In his attempt to excuse himself, he accuses his master. But there is nothing in the parable to justify a charge that the master is not just. In fact, there are contrary indications. The master can do whatever he pleases. He was under no obligation to entrust his wealth to servants. To entrust even one talent to servants was an extreme act of trust and generosity. The servant's own timidity, not the master's just demands, caused his downfall. Indeed, in Matthew's Gospel, fear is the opposite of faith, a characteristic demanded of Jesus' disciples. When Jesus sends out his disciples to preach the Gospel and perform miracles, he tells them repeatedly, "Do not be afraid" (10:26, 28, 31). On another occasion he says to them, "Take courage, it is I; do not be afraid" (14:27). Faith empowers deeds of loving kindness. There is no excuse for burying one's talent.

Jesus also tells his followers that "a good tree bears good fruit" (such as faith) and "Every tree that does not bear good fruit will be cut down and thrown into the fire" (7:18-19).

A master who expects "fruit" is just and good. It is up to the servant to know the master's will and do it. The third man resembles other characters found in Matthew's parables. Like the unmerciful servant of 18:23-35 who thought in terms of human justice and could not recognize unmerited forgiveness, this servant responds to an ill-conceived and false perception of his master. Even though he himself had been treated generously, he did not act with generosity or courage. In fear, he limited himself and thereby short-changed his master. Like those who labored the whole day in the vineyard (20:1-15), he seems to be more concerned with what the master should or should not do than how to appropriately respond to the master's trust. Jesus characterizes the reactions of both of these servants as evil, and in both parables the servants are dealt with severely (see 18:32; 20:15). One thinks of the petitions of the Lord's Prayer, "Deliver us from evil" (6:13). Reliable and wise servants follow the ways of the generous and just master they serve. It is from the master that they learn generosity and justice. The servants ought to imitate, not judge the master. Indeed, they show what master they serve by their actions.

Summary

Matthew presents us with three parables of servants and implies that the choice of what kind of servant we are, good or evil, is for us to make—but the time is short. The master will return and servants will be judged according to their behavior. The wise servant is contrasted with the evil one who becomes drunk and abuses the other servants. He is worse than a thief who would rob the house, for the thief would be a clear enemy. The evil servant is an insider, but she is a hypocrite and an imposter. She fails to provide for the delay of the parousia of the master. Instead she "sleeps" and has no "oil" like the foolish attendants of the bridegroom. Or finally, like the lazy servant of the third parable, he is condemned for hiding the considerable wealth entrusted to him by the absent lord. He has acted out of fear, instead of using the gift of his talent to produce profit for the master.

All three vigilance parables describe servants who are severely punished for their inattention to the values of the kingdom: the unfaithful servant, the foolish attendants, and the servant who hid his talent are harshly dealt with indeed. The time before the parousia of Jesus is, for Matthew, a time that must be used responsibly. The end of history will be a revelation of who has used the time well. Matthew stresses the revelatory function of the parousia. Before the end, Jesus had established the church, described by Matthew as a mixed reality, where the good and the bad will grow together (13:24-30, 36-43). Before the end is a time of tolerance and forbearance. But in these final three parables, Matthew warns against complacency. In a last great scene of cosmic judgment, Matthew concludes the public ministry of Jesus. Then attitudes and actions will be revealed and these will determine exclusion or inclusion in the kingdom.

The Final Judgment (Matt 25:31-46)

Matthew's last parable of final judgment pictures the coming of the Son of Man in glory and power, to judge the world. Readers will later recall this scene when, at the end of the gospel, Jesus instructs his followers to make disciples of all nations, teaching them all that Jesus has taught (28:16-20). The parable anticipates this final command of Jesus and assumes that it has been fulfilled. The king decides to make an accounting. All are assembled for judgment. They are separated, some on the right and some on the left. Those on the right are blessed and rewarded, while those on the left are condemned to eternal punishment. The final parable in Matthew appears like this:

> [31]"When the Son of Man comes in his glory, and all the angels with him, he will sit upon his glorious throne, [32]and all the nations will be assembled before him. And he will separate them one from another, as a shepherd separates the sheep from the goats. [33]He will place the sheep on his right and the goats on his left. [34]Then the king will say to those on his right, 'Come, you who are blessed by my Father. Inherit the kingdom prepared for you from the foundation of the world. [35]For I was hungry and you gave me food, I was thirsty and you gave me drink, a stranger and you welcomed me, [36]naked and you clothed me, ill and you cared for me, in prison and you visited me.' [37]Then the righteous will answer him and say, 'Lord, when did we see you hungry and feed you, or thirsty and give you drink? [38]When did we see you a stranger and welcome you, or naked and clothe you? [39]When did we see you ill or in prison, and visit you?' [40]And the king will say to them in reply, 'Amen, I say to you, whatever you did for one of these least brothers of mine, you did for me.' [41]Then he will say to those on his left, 'Depart from me, you accursed, into the eternal fire prepared for the devil and his angels. [42]For I was hungry and you gave me no food, I was thirsty and you gave me no drink, [43]a stranger and you gave me no welcome, naked and you gave me no clothing,

ill and in prison and you did not care for me.' ⁴⁴Then they will answer
and say, 'Lord, when did we see you hungry or thirsty or a stranger
or naked or ill or in prison, and not minister to your needs?' ⁴⁵He will
answer them, 'Amen, I say to you, what you did not do for one of
these least ones, you did not do for me.' ⁴⁶And these will go off to
eternal punishment, but the righteous to eternal life."

Matthew's text is rich in images and complex in background. A number
of commentators suggest that it is, in fact, not a parable. The only parabolic elements are that the Son of Man is pictured as a shepherd and as
a king, and those who are to be judged are likened to "sheep" and
"goats." Yet Matthew's love of symmetry suggests that this is a wonderful parable summarizing many of the themes previously found in the
gospel. The structure of the scene is simple and dramatic, with repetitious dialogue and parallelism. The authority figure is shepherd, king,
and judge, who decides to settle accounts once and for all. He exercises
universal power. All the nations, including Israel, are gathered before
him. The righteous and the wicked are separated into two groups representing opposite reactions to Jesus' teachings, specifically his identification with the little ones. There is blessing for some; others are cursed.
Matthew insists that all prophecy is fulfilled in Jesus. Matthew's Gospel
would not be complete without this parable.

Matthew once again shows his own tendency to allegorize using
symbols rather than realism. For example, there seems to be no realistic
rationale for the shepherd's separation of the sheep and goats, nor any
literal explanation for the precedence of the sheep over the goats. Perhaps
Matthew wants us to think back to the parable of the stray sheep. In
contrast, the "goats" may provide a better image for the wicked because
they are more independent and less vulnerable than sheep. Sheep and
goats are separated, one to the right and the other to the left. The "right
hand" refers to the strong side of the majority of people and therefore
symbolizes favor and honor. Fire represents unrelenting torment; along
with weeping and gnashing of teeth it is part of Matthew's stock apocalyptic description of misery reserved for the wicked.

There seems to be surprise in the sorting, the sheep as perplexed as
the goats at the way they are arranged. Previous categories and boundaries are eliminated. Judgment depends upon actions and reactions to
the "least ones." There is no security, complacency, or entitlement for
belonging to a particular group such as Israel or the church. The shepherd, king, and judge recounts the deeds of charity and mercy that con-

stitute justice. Such deeds are decisive for entrance into the kingdom of heaven. For those who have been attentive in hearing the Gospel, this judgment is really no surprise after all.

To this point in the gospel, Matthew has advocated tolerance with regard to the wicked who are mixed in among the righteous as weeds among the wheat. In this final scene, the wicked are condemned and sent away to "eternal" punishment, an indication that the grace period of patient forbearance is over. "Eternity" is an apocalyptic image indicating either unending fulfillment or unmitigated misery. Eternity is a manner of speaking about God's final victory over all evil. At last the righteous "inherit the kingdom prepared for you from the foundation of the world" (25:34). The scene brings together many of the themes we have already found in Matthew's earlier parables. It envisions a collage of Old Testament images and texts. Once more Matthew insists on the primacy of ethical action and the pastoral care of the "least" members of the community.

Matthew's picture of this last judgment draws on many passages from the Scriptures and includes several images for God and for God's agents. Listeners might think of Moses who gathered the people and laid out a choice for them of the ways of blessing or curse (Deut 30:15-20). There is a shift from shepherd to king, reminiscent of the oracles of the prophets about the leaders of Israel. Background for the image of the Son of Man can be found in Daniel 7:13-14 where the Ancient of Days hands on power and glory to the "one like a son of man" (originally meaning "one resembling a human being" but taking on additional levels of meaning through use by Christians). In this final parable of Matthew, the Son of Man exercises power over all people at the final judgment. Matthew emphasizes glory and power, especially the power to judge.

Matthew illustrates God's ultimate victory over evil. Jesus, the Son of Man, will separate those "blessed by my Father" from those accursed. God's invitation to righteousness was preached by Jesus and has been extended to all. The choice to accept it or reject it rests with each one. Jesus has repeatedly warned that the time is coming for judgment when all accounts will be settled once and for all. Matthew favors fulfillment and his gospel would not be complete without this warning coming true.

Jesus has continually committed the pastoral care of the "little ones" to his disciples. The "least brothers" or "least ones" refer to the most vulnerable members of the community or of society in general, like the Christians were. The basis of judgment is how one receives Jesus through his followers who proclaim the Gospel. In the mission discourse, Jesus identified with those he sent out to preach, saying "Whoever receives you receives me, and whoever receives me receives the one who sent me" (Matt 10:40). Thus, while Jesus is portrayed as judge, it is actually the righteous and the wicked who judge themselves by their actions, either in extending hospitality and justice to the "least," or in despising and rejecting them and ignoring their needs. Refusal to help the hungry and the thirsty, the imprisoned and the stranger, constitutes the great sin that merits eternal punishment. Conversely, the care of these least and vulnerable leads to blessing and everlasting life.

Conclusion

In his arrangement and presentation of parables, Matthew demonstrates the same characteristics that distinguish the rest of his Gospel. Matthew prefers organization and symmetry, often using parables as the centerpiece of Jesus' discourses, clustering them so that he emphasizes themes most basic to the gospel. For Matthew these themes include judgment based on true righteousness, care of the church entrusted to the disciples, the ethical implications of the Gospel, and the fulfillment of the Scriptures. Matthew's apocalyptic perspective is prominent in the parables that include warnings abou the ultimate destruction of evil and promises about the consolation and vindication of the just.

CHAPTER FIVE

Parables According to Luke

Introduction to Luke

Luke's Gospel was written around the middle of the eighth decade of the first century, about the same time as Matthew's. Luke had access to the same sources as Matthew, namely the Gospel of Mark and the sayings source known as Q. Whereas Matthew was writing for a predominantly Jewish-Christian audience, Luke was a Gentile writing for Gentile Christians. Luke follows the narrative outline of Mark, taking Jesus on a journey from Galilee to Jerusalem. But Luke extends the journey narrative and pictures Jesus earnestly instructing his followers along the way. The parables, often spoken in a meal setting, are a special part of Jesus' teaching as he travels to Jerusalem, the cross and the resurrection.[1]

Like the other evangelists, Luke focuses on *christology* and *discipleship*. Luke wrings some of the "mystery" out of Mark's identity of Jesus. Jesus is the "Lord" (*kyrios*) and "Savior" (Luke 2:11). His parables show that he is a sage speaking wisdom. Jesus is portrayed as a prophet and his disciples as witnesses to the prophet's message. The ministry of Jesus and the mission of his disciples expand and grow with astonishing results. This ministry is expressed in hospitality, forgiveness, and universalism, that is, the inclusion of all. Luke depicts Jesus instructing his servant-disciples on the high cost of discipleship on the way to Jerusalem (Luke 9:51–19:28) and the need for perseverance along the way.

Luke's view of the disciples is multifaceted and more positive than Mark's. The disciples are "the ones who, when they have heard the word, embrace it with a generous and good heart, and bear fruit through per-severance" (Luke 8:15). Jesus gives praise to his Father for his disciples, saying, "Although you have hidden these things from the wise and learned you have revealed them to the childlike" (10:21). Despite the disciples' shortcomings, Jesus says of them the night before he is to die, you are the ones "who have stood by me in my trials" (22:28). Luke omits some of the negative depictions of Jesus' followers found in Mark. In Mark, Jesus asked his disciples on more than one occasion, "Do you still not understand?" Luke, on the other hand, notes occasionally that they do comprehend Jesus and, despite any misgivings, follow him gener-ously and courageously. Most poignantly, when Jesus is arrested, Luke omits Mark's note that all his disciples fled and abandoned him.

Special Lukan Themes Found in the Parables

Some of the themes especially emphasized in the Gospel of Luke as a whole are also found in his parables. These themes include the *impor-tance of repentance* and the *reversal of this world's values* that characterize the kingdom of God. In Jesus' concern for the poor, the outcast, the dis-enfranchised, he reveals *the God of mercy and compassion*. Jesus not only advocates care for the poor and the downtrodden, but he personifies the compassion he demands of his disciples. The parables in Luke frequently stress the dangers of wealth and self-importance; the defenseless are vindicated and the complacent challenged.[2] Often Luke's parables are dramatic stories with character plots, and dialogue or soliloquy (talking to oneself). Luke stresses in particular the repentance (*metanoia*, i.e., change or conversion of heart) that is necessary to enter into the kingdom of God. This conversion must be expressed in following Jesus, table fellowship, faithfulness, and perseverance.

Prayer, joy, and praise are themes found in Luke's Gospel and especially prominent in the parables. Examples of prayer abound: Luke portrays Jesus' Mother praying at the annunciation of his birth and her visit to her kinswoman, Elizabeth. Jesus himself often goes off to pray and his disciples, seeing him, ask that he teach them to pray. According to Luke one of the robbers who was crucified with him turns to Jesus in prayer. Luke pictures Jesus' own prayer of trust and forgiveness as he died. The parables also put before us examples of women and men praying, as in the case of the persistent widow (18:1-8) and the humble but confident toll collector (18:9-14). The shepherd, the woman, and the father of the parables in Luke 15 exemplify the response of God and all of heaven when what had been lost is found.

Luke's parables are realistic, not allegorical as are many in Matthew. Believers are faced with a decision and a challenge to convert "today," here and now. Luke's themes are illustrations of wisdom that is practical, applicable to the everyday lives of believers. Luke is less interested in apocalyptic eschatology than in demonstrating the timeless presence of the reign of God. Some of Luke's "parables" are actually better categorized as "exemplary stories" in that they enable the reader to sample the kingdom of God that upends this world's values. Examples of this type of story are the good Samaritan and the prodigal father.

In addition to the themes Luke especially emphasizes, we find in the parables some literary techniques unique to the third gospel. For example, Luke pairs stories of men and women. Luke has a dramatic flair, and he includes more dialogue in his parables than the other gospel writers do. Hearers are directly challenged in Luke's parables as he oftentimes uses the second person, "You," as if pointing right at members of the audience. Sometimes the narrator interrupts the characters, as in the story of the rich fool when God speaks to the farmer, saying, "You fool" (Luke 12:20).

Luke extends Mark's occasional summaries and sometimes uses them as introductions to a series of parables. For instance, Luke introduces three parables about finding the lost by saying that the Pharisees and scribes were complaining because "tax collectors and sinners were all drawing near" to Jesus and eating with him (Luke 15:1; see 5:30). Repetitions in the details of such summaries give the reader the impression that these are typical occurrences. Jesus not only advocated mercy and compassion for the downtrodden, he modeled such behavior. And he did so as a direct product of his image of God he was trying to convey.

As Jesus makes his way to Jerusalem, he is accompanied not only by his disciples, women and men who follow him from Galilee, but crowds of people.[3] Luke often portrays large crowds who are mostly positive in their response to Jesus. In contrast to their leaders, who justify themselves or pose questions merely to "test" Jesus, the people praise God for sending them a prophet and rejoice in Jesus' power to heal and to teach. Luke involves Jesus' listeners, often addressing them in the second person with questions like, "What do you think?" or "Which of you . . .?" The implication is that they are identifying themselves either as disciples or as opponents. Luke also likes to contrast reactions to Jesus, providing stereotypic behavior on the part of those who reject him and his teaching as well as of those who accept them. These opposite reactions to Jesus implicitly ask the reader, "Which reaction is yours?"

Luke presents the progress of Jesus' journey to Jerusalem and his teaching along the way with a growing sense of urgency. As he makes his way to the city he calls the "killer of prophets" (see 13:34), Jesus' focuses on preparing the disciples for his death, which is the inevitable result of his preaching and his actions. Jesus gathers his disciples around and warns them of the sacrifices that will be demanded of them. He cautions them about the dangers and temptations they will face and of the perseverance, courage, and generosity that will be required of them.

Parables in Luke

The term parable occurs eighteen times in Luke, sometimes without having Jesus speak an actual parable.[4] So, for example, in Luke 4:23 we read: "He said to them, 'Surely you will quote me this proverb (*parabolē*), "Physician, cure yourself," and say, "Do here in your native place the things we heard were done in Capernaum."'" Luke also uses the word "parable" for a proverbial saying about patching an old cloak with new cloth.[5] Again in 6:39 we have only a short comparison called a "parable" by Luke: "And he told them a parable, 'Can a blind person guide a blind person? Will not both fall into a pit?'"

As his gospel unfolds, Luke will insert parables, some from his sources, Mark and Q, and many that are unique. Luke finds parables especially well suited to table exchanges in a meal setting. He will remind readers that Jesus was on his way to Jerusalem when he taught his followers in parables. Often Luke clusters parables, pairing them or presenting a series of three, as if to emphasize with their diversity many aspects of God and the kingdom of God.

In this chapter we will consider the parables Luke has in common with his source, Mark. We will note some of the changes Luke makes in the Markan parables, to bring out his own signature emphases. But first we will study a parable found only in Luke and inserted within the episode of the anointing of Jesus by the woman who loved much. This short parable provides a kind of case study for observing some of the typical characteristics of Luke's style and theology. This parable appears before Luke uses the initial parable in Mark and Matthew, the parable of the sowings.

A Lukan Case Study: The Parable of Two Debtors

Luke's first parable is found in 7:41-43, within the context of the story of the woman who anointed Jesus as he was at table. Jesus addressed the story of two debtors to his host, Simon the Pharisee, and concluded by asking Simon's opinion on which of the two "loved more"? As often is the case in Luke, Jesus uses parables as a way of getting people to see how different is the reign of God from our ordinary (i.e., unconverted) way of thinking. This short, three-verse parable provides a wonderful example of how Jesus uses parables in Luke as a way of challenging his listeners to see with new eyes, hear with new ears, and be converted and live accordingly. The parable hinges on challenging Simon to "see" both the woman and Jesus differently.[6] Here's how Luke tells the parable:

> [40]Jesus said to him in reply, "Simon, I have something to say to you." "Tell me, teacher," he said. [41]"Two people were in debt to a certain creditor; one owed five hundred days' wages and the other owed fifty. [42]Since they were unable to repay the debt, he forgave it for both. Which of them will love him more?" [43]Simon said in reply, "The one, I suppose, whose larger debt was forgiven." He said to him, "You have judged rightly."

The Setting in Luke

Jesus had been invited to the house of Simon the Pharisee, and when they were at table, a woman came in and began to anoint Jesus' feet and dry them. Simon saw this and began to talk to himself,[7] ruminating on the idea that it was well known that the woman was a sinner. Simon objected that if Jesus were a prophet he would know that the woman was a sinner (7:39). Therefore, Simon reasoned, Jesus could not be a prophet. As is often the case in Luke, Jesus is condemned for the company he keeps. But Luke shows that indeed Jesus is a prophet who has the power to forgive sins. When Jesus talks to him and presents him with this parable, Simon is able to judge rightly. Yet the question remains open whether he will adjust his behavior and begin to see and hear differently from that point on.

Just before the dinner at the home of Simon, Luke recounts Jesus challenging his listeners about why they went out to the desert. John the Baptist had provoked a divided response: "all the people," including tax collectors, accepted him eagerly, but "the Pharisees and scholars of the law" remained skeptical and unbelieving (see 7:29-30). There were two contrasting reactions to John. Similarly, in telling of the woman's anointing, the event that prompted this parable, Luke proposed two possible responses to Jesus. One is typified by Simon the Pharisee. The second response is that of the woman, who had been known as a sinner, but who now courageously and generously ministers to Jesus without reservation or fear. She is motivated only by great love.

The men, Jesus and Simon, dialogue about the action of the woman while she silently exemplifies through her ministry a disciple's response to forgiveness.[8] Jesus' words to Simon invite him to participate in the same kind of personal transformation that the woman had experienced. This short parable is a good example of how Luke uses parables to teach a different way of thinking and acting. The woman responds to Jesus wholeheartedly. Simon is stingy with his hospitality and suspicious of Jesus and his association with sinners. Simon uses false criteria to judge both the woman and Jesus. The woman, on the contrary, responds like a disciple and receives the greatest blessing of all when Jesus tells her, "Your faith has saved you; go in peace" (7:50).

The Choice:"Which of the Two Loved More?"

There really is no mystery involved in cracking the meaning of the parable. Simon gives Jesus the correct answer to the question, "Which of them will love him more?" The two debtors both respond with gratitude and love, but the one who experienced the greater forgiveness loved more. The next step would not be so easy for Simon to take. It would involve changing his mind and heart about Jesus as well as about the woman. As Barbara Reid so eloquently puts it, "The question that the story poses is, can Simon see differently? Can he see what Jesus sees: a forgiven woman who shows great love? If he can see her this way, then he may perceive Jesus aright: not only as a prophet, but also as the agent of God's forgiving love."[9]

Even though the parable's meaning may be apparent, we need to be open to its *surprise*: that is, the one who owed the more is made, through the power of forgiveness, the more blessed. She is the one who is enabled to love the more. The reversal of the parable upends the ordinary modus operandi of the world of debt. The greatest debtor becomes the most admired and her behavior the model for others.

A number of characteristics make this a good example of the Lukan use of parables. Luke's parables are often meant as examples of transformed thinking and consequent action. Luke's parables are realistic, showing how this transformation confronts listeners with a choice and affects human responses in the here and now. Luke often presents a choice between alternate reactions of people to a given situation and invites listeners to decide, "Which of the two?" exemplifies the appropriate response. Luke's language and examples often betray his concerns about the financial world: he speaks about "debt" and wealth and frequently features the poor and the outcast as more adept at hearing Jesus' message and responding than those in positions of authority, prestige, or wealth.

Parables Luke Adapts from Mark

In all, Luke borrowed and adapted only a very few parables from Mark: the parable of the sowings and the image of the lamp in chapter 8; the parable of the mustard seed in chapter 13; and the final parable, that of the wicked tenants, in chapter 20.[10] In Luke, parables simply appear to be Jesus' usual way of speaking. Luke draws attention especially to the meal context and to the journey context as appropriate for Jesus' parables. Thus Luke gives dramatic context to Mark's claim that Jesus taught using parables and "without parables he did not speak to them" (Mark 4:34).

The Parable of the Sowings in Luke (8:4-8)

The first speech in parables appears in Luke 8. Luke's context is different than Mark's. Luke constructs the discourse as a commentary on discipleship. Many hear the word Jesus the prophet speaks. And many respond positively, with faith. Luke introduces the parables saying that Jesus was traveling from one town and village to another preaching the Gospel and announcing the coming of God's reign. The parable of the sowings is an example of this preaching. Here's how the parable appears in Luke:

> [4]When a large crowd gathered, with people from one town after another journeying to him, he spoke in a parable. [5]"A sower went out to sow his seed. And as he sowed, some seed fell on the path and was trampled, and the birds of the sky ate it up. [6]Some seed fell on rocky ground, and when it grew, it withered for lack of moisture. [7]Some seed fell among thorns, and the thorns grew with it and choked it. [8]And some seed fell on good soil, and when it grew, it produced fruit a hundredfold." After saying this, he called out, 'Whoever has ears to hear ought to hear.'"

The Setting in Luke

From Luke we learn that a "great crowd of his disciples and a large number of people from all Judea and Jerusalem and the coastal region of Tyre and Sidon came to hear" Jesus (Luke 6:17). In Luke it appears that Jesus is hardly ever lacking a large audience for his teaching. They are not only taught, but healed. Teaching and healing are traits of the prophet and evidence of the coming of God's reign. Whereas Mark (and

Matthew) picture Jesus giving a long, unique discourse in parables, Luke uses parables as examples of Jesus' "preaching and proclaiming the good news of the kingdom of God" (Luke 8:1). Luke's emphasis on the word of God is reinforced in the sayings that follow the parable of the sowings, namely, the image of the lamp, the saying on revelation (vv. 16-18), and Jesus' saying about true relatives (vv. 19-21). The common theme of all these units from 6:17–8:21 is that Jesus preaches the word of God and his true disciples hear, believe, and continue to follow him.

The parable of the sowings is not specifically identified in Luke as a kingdom parable, but the context suggests that it is. God's kingdom is made up of those who hear God's word and act on it. In the course of his journeys, Jesus attracts people who decide to follow him, like Mary Magdalene, Joanna, Susanna (8:1-3), along with the Twelve, including also his mother and brothers (8:19-21). People as diverse as Simon the Pharisee and the woman who anointed Jesus are drawn to him and his message. Some hear and follow. Some others listen for awhile and then go their separate ways. The way gets steeper, as this parable of the soil illustrates. People gather around Jesus, coming from all the towns where he has preached, to hear more. Jesus gathers followers from all Galilee. Luke tends to be much more positive about the reaction of the crowds than the other gospels.

Luke omitted Mark 3:22-30, with its reference to Jesus' kinspeople thinking he is out of his mind. Instead, in Luke the shortened speech in parables is followed by the episode of Jesus' family seeking to join him and Jesus' redefinition of his mother and brothers as "those who hear the word of God and act on it" (8:21; see also 8:15). Instead of separating believers from unbelievers as in Mark and Matthew, the parables in Luke function to illustrate the need for faith. All initially hear the parables. But only those who ponder their meaning and persevere in bringing forth the fruit of faith are saved.

Luke's Changes to the Sowings Parable

Luke simplifies the parable and includes some of the changes and emphases characteristic of him. Luke places more stress on the word of God and generalizes the challenge of Jesus to hear the meaning of the parable and produce the fruit of the word. Luke's version of the parable's interpretation stresses the need for faith and its link to salvation.

There are small but cumulatively significant changes in the telling of the parable. The sower went out to sow "his" seed; Luke keeps Mark's singular, seed, whereas Matthew used the plural, seeds. Luke says in 8:6 that the seed that fell on rocky ground withered for "lack of moisture," a more precise cause of failure than Mark's or Matthew's "had no roots." Luke adds that the good soil produced a "hundredfold," omitting the lesser yields of thirty- and sixty-fold. Luke thus simplifies the conclusion and emphasizes the overwhelming contrast between the small seedlings and the amazingly huge yield.

The Sowings Parable Explained (Luke 8:9-15)

As in Mark and Matthew, Jesus proceeds to explain this parable. Luke omits Mark's confusing change of setting with the disciples asking in private about the parable's meaning. Luke simplifies the whole scene, picturing the "disciples" as those who follow up on Jesus' teaching, asking questions so that they may understand and act accordingly. Here is how Luke presents the explanation:

> [9]Then his disciples asked him what the meaning of this parable might be. [10]He answered, "Knowledge of the mysteries of the kingdom of God has been granted to you; but to the rest, they are made known through parables so that 'they may look but not see, and hear but not understand.' [11]This is the meaning of the parable. The seed is the word of God. [12]Those on the path are the ones who have heard, but the devil comes and takes away the word from their hearts that they may not believe and be saved. [13]Those on rocky ground are the ones who, when they hear, receive the word with joy, but they have no root; they believe only for a time and fall away in time of trial. [14]As for the seed that fell among thorns, they are the ones who have heard, but as they go along, they are choked by the anxieties and riches and pleasure of life, and they fail to produce mature fruit. [15]But as for the seed that fell on rich soil, they are the ones who, when they have heard the word, embrace it with a generous and good heart, and bear fruit through perseverance."

In Luke, the disciples approach Jesus and ask the meaning of this parable in particular, whereas Mark and Matthew say that the disciples ask why Jesus speaks in parables in general. Before explaining the parable, Jesus asserts that the disciples have been granted "knowledge of the mysteries of the kingdom of God" (Luke 8:10).[11] The disciples are given an explanation whereas others must be satisfied with a message in code. Jesus adds, but for others the secrets are in parables so that "they may look but not see, and hear but not understand." Luke vaguely alludes to Isaiah 6:9, but lacks the rejection motif present in Mark or the hardening idea of Matthew. Luke simply means that without the knowledge granted to the disciples, the others do not understand what they hear.

The secrecy motif that is so prominent but obscure in Mark is almost absent from Luke. Indeed, Jesus will express praise to God for "although you have hidden these things from the wise and learned you have revealed them to the childlike" (Luke 10:21). And this realization prompts Jesus to remind his disciples of the blessing they have received. Luke continues, "Turning to his disciples in private he said, 'Blessed are the eyes that see what you see. For I say to you, many prophets and kings desired to see what you see but did not see it, and to hear what you hear, but did not hear it'" (10:23-24).

Luke's interpretation of the parable is consistent and clear. He does not stress the differences between insiders and outsiders as Mark and Matthew did; rather, Luke focuses more attention on the sayings that follow the interpretation, showing that it is possible to lose what one has initially been given or thinks one already has (vv. 12-13).[12] All kinds of "soil" receive the word but only the "rich soil" that embraces it with a "generous and good heart" and bears its fruit through perseverance (8:15) is saved. Perseverance and faithfulness are characteristic of true hearing. In sum, the changes Luke makes illustrate the meaning of acceptance by the disciple. Luke emphasizes three elements: (1) Jesus the prophet preaches the Word of God, which is closely connected with salvation; (2) the diverse responses in terms of hearing and faith; and (3) the enduring character of faith.

Jesus the Prophet Preaches Salvation

Jesus, as the prophet of God's word, begins his explanation, "The seed is the word of God." Only Luke makes explicit this connection between faith in the word of God and salvation (8:11, 12). This is not the first time Luke has made this connection. In speaking to the woman who anointed him in Simon's house, Jesus had assured her that her faith had saved her (7:50). When he saw their faith, Jesus healed the paralytic and forgave sins (5:20). People respond to Jesus' works and words, some with faith that leads to salvation and others with disbelief and eventually rejection.

Faith is not a matter of hearing only, but of keeping the word, producing its fruit, and persevering. The receptive soil is a symbol for the disciples who are, throughout the gospel, described in just such terms as these. Of Mary, for example, Luke says, she "kept all these things in her heart" (Luke 2:51). The disciples will be persecuted and will suffer many things, Jesus warns, but he promises, "By your perseverance you will secure your lives" (21:19). Luke softens or omits some of Mark's allusions to the failures of the disciples. Rather, in Luke, Jesus reminds them at the Last Supper, "It is you who have stood by me in my trials" (22:28).

Faith and Perseverance

Disciples must persevere through temptations, trials, and suffering. Some will initially hear the word but they will be tempted by the devil who will "take away the word from their hearts that they may not believe and be saved" (8:12-13).[13] The devil vies for power over human hearts. The disciples follow their master, Jesus, who was himself tempted by the devil from the beginning of his mission. For Luke this was not a one-time thing. The devil departed from Jesus only "for a time" (i.e., *kairos*, 4:13), until the opportune moment presents itself. Then the devil will unite with Judas and seek the opportune moment to betray Jesus (22:3, 6). Satan will ask for Peter, to "sift [him] like wheat," but Peter will be reconverted and strengthen the other disciples because of his experience (22:31-32). The moment of Satan's greatest power will come when Jesus is arrested and led away to be condemned to death (22:53).

Some receive the word with joy, but have no root; they believe only for a time (*kairos*), but fall away in time (again, *kairos*) of trial (8:13). Here Luke gives *kairos* its fullest meaning, suggesting an opportunity or decisive moment for either good or evil. For Luke, suffering or obstacles are often opportunities for temptation against faith. People may believe for a while and they may be filled with a sense of joy and enthusiasm. But when they meet suffering or opposition, they lose faith and courage. Lacking roots, they abandon faith. Faith is useless without perseverance, especially in the face of suffering.

Luke makes acceptance of the word a matter of "faith." He omits the reference to "tribulation and persecution" (see Mark 4:13 and Matt 13:21), using instead "time of trial" (8:13), which relates the disciples' experience to that of Jesus. Luke sticks to an image of plant life fading or losing its color in the process of dying, substituting "fade away" for "stumble" (*skandalizomai*) found in Mark 4:17 and Matthew 13:21.[14] Luke also accentuates the active aspect of faith, stressing the plant's ability to produce ripe fruit, rather than simply "bearing" it as in Mark and Matthew.

Another obstacle to true faith is represented by "anxieties and riches and pleasures of life" (8:14). Luke drops two terms from Mark and adds another signified by the seed choked by thorns. He omits Mark's "worldly" when describing anxieties, and speaks of wealth itself rather than its "lure." Anxieties and wealth threaten faith. Luke adds "the pleasures of life" to the list, leaving the cumulative impression that the real danger to faith lies in life's supposed comforts rather than in its burdens. Jesus teaches a similar lesson in the parable of the rich fool in 12:16-21, and in the eschatological discourse of 21:34, where he says, "Beware that your hearts do not become drowsy from carousing and drunkenness, and that day catch you by surprise like a trap" (21:34-35a).

The seed that falls on good soil is received with a "generous and good heart" (8:15). Use of "heart" echoes verse 12 that said the devil removed the word from the hearts of those represented by the seed that fell along the footpath. The combination "generous and good," found only here in the New Testament, expresses the Greek idea of noble generosity. These disciples will "protect" (*katecho*) the word and nurture it to bring forth its fruit. The verb *katecho* suggests cherishing a prized possession; taken with perseverance or endurance it expresses fidelity especially in the face of adversity and sacrifice. The same idea is expressed in Luke 21:19: "By your perseverance you will secure your lives."

Three Proverbs about Witness (8:16-18)

Basically, Luke follows Mark in combining the image of the lamp with this parable of sowings, although Mark's parable discourse is significantly longer. In response to the disciples' question about the meaning of the sowings parable, Jesus indicated that knowledge of the mysteries of the kingdom of God had been granted to the disciples. The image of the lamp continues and extends the idea of enlightenment. The proverb about secrets becoming manifest links "light" to "witness." A third statement indicates the paradox of having and sharing versus hoarding and losing. Here's Luke's version of these sayings:

> [16]"No one who lights a lamp conceals it with a vessel or sets it under a bed; rather, he places it on a lampstand so that those who enter may see the light. [17]For there is nothing hidden that will not become visible, and nothing secret that will not be known and come to light. [18]Take care, then, how you hear. To anyone who has, more will be given, and from the one who has not, even what he seems to have will be taken away."

Luke presents three proverbs as a unit with only minor alterations of Mark 4:21-25.[15] These sayings, which might have been independent, appear to reflect secular wisdom and might not have been original with

Jesus. They rely on common sense and ordinary experience. Obviously, light is most effective when put in a prominent place rather than hidden. Often secrets become common knowledge. The "haves" get more, while the "have-nots" continue to lose even their meager possessions. The combination of these sayings serve Luke's emphasis on the importance of maintaining faith even in the face of suffering, and giving witness to others so that they also will believe in Jesus and the Gospel he preaches.

Only Luke adds the phrase in 8:16, "so that those who enter may see the light," the obvious effect of lighting a lamp. More importantly, this phrase helps to link the image with the following saying about things hidden becoming visible. Luke omits Mark's reference to the measure (Mark 4:24).[16] Luke also tones down the apocalyptic dimension of Mark's warning, "Anyone who has ears to hear ought to hear" (Mark 4:23). Rather, Luke cautions, "Take care, then, how you hear."

In the preceding passage (8:11-15), Luke contrasted those who initially hear "with joy" but "fall away in time of trial" (v. 13) to those who "[hear] the word, embrace it with a generous and good heart, and bear fruit through perseverance" (v. 15). With the image of the "light," Jesus stresses the need to bear witness and shine that others may "see the light" (v. 16). What was formerly secret comes to light. Luke links this proverb to the light saying to show that one cannot be silent about what she knows through experience, what she has seen and heard. Thus the disciple is one who has heard the word, embraced it generously, and pondered and retained it even in the midst of and despite suffering. The disciple brings forth the fruit of the word that was sown. The disciple's faith is manifest in witness, for if faith is not shared with others, it was never really experienced or possessed.

If hearing does not lead to enduring faith, Luke says, even what one seems to have will be taken away. Luke's version notes that often a person thinks he possesses something but finds that he does not, that what one thought he possessed was an illusion. Luke is consistent with the idea that initial or partial faith that cannot or does not withstand time, opposition, temptation, and suffering is actually no faith at all.

Summary

Luke uses the parable and explanation of the sowings as a commentary on discipleship. Disciples must not only hear the word but nurture it, even in times of suffering and tribulation. They must endure hardship and let the light of what they have seen and heard shine for others. Hearing, perseverance, bearing fruit, and witness are all required of the disciples. This is a significant part of Jesus' teaching as he makes his way to Jerusalem.

Three Parables of Productivity (Luke 13:6-9, 18-21)

In chapter 8 Luke significantly abbreviated Mark's parable discourse (Mark 4: 1-34). This is in contrast to Matthew who had expanded it into a "day of parables" (Matthew 13). However, Luke follows Mark in combining parables in pairs or in a series, often in three. Luke usually recounts a pair of parables or offers, as he does in chapter 13, a combination of the images: the barren fig tree (Luke 13:6-9), the mustard seed (13:18-19), and the leaven (13:20-21.[17]

The Barren Fig Tree (Luke 13:6-9)

As Jesus and his entourage made their way to Jerusalem, Luke tells us, reports reached them about the deaths of Galileans, some who had been put to death by Pilate and others who were killed in a tragic accident (Luke 13:1-5). Many thought these deaths were punishment for sin. But Jesus gives these events a prophetic interpretation, using them to warn his followers of the need for repentance while there is still time. Mark had told the story of Jesus and the withered fig tree as one of the events leading up to the passion (Mark 11:12-14; see also Matt 21:18-19). Mark, followed by Matthew, said that after he arrived in Jerusalem, Jesus searched a tree of figs but found none. He then cursed the fig tree and it withered immediately. A parable, probably originating with the same tradition as the event in Mark, is unique to Luke and exhibits some distinctly Lukan characteristics. Possibly Luke transformed the miracle story of the cursing of the fig tree into a parable. Here's is how Luke uses the image:

> [6]And he told them this parable: "There once was a person who had a fig tree planted in his orchard, and when he came in search of fruit on it but found none, [7]he said to the gardener, 'For three years now I have come in search of fruit on this fig tree but have found none. [So] cut it down. Why should it exhaust the soil?' [8]He said to him in reply, 'Sir, leave it for this year also, and I shall cultivate the ground around it and fertilize it; [9]it may bear fruit in the future. If not you can cut it down.'"

The "parable," a term used here in the sense of "lesson," of the fig tree follows Jesus' warning, "If you do not repent, you will all perish as they did!" (13:5). Repentance is a theme characteristic of Luke. The events in

Galilee reminded people that death can come at any moment. Jesus reminds them that the best preparation for death is a life of conversion and repentance. The owner of the fig tree planted it with the expectation that it would bear fruit. He has visited the fruitless tree and his patience was wearing thin. The gardener bargains for a little more time. The question of whether the fig tree will yet produce is left open. The prophet, Jesus, is challenging people to use their reprieve as an opportunity to change and to produce fruit. "Fruit" is an image for actions that manifest the kingdom of God present in the world.

Luke follows this short parable with the story of Jesus curing a woman crippled for more than eighteen years (13:11-13).[18] This healing illustrates the values and demands of the kingdom of God. It may seem as if this healing episode interrupts Jesus' instruction to his followers. But Luke, ever the dramatist, reinforces his lesson on living according to the values of the kingdom of God with this story of healing and two diverse reactions to it as represented by the woman herself and the leader of the synagogue. She glorifies God while the leader becomes indignant because Jesus has worked a miracle on the Sabbath. Luke pictures Jesus as the prophet visiting God's people. With great irony, the synagogue leader acts like the fruitless tree that fails to respond to the time of the owner's visit. The leader wrongly considers the Sabbath moment no time for healing or miracles.

Just as the reaction of the woman is in stark contrast to the indignation of the leader of the synagogue, there are two typical but diverse reactions to this series of events and sayings. With an example of Lukan hyperbole, we learn that "all his adversaries were humiliated; and the whole crowd rejoiced" at Jesus' words and deeds (13:17). Luke continues to picture Jesus traveling to Jerusalem followed by a mix of disciples and opponents. Luke keeps his readers open to the choices they face as they hear Jesus tell of the arrival and the growth of the reign of God among them.

The parable of the fig tree functions as both encouragement and warning. Jesus encourages his followers to recognize the time of their visitation by God's prophet, heed his message, repent and convert their lives, and act according to the values of the kingdom of God, including showing mercy to the needy. The parable also serves as a warning that believers use the time of reprieve productively. Whether Jesus' hearers will learn the lesson of the fig tree is left an open question. The story of the cure of the crippled woman links the fig tree parable to two other parabolic images that stress the unfettered growth of the kingdom of God despite its small, unpromising beginnings.

The Parables of the Mustard Seed and the Leaven (Luke 13:18-21)

Two short parables become encouragement to Jesus' followers that the kingdom of God has begun among them and will continue to grow, fed with God's power. Like the healed woman who had been overlooked and "hidden" in the midst of those considered more important and powerful, the small seed and the leaven are signs of the presence of the kingdom of God. Likewise, what Jesus has begun in his ministry as exemplified by his teaching and healing, the disciples will continue. And faith will grow and spread. Here is how Luke presents the two parables of the mustard seed and the leaven:

> [18]Then he said, "What is the kingdom of God like? To what can I compare it? [19]It is like a mustard seed that a person took and planted in the garden. When it was fully grown, it became a large bush and 'the birds of the sky dwelt in its branches.'" [20]Again he said, "To what shall I compare the kingdom of God? [21]It is like yeast that a woman took and mixed [in] with three measures of wheat flour until the whole batch of dough was leavened."

Luke deliberately places the small parables of growth within a highly charged context of conflict. These parables are commentary on the healing of the woman, suggested by Luke's transition: "Therefore he began to say." A couple of contrasts are built into the images: small beginnings are contrasted with powerful results, and the hidden is in contrast to what is manifest. Limits and obstacles to growth are being overcome. Will people recognize the kingdom of God present among them in time?

With the image of the mustard seed, Jesus shows how from a small beginning the kingdom of God grows into a "large bush" which provides shelter for the "birds of the sky." Luke does not allude to the small size of the mustard seed as Mark (and Matthew) did, nor the exaggerated claim that the seed becomes the "greatest" of shrubs. But Luke, like Mark and Matthew, does contrast the inauspicious beginnings of the small seed with the "large bush" it produces that is big enough to provide shelter for many birds. For Luke, Jesus' healing and preaching are signs of the presence of the reign of God that is growing and becoming a great force in human history. There is also a direct connection between the small beginnings of faith such as that of the healed woman and the disciples, and the future fullness of the kingdom of God impacting the world in power.

Luke also compares the reign of God with leaven hidden in the dough. The yeast, while its quantity is negligible, is actually the most important ingredient. The flour may be important and more abundant and more visible. But without leaven, there would be no bread. Although hidden, the yeast is essential for the dough to rise and become bread. Moreover there is a subversive quality of the "hidden" yeast. It is the catalyst that changes everything and, once added, cannot be eliminated. This ingredient in the hands—and intent of the woman—permeates the entire "three measures of dough," an exceedingly abundant amount of flour, and produces something totally new and different. Similarly the seemingly insignificant leaven of the kingdom of God present already in the ministry of Jesus and his disciples has the power to change the whole world.

Summary

Luke combines three parables in chapter 13 to provide commentary on current events such as Pilate's cruelty to some Galileans, as well as on Jesus' healing of the crippled woman. Luke uses the parables to convey several lessons. The fig tree, a symbol of God's people, is given a reprieve from being cut down so that it may bear fruit. The parable serves as a warning to repent. The mustard seed and the leaven illustrate how, despite small and hidden beginnings, the Gospel will spread through the power of God.

The Parable of the Wicked Tenants (Luke 20:9-19)

Luke recounts the parable of the wicked tenants much like Mark does. This is the last parable of the Synoptic Gospels. Events have taken a dangerous turn. In Jerusalem, Jesus encounters great animosity and resistance from the leaders of the people who seek an opportune moment to destroy him. And from the "hour" that he spoke this parable (Luke 20:19), they were intent on doing so. Although it is Jesus who is in danger, it is the leaders who are afraid. They fear the people who continue to flock around Jesus. The leaders will not repent. They are intent upon putting Jesus to death. Not long after speaking this parable with its veiled threat, Jesus will more openly warn that they will receive "a very severe condemnation" because of their practices.

Jesus addresses the parable to the "people" (Luke uses *laos* whereas Mark used "crowds"), but the leaders are very aware that it is spoken with them in mind. It is an accusation and they know it. For once they get the meaning of the parable. But it is also clear that they will not convert their minds and hearts. They are closed to the message of the prophet, Jesus. Here is how Luke tells the story:[19]

⁹Then he proceeded to tell the people this parable. "[A] man planted a vineyard, leased it to tenant farmers, and then went on a journey for a long time. ¹⁰At harvest time he sent a servant to the tenant farmers to receive some of the produce of the vineyard. But they beat the servant and sent him away empty-handed. ¹¹So he proceeded to send another servant, but him also they beat and insulted and sent away empty-handed. ¹²Then he proceeded to send a third, but this one too they wounded and threw out. ¹³The owner of the vineyard said, 'What shall I do? I shall send my beloved son; maybe they will respect him.' ¹⁴But when the tenant farmers saw him they said to one another, 'This is the heir. Let us kill him that the inheritance may become ours.' ¹⁵So they threw him out of the vineyard and killed him. What will the owner of the vineyard do to them? ¹⁶He will come and put those tenant farmers to death and turn over the vineyard to others." When the people heard this they exclaimed, "Let it not be so!" ¹⁷But he looked at them and asked, "What then does this scripture passage mean:

'The stone which the builders rejected
has become the cornerstone'?

¹⁸Everyone who falls on that stone will be dashed to pieces; and it will crush anyone on whom it falls." ¹⁹The scribes and the chief priests sought to lay their hands on him at that very hour, but they feared the people, for they knew that he had addressed this parable to them.

The Setting in Luke

In a summary characteristic of him, Luke once again asserts that Jesus' teaching in the Temple met with two opposite reactions. The "chief priests and scribes" sought to destroy him, but he was highly popular with the people. Indeed, fear of the people frustrated the authorities so that the most they could do was challenge Jesus' authority. They ask Jesus, "[W]ho is the one who gave you this authority" to teach (20:2)?

The meaning of the parable, based on the image of the vineyard from Isaiah, is clear, as the leaders themselves recognize. Although Luke hardly deviates from Mark in the telling, there are a few deliberate changes that bear Luke's signature and call for comment. Luke uses the word *kyrios* (Lord) for the owner of the vineyard (vv. 13, 15). Only Luke has the people interject their horror when the owner decides to take the vineyard away from the tenants (v. 16). And finally, Luke overlays meanings to the "stone" image and imbues it with an implied threat (v. 18).

The Vineyard Owner Is *Kyrios*

Isaiah had stated that the vineyard belonged to God (*kyrios*). Like the fig tree owner in Luke 13:8, the *kyrios* is powerful and has the authority to cut down the tree or slaughter the unproductive servants (20:16) if he chooses. The title is clarified when readers relate Jesus' parable to Isaiah 5:7, the passage Matthew explicitly cites in this regard. This title is linked to the "beloved son" who is sent last of all to reason with the tenants. Readers would connect this phrase with Isaac, the beloved son of Abraham. Luke's readers might also be reminded of the only other two times Luke uses the word "beloved" (*agapētos*) identifying Jesus as God's beloved Son, at his baptism (3:22) and at his transfiguration (9:35).

"Let it not be so!"

Only Luke's parable has the response of the people when they hear that the owner will turn over the vineyard to others: "Let it not be so!" (20:16). Once again Luke contrasts the responses: the people who recoil in horror at the judgment against the tenant farmer, versus the leaders who continue to conspire to kill Jesus. The people (*laos*) speak with one voice, like a chorus in Greek plays. Luke often pictures bystanders exclaiming a positive response in praise or joy (see 1:58, 66; 4:15, 22, 36-37; 5:26; 7:16-17, 29; 13:17; 18:43; 19:38, 48). The vineyard represents the kingdom of God. It has been promised and the people are longing for its coming. The people, having waited expectantly and with hope, are portrayed as much more open and receptive to Jesus than their leaders.

The "Stone"

The parable of the wicked servants serves as a critique to the authorities because they did not return fruit from the vineyard to the Lord. Although the leaders know the parable is meant for them, as Luke mentions in 20:19, they reject its demand for conversion. In fact, a verse found only in Luke (v. 18) becomes a threat: the cornerstone the "builders" or leaders rejected could fall on them. Luke seizes on the notion of a "stone" or "rock" and layers it with meaning. For Luke it is the cornerstone, a stumbling block, and a rock that could fall and crush them.

Luke is influenced by three passages from the Old Testament: Psalm 118:22, Isaiah 8:14-15, and Daniel 2:34-35, 44-45. Luke explicitly quotes only verse 22 from Psalm 118, which reads: "The stone the builders rejected has become the cornerstone." This saying functions as a proverb meaning that what is insignificant to human beings is selected by God to become essential.[20] It expresses the reversal of human expectations contrasted with God's purposes. The "stone" may originally refer to the foundation stone or capstone of the Temple. The New Testament interpreted the verse as referring to the death and resurrection of Christ (Matt 21:42; Acts 4:11; see also Isa 28:16 and Rom 9:33; 1 Pet 2:7).

The cornerstone does not mean the brick adorned with a plaque that gives the year that the building was dedicated, as it often does today. Rather, the cornerstone is the one that bears the weight of two walls. It is the essential, most crucial stone of the building, the one that holds it up. This stone has to be carefully selected by the builders. But the New Testament writers argue that it is this stone that the builders, the leaders of Judaism, rejected when they condemned Jesus to death. The precious cornerstone image is combined with a warning about a stone that serves as an obstacle, with the suggestive reference to Isaiah 8:14-15, a passage that reads:

> [14]Yet he shall be a snare, an obstacle and a stumbling stone
>   to both houses of Israel,
> A trap and a snare
>   to those who dwell in Jerusalem;
> [15]And many among them shall stumble and fall,
>   broken, snared and captured.

The stone provides a multifaceted image. The cornerstone is crucial to the building; but when it is rejected by the builders, it becomes also a stumbling block or *skandalon* that will cause people to trip and fall. The word "scandal" also means that which gives offense or arouses opposition.[21] Luke had Simeon prophesy exactly this result of Jesus' preaching the very first time he was presented in the Temple (see Luke 2:34). In his response to the messengers of John Baptist, Jesus says, "Blessed is the one who takes no offense (literally "is not scandalized") at me" (see Luke 7:23). For Luke, those who are scandalized by Jesus, that is, those who reject and oppose him, are themselves to blame. They ought to hear these words from Isaiah as a prophecy and a threat. Luke is implying that this Scripture passage is fulfilled in the leaders' rejection of Jesus in Jerusalem.

Yet another aspect of the image seems to be derived from Daniel 2:34-35, 44-45. Rather than tripping on this stone, it could fall and crush people. Daniel describes the king's vision of a statue; it reads:

> [34]"While you looked at the statue, a stone which was hewn from a mountain without a hand being put to it, struck its iron and tile feet, breaking them in pieces. [35]The iron, tile, bronze, silver and gold all crumbled at once, fine as the chaff on the threshing floor in summer, and the wind blew them away without leaving a trace . . . [44]In the lifetime of those kings the God of heaven will set up a kingdom that shall never be destroyed or delivered up to another people; rather, it shall break in pieces all these kingdoms and put an end to them, and

it shall stand forever. ⁴⁵That is the meaning of the stone you saw hewn
from the mountain without a hand being put to it, which broke in
pieces the tile, iron, bronze, silver, and gold."

Daniel's allusion adds another layer of meaning to the "stone." It may
fall and crush anything in its path. Jesus is the prophet who comes to
fulfill all these descriptions of the "stone." He is the one rejected by the
leaders but chosen by God. He is a stumbling block to many because of
their obstinacy and refusal to repent. He will bring justice to the needy,
but he will crush the rich and the proud and the complacent.

The Urgent Importance of Jesus' Mission

Especially as Jesus has now arrived in Jerusalem, the urgent sense of
Jesus' mission in Luke is greater and the reality of the time of judgment
nearer than ever before. The leaders who would have been very familiar
with the Scriptures, realize the implications and the prophetic tone of
Jesus' words. Luke says that they would have laid their hands upon
Jesus and arrested him, but they "feared" the people (20:19). Soon they
will fall silent (20:26), and finally "they no longer dared to ask him anything" (20:40). But this does not mean that they have surrendered.

The scribes and the chief priests had challenged Jesus' authority to
teach (20:1) and he had silenced them with his own question about the
authority of John the Baptist (20:1-8). When they refused to answer Jesus'
question, he turns to teach the people as the leaders stand by helplessly.
The sense of foreboding, heightened danger to Jesus, and the paradoxical
fear on the part of the leaders who are so intent on putting him to death,
increases as Jesus faces down his enemies. They have refused to hear
this and all the other parables. Soon Jesus' teaching will be complete and
he will be condemned because of it. The leaders know that this parable
is intended for them or better, "against them." Luke conveys the meaning
of accusation. In this, the final parable of the gospels, Jesus will make
one last attempt before his death to get them to "hear." Although Luke
leaves open the question of whether they will convert their hearts, we
already have the sense that they will not.

This impression is reinforced as Luke's narrative draws to a close. Just
before the eschatological discourse of chapter 21, Luke will draw a final
diptych of two responses to Jesus' preaching to this point, including this
and all the other parables. Jesus denounces the scribes while he praises
a poor widow in Luke 20:45–21:4. Within hearing of "all the people,"
Jesus issues a final invitation and warning to his disciples to "be on

guard" against the scribes who "devour the houses of widows and, as a pretext, recite lengthy prayers. They will receive a very severe condemnation" (Luke 20:47). The prophets of old condemned those who took advantage of the poor, especially while excusing their conduct in the name of religion. For example, Ezekiel decries the sins of the Jerusalem leaders, accusing them of oppressing orphans and widows (Ezek 22:7). Similarly, Job warns of coming disaster because "You have sent widows away empty-handed" (Job 22:9). The scribes are leaders and teachers of the people. They are generally described as seeking out honors and showing false religious piety while they do not take care of the defenseless among them. They are warned of impending condemnation.

The image of the widow links former prophetic warnings with Jesus' observation of the poor widow who offered her whole life (*bios* in v. 4) in support of the Temple (21:1-4). From her poverty, her offering of two small coins represents a sacrifice much larger than those who give out of their surplus. She makes readers think of the prophet Anna who appeared at the beginning of the gospel, awaiting the redemption of Israel (2:36-38).

Luke thus stays true to form, featuring two opposite responses to the gospel, which is nearing its conclusion with Jesus' death and resurrection. Luke continues to draw in his readers with implicit encouragement to choose which reaction to Jesus they will identify as their own. Will they imitate the "scribes and the chief priests" who know that the parable is addressed to them but conspire to put Jesus to death anyway? Or will they follow the chorus of voices of the people who protest "Let it not be so!"?

Conclusion

In parables adapted and edited from Mark, Luke emphasizes some of the most important themes of his gospel. For example, the parable of the sowings challenges listeners to cultivate in themselves an open and generous heart to receive the word of God and to bring forth its fruit through perseverance. The image of the lamp illustrates the necessity of visible witness reflecting the way of discipleship for others to see and imitate. Similarly, the example of the fig tree shows the importance of bearing fruit and warns that, if not, the Lord will cut it down. The lesson of the mustard seed, like that of the leaven, is the hope that from inauspicious beginnings, God can and will give abundant growth. Finally, the parable of the wicked tenants functions as an urgent call to repentance; the Lord has sent his beloved Son in hopes that the tenants entrusted with the vineyard will repent. It is the Lord's will that they will respect and receive his Son.

Many of Luke's parables make clear that Jesus and his word are met with two opposing reactions: acceptance or rejection, transformation or resistance. The moment of decision and action has come with Jesus' entrance into Jerusalem. We have heard his proclamation of the kingdom and learned of the challenges and sacrifices demanded of those who wish to enter into it. With the realism typical of Luke, we are faced with the call for commitment "today," in the present, here and now.

CHAPTER SIX

Parables of Luke's Travel Narrative

The majority of the parables found in Luke appear in the course of Jesus' journey to Jerusalem. Luke extends the journey narrative he found in Mark (see Luke 9:51–19:28; Mark 8:22–10:52). Luke stresses that Jesus' journey is purposeful and reminds readers that his destination is Jerusalem (Luke 9:51; 13:22; 17:11), the city he indicts as killer of prophets (13:34). The terms "way" or "road" also appear within this travel narrative (9:57; 10:4) as do other periodic references to Jesus' movement from village to village (see 10:1; 11:53; 18:35; 19:1). Within the general framework of this travelogue, Luke inserts much of the material unique to him.

Although it is important to remember that Jesus is bound for Jerusalem, Luke is also concerned with the preparation of the disciples as witnesses who will be required to testify to all Jesus does and says. The "journey" theme loosely assembles Jesus' instructions to his disciples who accompany him. Along the way Jesus often dines with his disciples and a wide variety of others, including religious leaders like the Pharisees and scribes, as well as tax collectors and sinners. Through dialogue with his opponents and with his followers, Jesus was preparing his disciples to continue his ministry, spreading the Gospel despite obstacles, suffering, and the required sacrifice of themselves.

Most of Luke's parables are found in this elongated journey passage. Many of these parables are unique to Luke and illustrate the special themes so important and characteristic of the third gospel. Jesus' instruction is urgent, as if to emphasize that the way is tough and treacherous and will require faith, perseverance, and wisdom. The disciples are linked with Jesus in a very special way. His journey is their journey. His fate will be their fate. They face temptation and persecution. Instead of preaching to them through long sermons, Jesus teaches in simple stories that invite the disciples to catch a glimpse of life in the kingdom of God. Through his parables, Jesus warns them about temptations that come in various forms: for example, greed (rich fool), pride (Pharisee and publican), worldly ambition (the great banquet), false religiosity (good Samaritan). Also in parables Jesus emphasizes qualities such as hospitality, forgiveness, and reconciliation (the lost sheep, the lost coin, the lost son), the importance of sharing, and the justice of the kingdom (the rich man and Lazarus).

There are two types of parables especially distinctive to Luke: "example stories," and parables told in meal settings, both conveying the flavor of life according to the kingdom of God. These are mainly stories that are meant to guide the believing community's decisions about inclusiveness, hospitality, possessions, and justice. Since Luke has the greatest number of parables, we have to be selective and will focus on those that capture important Lukan themes. Many of these are found in the middle part of Luke's Gospel, chapters 10–16.

The Good Samaritan (Luke 10:29-37)

One of the most beloved of Luke's parables, the good Samaritan, is actually an example story that gives a feel for the compassion required in order to live as "children of the Most High" (6:35) who personifies mercy (6:36). This story is told in answer to a lawyer who approaches Jesus, to test him (10:25-29). The lawyer asks, "Teacher, what must I to do to inherit eternal life?" Jesus turns the question around and asks, "What is written in the law? How do you read it?" The legal scholar answers by combining the command to love God with the one to love neighbor. Jesus replies that he is correct in so answering. When the questioner wants to "justify himself" for having asked what he clearly knew already, Jesus tells the story of the good Samaritan.

> [30]"A man fell victim to robbers as he went down from Jerusalem to Jericho. They stripped and beat him and went off leaving him half-dead. [31]A priest happened to be going down that road, but when he saw him, he passed by on the opposite side. [32]Likewise a Levite came

to the place, and when he saw him, he passed by on the opposite side. [33]But a Samaritan traveler who came upon him was moved with compassion at the sight. [34]He approached the victim, poured oil and wine over his wounds and bandaged them. Then he lifted him up on his own animal, took him to an inn and cared for him. [35]The next day he took out two silver coins and gave them to the innkeeper with the instruction, 'Take care of him. If you spend more than what I have given you, I shall repay you on my way back.' [36]Which of these three, in your opinion, was neighbor to the robbers' victim?" [37]He answered, "The one who treated him with mercy." Jesus said to him, "Go and do likewise."

The Samaritan of this story represents a practical example of the radical demands on Jesus' disciples. The point of the story is conveyed not by some short moral formula but by the gist of the example itself. Jesus' response to the lawyer in the form of the parable of the Good Samaritan means that one cannot limit the object of love, compassion, or grace. The Samaritan is chosen to illustrate a subject whose range is unlimited, perhaps preparing for other passages in Luke, such as the grateful Samaritan of Luke 17:16 and Acts 8:4-8 with their positive picture of the Samaritans' reaction to the Gospel.

As he proceeds to Jerusalem, Jesus gives instruction about discipleship. He is followed by a mixed entourage: the usually positive crowds, the disciples, and the usually hostile opponents. Sometimes, as in the case of the good Samaritan story, questions occasion eloquent lessons on conduct worthy of the kingdom of God. Just prior to the scholar's question, Jesus offered this beatitude for his disciples: "Blessed are the eyes that see what you see" (10:23). The scholar's question gives Jesus the opportunity to paint a picture for his followers so they will not only "see" but "go and do likewise."

When he poses his seemingly benign "test," the scholar of the Law assumes the usual posture of a learner: he stands and asks Jesus the teacher what he must do to inherit eternal life. The "test" is not so much whether Jesus knows the answer as whether he will answer that one commandment of the Law is more important than another. Some rabbis taught that the greatness of the Torah stems from the fact that the smallest command is as important as the greatest, that every "jot and tittle" (see Matt 5:18), every detail, as God's instruction, is as significant as every other.

Luke inserts this parable into the context derived from Mark of an encounter between a scribe and Jesus (see Mark 12:28-31; also Matt 22:34-40). In Mark, this exchange takes place in Jerusalem when the scribe asks about the greatest commandment. Jesus' answer suggests a "first" (Deut 6:5) and a "second" (Lev 19:18) commandment, "like the first." Mark pictures the scribe pronouncing Jesus' answer correct and Jesus in turn praising the scribe, saying, "You are not far from the kingdom of God" (Mark 12:34). Mark only hints vaguely at the scribe's disposition, concluding this episode with the comment, "And no one dared to ask him any more questions" (12:34). Luke displaces this encounter by making it occur early, long before Jesus' arrival in Jerusalem. The motives of the lawyer are less benign. He comes to challenge Jesus and, when Jesus' answer is irrefutable, he attempts to "justify himself" (v. 29). When the lawyer is drawn into the story, he gives a begrudging answer to Jesus' question about who acted as neighbor to the victim. Apparently unwilling to name the Samaritan, the lawyer answered, "The one who treated him with mercy." Unless he overhauled his perspective, the lawyer could not have been pleased to hear the command from Jesus, "Go and do likewise." He was being told to imitate the hated enemy!

There is both a literal and a theological meaning to this story. To see and follow what Jesus is commanding his followers to do, we need to probe some of the elements of this example story to see what they meant in Jesus' time. Although a story with a timeless message, Luke's dramatic presentation presupposes at least a rudimentary knowledge of the significance of the roles of some of the starring characters such as priests and Levites, Samaritans, and neighbors.

The Characters

The distance from Jerusalem to Jericho is about eighteen miles, much of it a virtual no-man's land of inhospitable desert, with no respite along the way. People would not normally travel alone, but in groups. Any number of dangers threatened the traveler: animals, hunger, thirst, exhaustion, and accidents, not to mention the malicious intents of thieves and bandits waiting in ambush. Yet in Jesus' parable, a "certain man," presumably Jewish, appeared along this road by himself. In contrast, the robbers band together and overwhelm him. Jesus accentuates the victim's vulnerability listing the assaults he suffered: he was robbed, beaten, stripped, and left for dead. His wait for help only adds to the agonized suspense. His wounds were so severe that he could utter no cry for help when others did appear. All he could hope for was that someone noticed him and would respond with compassion.

The robbers had abandoned their prey and now the victim appears as a kind of bait awaiting the reaction of the passersby. Finally a string of people appears one by one. The priest and Levite may be coming from normal routine duties connected with the Temple in Jerusalem. They appear to be in haste, passing by the victim lying in the road. They both go out of their way to avoid him, passing by on the other side. They do not seem to identify with his situation, as if this could not have happened to them. The third traveler, a Samaritan, is really out of place along this road from Jerusalem. While the identity of the priest and the Levite offer them some degree of security, the Samaritan, conversely, is more at risk of abuse even than the victim himself. A little background on these passersby is in order.

Levites originally referred to descendants of the tribe of Levi, one of Jacob's twelve sons. Aaron, Moses' brother and a Levite, was considered the father of the priests. After the Exile in the sixth century B.C., there is a division between Levites and priests. The Jerusalem authorities did not accept Levites as priests and reduced them to a subordinate position because they suspected that the Levites had been tainted by pagan idolatry. Eventually Levites as well as priests had essential roles connected with the Temple and sacrifice but also were known for teaching. Yet both groups fell into disrepute at various times in the course of history. Many Levites did not return after being deported into exile in Babylon in the sixth century B.C. After that time it was difficult or impossible to trace the lineage back to Levi or to any of the twelve sons of Jacob. The priests were also overshadowed by the suspicion that their title was bought when Roman rulers named the high priest and interfered with religious functions and practices.

Despite all this, Levites and priests continued to enjoy a certain prestige, linked to each other and to the Temple. In Jesus' day, priests were entrusted with the Temple's liturgical sacrificial duties. Levites performed secondary functions such as cantors, musicians, and lectors. Both had responsibility under the Law to remain "clean," free of any defilement such as they could derive from contact with a corpse. This could be the background explaining why the priest and Levite, to avoid contamination, would have "passed by" the half-dead victim. In the story Jesus tells, a priest and a Levite are pictured leaving Jerusalem and probably their Temple duties and returning to Jericho. This is a credible detail of the story as many priests, it appears, lived in Jericho, a fairly convenient domicile for the performance of their occasional duties.

In contrast to the prestige of "priests and Levites," Samaritans were considered schismatics by the Jews. The role of the Temple was one important issue of disagreement between the Jews and the Samaritans. The Samaritan woman in John 4:20 succinctly sums up one of the principal sources of conflict: "Our ancestors worshiped on this mountain, but you people say that the place to worship is in Jerusalem." Yet the reasons for the hostility between the Jews and the Samaritans were long-standing, going far beyond the Temple. They were ethnic and religious in nature. The region of Samaria was between Galilee and Judea; oftentimes Jewish people traveling from north to south took pains to avoid going through the area of the Samaritans for fear of harassment. The town of Samaria was the capital of the northern kingdom of Israel from the time of the reign of Solomon's son to the fall of the North in 722 B.C. Even before this time, there was tension between the South and the North, where many important shrines dating back to the patriarchs were located. Certainly after the building of the original Temple in Jerusalem, and more so after its rebuilding, when the people returned from the exile in Babylon, the Jews and the Samaritans mutually avoided and even hated one another.[1]

The terms "Samaria" or "Samaritan" occur twenty-two times in the New Testament,[2] the majority of the references in John and Luke, many with a positive connotation. This is somewhat surprising given the mutual hostility between Jews and Samaritans. As a Jew, Jesus himself probably would have shared some of the typical suspicion about Samaritans; but the overall picture that emerges from the New Testament is that the Samaritans were open to the message of Jesus and became representative of those who received his message eagerly early on.

The figures of the priest, Levite, Samaritan, and neighbor are used by Jesus to stretch the limits of the lawyer's guarded question. Priests and Levites had a legal right to "pass by." Religious responsibilities provided implied excuses for neglecting the needs of the robbers' victim. But in the parable, by implication, the priest and the Levite are indicted not for any violence or lawlessness on their part, but for their startling indifference to the wordless pleas of the man left for dead at the side of the road. More basic than the Law's demands, Jesus intimates, is the human condition the victim shares with all others in this story. Neither Jesus nor the lawyer have to condemn the priest's and the Levite's inaction on behalf of the victim. Human solidarity itself indicts them.

Indeed, even the Samaritan, who held the same Pentateuch as the priest and Levite, could have invoked religious duty and passed by. He could have excused himself, citing that the victim's plight was none of his business. But he did not consider his own safety, the business that brought him to that road far from home, nor any self-justification to support his passing by. Rather, he makes himself "neighbor" to the victim in the ditch. Luke multiplies the verbs used to describe the Samaritan's extraordinary compassion. Not only does he stop to help the man and bandage his wounds, he lifted him up, put him on his own animal, took him to an inn, cared for him there, and finally incurred a debt with the innkeeper on the man's behalf. The extraordinary effort on the Samaritan's part goes way beyond anything that can be measured or legislated. Their common humanity binds the Samaritan and the victim and illustrates the power and abundant generosity of sharing God's own life of mercy.

Now the lawyer's response does not seem so surly. The Samaritan has a new identity as "the one who showed mercy." And "neighbor" has a new possibility as a symbol of openness rather than restriction. The honor accorded the priest and Levite is no longer a cover for failing to respond to those in need. The animosity formerly shown to outsiders is converted into respect by this story that makes "Samaritan" synonymous with "good." The victim is never further described and so represents anyone encountered along the way whose need appeals to our humanity and expands it with the life of God in the form of compassion and generosity.

Luke 10:34-35 describe at length everything the Samaritan did for the man who fell among robbers. As the priest and Levites poured out the oil and wine on the high altar before God (oil and wine were used in the Temple services for the burnt offerings), so the Samaritan now pours oil and wine on the man's wounds, thus pouring out the true offering acceptable to God. The words, "poured out," and "bind up" belong to the language of worship. The parable would suggest that the Samaritan, not the priest and Levite, offers the right kind of worship to God (see Hos 6:6; 2 Chr 28:8-15). The Samaritan did not rely naively on the charity of the innkeeper, but paid him two denarii, the equivalent to two days' wages. The Samaritan then assured him that he would settle any further accounts upon his return. He took all necessary precautions to assure the well-being of the wounded man.

Initially the lawyer asked, "And who is my neighbor?" By means of the parable the question has undergone a transformation, and it now asks, "Who became (or who made himself) neighbor to the man who fell among the robbers?" The change in the form of the question corresponds to a change of perspective. The lawyer placed his own ego at the center of his question; the center ought to be the person in need. Therefore, the question is turned upside down, or rather, inside out. While the lawyer initially raised the question concerning the limits of love of neighbor, the story made it clear that there is no limit to whom we must act as neighbor.

The difference between the beginning and the end of the parable is basically the distance between two very different perspectives. The new perspective, that of Jesus and the kingdom he preaches, fully illustrates that love of neighbor is primary and universal. The story of the Good Samaritan shows that one cannot define or describe one's neighbor; one can only *be* a neighbor. Love does not begin by defining its objects; it discovers them. Again the lawyer is forced to answer his own question, which, however, has been reformulated in the light of the parable. The answer is unavoidable. With these final words, "Go and do likewise," Jesus answers the lawyer's initial question, "What must I do to inherit eternal life?"

The parable of the Good Samaritan is timeless. The parable is not a story of someone who does a good deed. It is an indictment against anyone who raises protective barriers in order to live a sheltered life insolated from others' needs. The parable claims that love is not words, but deeds. And these deeds involve risks, sacrifices, and sharing one's possessions. The parable's directive, "Go and do likewise." is not an invitation, but an imperative. Significantly, the only other time that Jesus issues the directive "do this" is during the Last Supper when he says, "do this in memory of me" (Luke 22:19) Especially in Luke, the Eucharist was the probable setting for remembering many of Jesus' parables and other teachings. Luke's church wrestled with questions about inclusion. This parable is a story about true worship, which for Luke means being compassionate, offering hospitality and healing to anyone in need. Through this parable, disciples are urged to become one with the compassionate and hospitable God by breaking open their lives and caring for the needs of others as God has cared for them.

The Meal Parables of Luke 14–16

Some of the most vivid and memorable parables are told in the meal setting featured in the middle of Luke's journey narrative. In chapters 14–16 Luke portrays Jesus at table with a mixed company of Pharisees and scribes (14:1-3, 7, 15; 15:2), toll collectors, and sinners (15:1), as well as disciples (16:1), and sometimes "crowds" (14:25) gathered around him. The meal setting, which extends uninterrupted from Luke 14:1 to 17:10, provides the context for many parables. These parables describe what table fellowship with Jesus entails, or what is involved in "dining in the Kingdom of God." In a series of parables, Jesus speaks of the inclusiveness of a great banquet (14:15-24), the celebration and joy at finding what had been lost (chapter 15), the importance of prudent stewardship (16:1-13), and the responsibility of the rich to show hospitality and care to the poor and the ill (16:19-31).

Typical Lukan elements characterize these parables. Luke includes everyday scenes and incorporates dialogue that gives a realistic dimension to Jesus' images. The supposed listeners are people of every stripe—the righteous and the lowly, disciples and opponents. They are all challenged by the reversals in Jesus' stories. It is as if Luke invites his readers to identify with one or the other and choose to become witnesses to the truth Jesus teaches. If they do not, they will be revealed as hypocrites and betrayers, for these lessons are offered in a context of intimacy, with Jesus at table, sharing food and life with others.

Hospitality, Sign of Life in the Kingdom

In chapter 14, three episodes highlight hospitality as a centerpiece of Jesus' instruction to his disciples. All take place in the home of a Pharisee Jesus visited. First, the cure of the man with dropsy (14:1-6)[3] pairs with the cure of the crippled woman (see 13:10-17) and provokes the same criticism from Jesus' host that he is dishonoring the Sabbath and violating the Law. Then Jesus offers instruction about conduct at table in the form of an observation about guests and hosts (15:7-14). And finally Jesus pronounces the parable of the great banquet (14:15-24). Jesus' teaching advocates a change of heart about honor and about the appropriate reception and response to the prophet. The table setting probably indicates the central importance of the Eucharist as the context for rethinking participation in the kingdom and the basis for discerning attitudes and actions of authentic discipleship.

Hospitality plays a central role not only in Jesus' teaching with words, but also in his example. Jesus associates with the leaders of the people as well as with toll collectors and sinners (14:1-3; 15:1-2). Jesus is presented as a prophet who invites people to repent of their former values and behavior and adopt a new standard. As the host of God's banquet, Jesus is the savior who is Christ and Lord. In sharing table fellowship, Jesus extends his invitation and his challenge to become participants in the reign of God. Jesus observes the customs of courtesy and etiquette and ties these issues of daily protocol to a lesson about the kingdom. Above all the kingdom involves a whole new set of priorities and values: "everyone who exalts himself will be humbled, but the one who humbles himself will be exalted" (Luke 14:11; see 18:14).[4] Jesus is featured as holding a symposium in the context of a meal. He teaches lessons in the course of this symposium. He had posed a question to his host, other Pharisees, and scholars of the Law about the cure of the man and they had refused to answer (14:6). Then Jesus broadened his perspective to include the guests at table, observing their views about honor and the related conduct produced by these views. In a "lesson" (called a parable in 14:7, but an observation rather than a story), Jesus will propose an alternative way. This observation provides the context for the parable of the great banquet that follows.

Participants usually reclined at a table that was t-shaped or perhaps somewhat of a horseshoe. Hosts and guests usually reclined on their left sides, leaving their right hands free for dipping and eating. The place of honor would have been directly perpendicular to the host so that the honored guest could talk directly with the host. Succeeding places of honor continued along the crossbar and down the left side, with the lowest places situated at the end of the left extension; the guest placed here would have to constantly readjust position in order to converse even with those in the lowest places. What Jesus notices, therefore, is a stream of guests jockeying for the spot near the host while avoiding anything close to the "last place."

In an honor-shame culture of the Mediterranean world of Jesus' time, the experience of overstepping one's station and being told to move down would have been more than extremely embarrassing. Conversely, the invitation to come up higher would have been very enviable. At first Jesus seems to simply advocate prudential good manners that could lead not only to avoiding disgrace, but winning honor and approval. But this first instruction reveals the very different value system of the kingdom of God. Underlying just about everything in the Roman world was a patronage system by which the rich and powerful maintained favor among their constituencies with banquets and gifts meant to bolster their reputation and influence as generous benefactors. Jesus advocates investing in people who could not possibly make any return. The "banquet" is an image for a forum in which the grandiosity of the rich and the powerful can be displayed. If they lavish their wealth and power on those who "repay" them, Jesus points out, they will have already received their reward. But if they are generous to people who could not possibly reciprocate, they are "blessed" indeed by God (14:14). Jesus promises them they will receive the resurrection of the righteous.

The Parable of the Great Banquet (Luke 14:15-24)

Prior to the parable of the great banquet in Luke, Jesus blessed those who invited the poor, the crippled, the lame, and blind to a feast (14:13-14). Hearing this blessing of Jesus, a fellow guest speaks up with the confidence of a participant in a banquet in the kingdom of God.

The guest's words set the stage for the parable of the great banquet in 14:15-24:

> [15]One of his fellow guests on hearing this said to him, "Blessed is the one who will dine in the kingdom of God." [16]He replied to him, "A man gave a great dinner to which he invited many. [17]When the time for the dinner came, he dispatched his servant to say to those invited, 'Come, everything is now ready.' [18]But one by one, they all began to excuse themselves. The first said to him, 'I have purchased a field and must go to examine it; I ask you, consider me excused.' [19]And another said, 'I have purchased five yoke of oxen and am on my way to evaluate them; I ask you, consider me excused.' [20]And another said, 'I have just married a woman, and therefore I cannot come.' [21]The servant went and reported this to his master. Then the master of the house in a rage commanded his servant, 'Go out quickly into the streets and alleys of the town and bring in here the poor and the crippled, the blind and the lame.' [22]The servant reported, 'Sir, your orders have been carried out and still there is room.' [23]The master then ordered the servant, 'Go out to the highways and hedgerows and make people come in that my home may be filled. [24]For, I tell you, none of those who were invited will taste my dinner.'"

The proposed excuses are actually plausible ones, except that the guests had already accepted the invitation. Now their refusal to attend is an insult to the host, jeopardizing their standing, reputation, and perhaps even their lives in a society that was governed on all levels by a patronage system. In fact, the last-minute excuses shift the focus to the dinner itself. Accepting the invitation requires setting the priorities right. Participants must value the kingdom of God above all else. Those who refused to attend the banquet demonstrate that they regard the daily affairs of this life as more important than the demands of participating in the kingdom of God. This is an excuse Luke considers very dangerous and the one he consistently warns against.

Whereas the wealthy rejected the summons to the banquet, the poor and needy eagerly accept the gracious invitation extended to them. When there is still room at the table, the servant is ordered to fill the master's home with guests from the "highways and hedgerows," that is, from outside the parameters of the town. Strangers will dine at the places originally set for friends. Luke's parable becomes an allegory demonstrating one of his favorite themes, hospitality. Invitations to the eschatological banquet were first issued to Jews and only eventually to Gentiles. Those who refused to attend are excluded only by their own resistance and rejection. Luke consistently emphasizes that it was the poor who were open and readily accepted Jesus and the kingdom he inaugurated.

The master's concluding comment is a solemn warning: "For, I tell you, none of those who were invited will taste my dinner." Jesus dramatically warns the smug and self-righteous who presume their own merit or the indulgence of the patron, taking for granted his protection despite their careless refusal. They are in for a rude awakening when they find they have abused his generosity and patience.

Luke is far more subtle in his use of the Scriptures than Matthew or even Mark. Yet Luke certainly could have been inspired by Isaiah 25:6-10 for this depiction of the banquet as metaphor for the messianic age. Isaiah pictures a lavish feast of rich food and choice wines with room for everyone. There will be no more death or tears. All will be filled and satisfied. The banquet is the sequel to the enthronement scene of Isaiah 24:21-23, celebrating the divine kingship. Mourning is over. Yahweh is enthroned as King and is victorious: "he will swallow up death." Rest, food, water, are all symbols of satisfaction and refreshment, and also previews of eschatological joy and peace.

Luke consistently alternates sayings of rejection and calls to conversion with teachings on discipleship. With this parable, Jesus is correcting the false ideas about participating in the kingdom of God and substituting his prophetic challenge. Jesus told this parable of rejection, showing how overinvolvement with possessions and relationships distract those invited to the banquet. Then Luke has Jesus turn to the crowds who were following him (14:25) and repeat the same kind of warning. Disciples may be required to relativize all previous relationships (14:26), in contrast to the man of the parable who married a wife and could not come to the feast. The requirement to relinquish all possessions (14:33) contrasts with those who refused the invitation because of field and cattle (14:18-19). Between these stark requirements, Luke includes the two images unique to his gospel: the man who wanted to build a tower and the king who wanted to wage a battle (14:28-32). Both state the simple lesson: Don't start what you can't finish. The priority of following Jesus is the most fundamental and radical lesson of all. Discipleship means bearing one's own cross and following the path of the prophetic Messiah (14:27).

The parable of the banquet and the demands of discipleship make the same point: the call of God issued by Jesus must take precedence over all else. The parable shows how entanglement with persons and things can in effect be a refusal of the summons to the banquet. The decision to become Jesus' disciple may require detachment from possessions and even people. There is little that is gentle or reassuring in this. But as the final saying on salt suggests (14:34-35), any disciple who wavers because of possessions or wealth or family ties will be like salt without savor, fit for nothing. "It is thrown out" (14:35).

Parables of Joy in Finding What Was Lost (Luke 15)

Three parables appear as a unit in Luke 15. These three parables have been called "the heart" of the Gospel of Luke.[5] The three were probably not spoken together by Jesus. Rather, Luke himself created a unit of the three. They are an eloquent expression of one of Luke's major themes, namely, God's steadfast love and mercy for sinners. Luke uses these parables in particular to show that Jesus' pastoral strategy is consistent with and a product of the image of God he is constantly trying to convey.[6] God seeks out the lost. God, represented by the main character in all three parables, experiences "joy" when the lost are found (15:7, 10).

While showing the positive response Jesus receives from the outcasts and the downtrodden, Luke also stresses the resistance that characterizes the religious leaders' response to Jesus. As tax collectors and sinners gathered around Jesus, the "Pharisees and scribes" remained at a distance and complained about the company he kept. Hearing their grumbling, Jesus proposed a parable to them, Luke says. Then he proceeds to lay out not one but three parables about the joy of finding what had been lost. Only the first parable, that of the found sheep, appears elsewhere, in Matthew; its source is Q. The parables of the coin and the son who had been lost and were found are unique to Luke. Together the three parables represent a meditation on the nature of God. The main character in each of the parables helps Luke portray the God of Jesus.

Once again Jesus gives important instruction on discipleship in a meal setting. This magnificent sermon is presented by Luke as a kind of dialogue, although Jesus is the main speaker. He is responding to criticism about his companions, and the meal becomes a symposium on the nature of God. Already in the setting of these parables, Luke is showing how the Gospel reverses human categories and turns expectations upside down. Toll collectors and sinners draw near to Jesus while the Pharisees and scribes distance themselves from him.

The Characters

The gospels associate "tax collectors" with "sinners" in several places, a combination that hints at the ill repute of both groups. The term *telonai*, often translated as "tax collectors," has given people who provide a legitimate and necessary service a bad name. "Toll collectors" may be a better translation because it helps to convey the special circumstances of first-century Palestine that shed light on why this group would be mistrusted and easily associated with "sinners."[7] In this context, the term refers to Jews who were responsible for collecting tolls from various areas in Palestine for the Romans. The job of chief toll collector went to the highest bidder who paid the Romans in advance the sum to be collected. They subcontracted the collections to other agents and all derived their respective profits from the amounts they collected. The system was open to every kind of abuse and dishonesty. Their reputation for extortion is echoed in the Baptist's counsel to them (3:12-13),[8] as well as the Zacchaeus episode (19:1-10). In Matthew, toll collectors are associated with "Gentiles" (Matt 18:17) and with "harlots" (Matt 21:32). These toll collectors were generally disliked and distrusted, and considered as dishonest as robbers (see Luke 18:11). They were deprived of civil rights, such as holding office, or bearing witness in legal proceedings.[9] As disreputable persons, they were usually avoided.

There were all sorts of taxes. The main taxes were the poll and the land tax, and the Romans tried with difficulty to collect these directly. There were also a number of indirect taxes, especially on the transport of goods, and the collection of these was often left to local Jewish toll collectors. These toll collectors appear at commercial centers such as Capernaum and Jericho where there were "customs houses" (*telonia*) such as where Jesus had found Levi at work (see Luke 5:27). In addition to all such tolls, Jews were obliged to pay religious taxes, such as the Temple tax, and tithes on produce to support the Jerusalem priests. Of course, these Jewish taxes were also collected by Jews.

The category "sinners" referred to people ostensibly leading immoral lives (e.g., prostitutes, adulterers, swindlers) and also those whose trade put them beyond the boundary of religious or social approval. The Pharisees express their disapproval that in consorting and eating with these people, Jesus is engaging in irreligious behavior.

The charge of eating and drinking with toll collectors and sinners is first made against Jesus by the Pharisees in 5:30 and repeated in 7:34. Peter, although he referred to himself as a "sinner," was called by Jesus and followed him (5:1-11). Similarly, Levi the toll collector also left everything and followed Jesus (5:27-32). In fact, according to Luke, "Levi gave a great banquet" for him and a "large crowd of tax collectors and others were at table with Jesus," which provoked the same complaint from the

Pharisees and their scribes: "Why do you eat and drink with tax collectors and sinners" (5:30)? Luke connects the very identity of Jesus with his association with sinners. Conversely, those who reject Jesus because of his attraction and association with sinners fail to recognize either Jesus or the kingdom of God, a kingdom of compassion and mercy that Jesus inaugurates.

Pharisees and Scribes

While Jesus is attractive to sinners and tax collectors, the Pharisees come to him to complain. Those who complain that Jesus draws sinners and goes too easy on them are actually taking themselves out of the realm of the sinners in need of mercy. Luke indicates two groups of opponents, the scribes and Pharisees (see also 5:21, 30; 6:7; 11:53), just as he identified two groups of those who came to hear Jesus, the toll collectors and sinners. The scribes (literally "writers") were probably a literate group of experts among the Pharisees. Scribes were also associated with other parties of the Jews, such as the Sadducees who were connected with the Temple and appear later when Jesus reaches Jerusalem. As religious leaders, the Pharisees and Sadducees and their scribes had their own ideas about the identity of the Messiah. Although they did not usually agree among themselves, they seem to be of one mind when it came to rejecting the Gospel Jesus preached and its implications.

The Pharisees were the teachers of the Law of Moses. They held important positions in the synagogues, which were the houses of worship and instruction in all the important Jewish towns around Palestine. Particularly in the two hundred years before Jesus and two hundred years after, the Pharisees' role in the formation of rabbinic Judaism was key. The Pharisees' prestige as teachers was spread by the number and importance of the disciple-students they attracted. Jesus' own success as a teacher no doubt stirred jealousy and competition among the other teachers of his day. To the extent that Jesus' teaching was considered erroneous and even dangerous, religious leaders such as the Pharisees, opposed him. While the gospels' presentation of the Pharisees is usually negative and biased to some extent, it does convey the sense of competition between the various factions of Judaism experienced during this time between the composition of the Old and the New Testaments.

Luke explicitly indicates that Jesus addressed the parables of chapter fifteen to the Pharisees and scribes, although they do not appear disposed to "hear" what Jesus has to say. By contrast, Luke mentions that the tax collectors and sinners came to Jesus for the purpose of "listening" to him. This is the attitude of the disciple. It corresponds with Jesus' challenge at the end of chapter 14: "Whoever has ears to hear ought to hear" (14:35). Thus Luke describes the outcasts responding to Jesus, eating with him and persevering in his company as he continues his journey toward Jerusalem. Even if the parable is not "directed" to them, Luke insinuates that they were willing and eager to hear it and learn its meaning.

The scribes and the Pharisees represent the hard-hearted who have too much to lose to accept Jesus' teaching about God and about sinners. Their prestige is built upon the separation they maintain from the unclean and the unholy. In chapter 14 they had turned an occasion of hospitality into an opportunity for spying on Jesus (14:1-6). They observe Jesus with suspicion (6:7; 14:1), and conspire against him (11:53). Later the Pharisees are further described by Luke as "loving money" (16:14). In contrast to the "toll collectors and sinners" who drew near to Jesus, after the Pharisees "heard" what he had said, they "sneered" at Jesus in rejection of his message (16:14).

The Parables of the Shepherd and the Woman (Luke 15:4-10)

While the three parables of Luke 15 form a unit telling of what had been lost and now was found, the first two have been called "twin parables," and they ought to be considered together. A single conclusion (vv. 7 and 10) is drawn from the experiences of the shepherd and the woman, both of whom are representative of God (15:7 and 10): "In just the same way," Luke says, there is rejoicing in heaven over a single sinner who repents. The fact that the first story is found in Matthew (as well as the Gospel of Thomas) tells us that Luke obtained this story from Q.[10] It is typical of Luke to pair a story of a man with that of a woman as he does in this case, adding the parable of the coin that is lost and found to that of the sheep. Here is how Luke tells these stories:

> [4]"What man among you having a hundred sheep and losing one of them would not leave the ninety-nine in the desert and go after the lost one until he finds it? [5]And when he does find it, he sets it on his shoulders with great joy [6]and, upon his arrival home, he calls together his friends and neighbors and says to them, 'Rejoice with me because I have found my lost sheep.' [7]I tell you, in just the same way there will be more joy in heaven over one sinner who repents than over ninety-righteous people who have no need of repentance.
>
> [8]"Or what woman having ten coins and losing one would not light a lamp and sweep the house, searching carefully until she finds it?

> [9]And when she does find it, she calls together her friends and neighbors and says to them, 'Rejoice with me because I have found the coin that I lost.' [10]In just the same way, I tell you, there will be rejoicing among the angels of God over one sinner who repents."

With his characteristic realism, Luke tells of the common experience of losing something valuable followed by the overwhelming joy of finding it again and sharing that joy with others. The pattern of these parables is similar: losing, searching, finding, rejoicing, celebrating. In the first parable, the shepherd loses one of the sheep, whereas Matthew pictured the sheep wandering off. Luke has the rest of the flock left "in the desert" rather than Matthew's "in the hills," and has the shepherd seek until he finds it, whereas Matthew makes the finding more hypothetical (Matt 18:13) by saying, "if he finds it." Matthew lacks the picturesque detail that the shepherd put the sheep "on his shoulders," a note that could well reflect actual practice. Luke is often very dramatic in the telling, as we see in most of his parables.

Jesus introduces both parables with the rhetorical question, "What man among you . . ." or "What woman . . ."? Listeners recognize a universal experience of having more joy at the finding than in originally possessing something. The shepherd and the women finally gather "friends and neighbors" to celebrate the finding. This phrase echoes the "friends and wealthy neighbors" from the preceding chapter when Jesus cautions about whom not to invite to a banquet (14:12). Both the shepherd and the woman, like the father in the following parable, are images for God. Two distinctive themes of Luke are combined in all three parables: the exhortation to others to join in the celebration as well as the theme of repentance (15:9, 23-24). The joy in human fellowship, especially because of repentance, mirrors that in heaven. As early as 5:32 Jesus had expressed his mission as a call to repentance: "I have not come to call the righteous to repentance but sinners" (5:32).

Jesus tells us that the woman had "ten coins" (15:8): this is the only time in the gospels that the term "drachma" appears. The drachma was an ancient silver coin whose value is difficult to estimate. It was roughly equivalent to the denarius, that is, a day's wage.[11] Some interpreters suggest that the ten drachmas were part of the woman's dowry, which was sometimes displayed in her headdress. In any case, this is a poor woman who would be much distressed to have lost a tenth of her worth. The shepherd with a hundred sheep is rich in comparison to this woman. At first reading, it may seem surprising that when she finally finds the lost coin, she seems to squander it by throwing a party for all her friends and neighbors. But this would miss the point that her find is much greater than her loss. The restoration of her coin makes it all the more precious. Jesus shows that, like the shepherd, the woman's entire focus is on finding what is lost and restoring it to its rightful place among her treasures.

The story of the woman's search, although very brief, is detailed: she "lights a lamp, sweeps the house, searches carefully." The woman is focused. She cannot interrupt her search until she finds the coin and puts it back with the others. Just as Jesus' listeners can imagine her overflowing gratitude for finding what had been lost, so, we are told, "there will be rejoicing among the angels of God over one sinner who repents" (Luke 15:10). The apparent passivity of the lost sheep and the lost coin is striking. Commentators have noted that "repenting" here in Luke seems to indicate the mere act of being found.

The Prodigal Father (Luke 15:11-32)

Next, Jesus tells the story of the father who, like the shepherd and the woman of the preceding parables, experiences loss and the great joy at the "finding." The story begins, "A man had two sons . . ." Our attention should remain on the father who tries to restore both his sons to kingdom thinking and acting. The story has two parts: the first (15:11-24) follows the pattern of the previous two parables about losing, searching, finding, rejoicing, and celebrating, though it is longer and more detailed. The second part of the story (15:25-32) is open-ended in its hope of the elder son ultimately "finding" himself and his right relationship with his father, a reason to join in rejoicing and celebration. Some commentators have suggested that the original parable might have been the story of the younger son and his return. By adding the second part, Luke turned this parable into a subtle criticism of the scribes and Pharisees mentioned in verse 2. At the same time, Luke also provided a bridge to chapter 16 where Pharisees sneered in reaction to Jesus' parable about the enterprising steward (16:1-16). This fuller Lukan context relates the attitude of the elder son to the grumbling Pharisees and scribes. Here is how Luke relates the parable of the prodigal or generous father:

> [11]Then he said, "A man had two sons, [12]and the younger son said to his father, 'Father, give me the share of your estate that should come to me.' So the father divided the property between them. [13]After a few days, the younger son collected all his belongings and set off to

a distant country where he squandered his inheritance on a life of dissipation. [14]When he had freely spent everything, a severe famine struck that country, and he found himself in dire need. [15]So he hired himself out to one of the local citizens who sent him to his farm to tend the swine. [16]And he longed to eat his fill of the pods on which the swine fed, but nobody gave him any. [17]Coming to his senses he thought, 'How many of my father's hired workers have more than enough food to eat, but here am I, dying from hunger. [18]I shall get up and go to my father and I shall say to him, "Father, I have sinned against heaven and against you. [19]I no longer deserve to be called your son; treat me as you would treat one of your hired workers." [20]So he got up and went back to his father. While he was still a long way off, his father caught sight of him, and was filled with compassion. He ran to his son, embraced him and kissed him. [21]His son said to him, 'Father, I have sinned against heaven and against you; I no longer deserve to be called your son.' [22]But his father ordered his servants, 'Quickly bring the finest robe and put it on him; put a ring on his finger and sandals on his feet. [23]Take the fattened calf and slaughter it. Then let us celebrate with a feast, [24]because this son of mine was dead, and has come to life again; he was lost, and has been found.' Then the celebration began. [25]Now the older son had been out in the field and, on his way back, as he neared the house, he heard the sound of music and dancing. [26]He called one of the servants and asked what this might mean. [27]The servant said to him, 'Your brother has returned and your father has slaughtered the fattened calf because he has him back safe and sound.' [28]He became angry, and when he refused to enter the house, his father came out and pleaded with him. [29]He said to his father in reply, 'Look, all these years I served you and not once did I disobey your orders; yet you never gave me even a young goat to feast on with my friends. [30]But when your son returns who swallowed up your property with prostitutes, for him you slaughter the fattened calf.' [31]He said to him, 'My son, you are here with me always; everything I have is yours. [32]But now we must celebrate and rejoice, because your brother was dead and has come to life again; he was lost and has been found.'"

This is an "example story" contrasting two types of responses to a situation. Luke likes to present his readers with a choice, challenging their attitudes and implying the question, "Which one are you?" Readers often note ruefully that they can identify with the complaint of the elder son who points out that he has never left his father, nor squandered his inheritance, yet no party was given for him. The elder son feels underappreciated. All the more reason to insist that the central character of this story is the father who shows both his sons generous and compassionate love and acceptance. The attitudes of both sons need to be converted to reflect the values of the kingdom of God. They both need to repent before there can be true rejoicing. Luke uses this story of one of the most universal and poignant experiences of humankind, that of family love, honor, and devotion, as well as disappointment and feelings of betrayal and injustice, to convey the unconditional, unlimited love of God.

The moral of the first part of the story about the younger son seems self-evident. After losing everything, his possessions as well as his self-respect, he returns remorsefully to his father who, almost predictably, welcomes him with open arms. The moral of the second part of the story about the elder son is more challenging and open-ended. The second part of the story makes plain the paradoxical nature of divine forgiveness. It poses the question to all readers: "Do we really think of ourselves correctly if we are unaware that we, too, are forgiven sinners?" Is self-righteousness so blinding that it makes us think it is unfair that others are forgiven or included if they came to forgiveness by another route than we did? The elder son complains that he served his father much as a slave would have and had not been rewarded by so much as a goat for his trouble. We can think of Cain's unhappiness when God received the sacrifices of Abel. God responds to Cain: "Why are you so resentful and crestfallen?" (Gen 4:6). Or as the landowner asked the laborers who complained that they had received the same wage as the lately hired: "Is your eye evil because I am good?" (Matt 20:15; author's translation).

The idea that the story has two parts should not distract the reader from maintaining focus on the father. He is the one who has experienced the loss and, in the case of the younger son at least, the restoration. He is the one cajoling the elder son to embrace his brother and stop thinking of himself as a "slave" because he is dutiful and productive. This story might also be seen as a correction to the notion of patriarchy operative at the time. In this story Jesus challenges the laws governing the rights and distribution of property among heirs, as well as the restrictive expectations of a father's behavior toward sons.

The parable begins well enough with Jesus saying, "A man had two sons." But with the description of the disrespectful demand by the younger son, Jesus' audience would have been repelled. When the Father daily scans the horizon for the delinquent son and then runs to meet him, the audience would have become indignant. Jesus would seem now to be undermining the very last bastion of family honor, one of the last values that ought not to need defending. The ideals of patriarchy provided the foundation of society and contributed to good family values

and virtues. Jesus implies that God was nothing like the limited, re-
stricted notions of patriarchy as it was generally practiced in Jesus' day.
In fact, in his response to the criticism of the scribes and Pharisees, Jesus
is correcting their understanding of God and challenging them to see
God and themselves in a new relationship built on compassion, forgiveness, and unconditional love. God is not like human patriarchs were
supposed to be in Jesus' day. Rather, this parable offers a totally new
way of imagining God.

The Father and the Younger Son

The story of the younger son follows the pattern of the stories of the
shepherd and the woman who search for what is lost and finally find it.
What helps to make this story even more compelling than the other two
is that it adds the personal dimension—of freedom and youthful irre-
sponsibility, personal estrangement and remorse, parental anguish and
generosity, longing and a tearful homecoming. These are universal
human experiences. Luke adds to the realism of this story also with his
use of dialogue and detail. The son rehearses his apology, saying, "Father
I have sinned against heaven and against you." The Father catches sight
of him from a distance and runs to meet him. He clothes his son with a
robe, a ring and sandals, and then ordered the fattened calf to be slaughtered so that the celebration can begin.

Luke hardly spares any aspect of the younger son's reputation. His
request for his portion of his inheritance while his father is alive is an
insult amounting to disinheriting his family. The Law allowed for an
early distribution, providing the oldest son a double portion to the individual inheritances of the others. In the case of two sons, the younger
could receive one-third while the older would receive two-thirds. The
boy hastily converts his share to cash and goes off to live among Gentiles,
a detail signified by the fact that he went to a distant country and eventually was hired to tend pigs. First he squandered his inheritance and
then, after a famine struck, he sold himself. His new status as swineherd
clearly illustrates his degradation. Jesus' Jewish audience could hardly
have imagined anything more horrific, especially in relation to their
children.

At last he comes to his senses, indicating that he remembered who he
was. Once again Luke pictures a character of his parables talking to
himself, this time in a positive way. The boy remembers his father and
his home and begins to regret his misdeeds. He resolves to return to his
father, his remorse the first step toward repentance and reconciliation.

He vows to arise and go to his father and admit his sin. He realizes that in sinning against his father he has sinned against God, too. He goes further. In demanding and then accepting his inheritance, he has already severed any further claim to his father's grace or favor. He can no longer expect to be treated as a son. But he resolves to ask humbly only to be considered like a hired worker would be. He can have no expectation of merit nor certainly of privilege. His rehearsed words of remorse are like the prayer of the tax collector who could only beat his breast and plead for mercy (18:13).

The lad then puts his resolve into action. He got up and returned to his father who takes over from this point on in the story. Even while the son is yet a long way off, the father spies him and, filled with compassion, runs to meet him. Implied is the idea that the father is distracted with longing and constantly searching for any sign that his wandering son will come back home. The father is motivated by compassion.[12] The restorative actions of the father who ran, embraced, and kissed his son preceded any words of remorse from the son. The father does not hesitate nor does he even let his son finish his confession. The pace of the story quickens toward a full-scale celebration before the son has even finished speaking. From a position of authority, the father "orders" his son to be rehabilitated, giving him a robe, a ring, and sandals to wear. The robe is "the first robe," meaning of the best quality (see Ezra 27:22; Amos 6:6), and the ring could signify the son's restoration as an heir, with authority and honor. These gifts represent the extravagance of the father's compassion. A feast is prepared. The father concludes his orders, talking to himself, "Let us celebrate a feast because this son of mine was dead, and has come to life again; he was lost and has been found."

The father proposes a feast and makes it happen. Readers might think of the rich fool who, with a very different disposition, talked to himself and, apparently in solitude, decided to "eat, drink and be merry" (12:19). The phrase also anticipates the father's dialogue with his elder son in verse 32: "But now we must celebrate and rejoice." Nothing could dictate such festivity more than having a dead son come back to life again, having a lost child return! There is no joy comparable to this. The household simply cannot hold back its celebration. And so it is done as the father says.

The Father and the Elder Son

The universal appeal of this story is in large part due to the realism and poignancy of the exchange between the father and elder son. Luke's vivid details picture this son returning home after working all day in the fields, only to hear the sound of music and dancing as he nears home. Readers sense his indignation mounting as he inquires about the cause of the merriment. In contrast to what is going on inside, the elder son obstinately refuses to enter the house and join in the celebration. When his father comes outside to plead with him, Luke conveys the extent of this son's alienation through the dialogue he supplies.

The elder son does not use familial language with regard to himself, his father, or his brother. The son complains that he has "slaved" for his father, a more accurate translation than "served" his father, and has been obedient to his every command, but has never even been offered a goat (a far less valuable gift than a fatted calf) to celebrate with his friends. He does not include his father as one he would have liked to celebrate with, an indication that he did not feel much affection for him. His indignation mounts as he gathers steam and begins to exaggerate what he could possibly know of the younger son's sins. He accuses him of wasting his inheritance and indeed his "life" (the Greek word used is *bios*) with prostitutes.[13] He contrasts his own behavior with that of "your son." His father's reply tries to correct the son's perspective and reconnect with his firstborn. He addresses him, "My Son," and speaks of "your brother." By so doing, the father urges his eldest to reconcile himself with his family to enter his home, and take his place as a well-beloved son.

The father reminds his child, "Everything I have is yours." Such sharing also implied a common outlook. The father is appealing to his son to act with integrity, to reaffirm his identity as a son and a brother. Although the son may perceive his relationships as fractured, the father does not, either with him or with his brother. The father will not allow the limited, even stingy perspective of the elder son who would accept the "death" of the younger son as the final word, to stifle his own hope and love for both his sons. Even if the father is disappointed with the bitterness of the elder son, he reaffirms his love for him, accepting the son's avowal of faithfulness at face value. "You are here with me always," he tells his elder son, as if to confirm their relationship past, present, and future. On the basis of what the son has said, they both (or better all three) have a lot of reconciling work to do; on the basis of the father's response, they have the time and motivation to do it.

The father tells his son that it is necessary to celebrate. This is a fairly common construction in Luke who shows, for example, the necessity for Jesus to suffer and so enter his glory (24:26), just as it was necessary to liberate the woman crippled for eighteen years from the power of

Satan (13:16). Similarly, it is necessary for disciples to celebrate and rejoice when God's power is made manifest, as in the case of the return of one who was lost. The kingdom of God is founded on repentance and conversion.

The original parable of the son who returns culminates the examples of the lost sheep and the lost coin. The emphasis is on the joy of finding what is lost, whether it is a sheep, a coin, or a child. But above all there is joy if what one not only lost, but thought dead, was restored completely. The second part of the parable is best understood within the Lukan context fixed by the introductory verses, 15:1-2, which relate the parable to the criticism of the Pharisees and scribes. Their slavish obedience to the Law is beside the point. It seems only to have rendered them judgmental of others and unable to identify themselves as children of God. In begrudging God's generous forgiveness to sinners, they fail to see themselves as beneficiaries of God's patrimony and grace. The father is a symbol of God's unconditional and unlimited mercy, forgiveness, and love of all. To deny another sinner such love is to put oneself outside its scope. From the beginning of his ministry, Jesus has said that he has come to bring the Good News of salvation to those who are in need of it, represented by the poor, the sick, the downtrodden, the sinners. There is cause—or better—need, for celebration and joy, not grumbling and self-righteousness.

The parable of the prodigal father is left open-ended. Readers wonder whether the elder son went inside the home he shared with his father and brother and joined the party. Or perhaps he remained outside the house, a slave to his bitterness, self-righteousness, and envy. Like a good parable, the one of the prodigal father does not tidy up the loose ends but leaves readers hanging and pondering their own reactions. Yet Luke hints that even the image of the father in this story was not enough to change the hearts of some who were angered by Jesus' association with the poor and the outcasts. Jesus went on to tell yet another parable that was met by the Pharisees' sneers (16:14). Apparently they were not convinced by the image of God Jesus was presenting. Rather, they continued to deride and reject Jesus and his message.

The Parable of the Master Who Praises Ingenuity (Luke 16:1-8a)

Luke follows up the lost-and-found stories with another parable in 16:1-8a. This time Jesus specifically addresses his disciples and presents to them the image of a steward called to give an accounting to the master of the household. A number of elements in this story link it to the preceding one of the father and his two sons; for example, the master of a household is faced with a crisis caused by the squandering of resources. The steward, like the younger son, undertakes a course of action because his way of life forces him to change.[14] Here is what Luke says:

> [1]Then he also said to his disciples, "A rich man had a steward who was reported to him for squandering his property. [2]He summoned him and said, 'What is this I hear about you? Prepare a full account of your stewardship, because you can no longer be my steward.' [3]The steward said to himself, 'What shall I do, now that my master is taking the position of steward away from me? I am not strong enough to dig and I am ashamed to beg. [4]I know what I shall do so that, when I am removed from the stewardship, they may welcome me into their homes.' [5]He called in his master's debtors one by one. To the first he said, 'How much do you owe my master?' [6]He replied, 'One hundred measures of olive oil.' He said to him, 'Here is your promissory note. Sit down and quickly write one for fifty.' [7]Then to another he said, 'And you, how much do you owe?' He replied, 'One hundred kors of wheat.' He said to him, 'Here is your promissory note; write one for eighty.' [8]And the master commended that dishonest steward for acting prudently."

With this new parable the theme changes from joy over finding what was lost to the proper attitude toward material possessions, a theme also found in the next parable about the Rich Man and Lazarus (16:19-31). Yet Luke is continuing to link behavior in this world with the standards of the world to come, the fullness of the kingdom of God. We have already heard about debtors and stewards. Now Luke tells of a steward who acted "wisely" when faced with a crisis of his own making; the master, hearing about the steward's misconduct, demands an accounting that will terminate his career. The steward's wisdom is in promoting his own security after he is dismissed. In the end, the "master" (referring either to the rich man of this parable or to Jesus) commends the steward and advocates that the disciples act as wisely in view of the accounting that will be demanded of their stewardship.

There are a number of debatable issues regarding this parable. Commentators have argued about where the parable actually ends and how much of the following material ought to be considered part of the original application of the parable. Readers wonder how Jesus could appear to commend the apparent dishonesty of the servant who, at the very least squanders his master's wealth and then, apparently arbitrarily, instructs debtors to reduce the amount owed. The steward resorts to self-help so he can rely on "friends" when he no longer has a job. So what are the listening disciples to learn from this example? Without going into the details of each of these questions, we will try to understand this passage and what it might have meant in its Lukan context.

The relationships described in the parable presuppose a situation common in the Palestine of Jesus' day. An absentee landlord entrusts the care of his property to a "steward" (the Greek word is *oikonomos*, only found in Luke among the evangelists; see Luke 12:42; 16:1, 3, 8). The householder is designated as a "rich man" (16:1) as is also the case in the next parable (16:19). He is also called master (i.e., *kyrios*) in 16:3, 5 and probably also verse 8.[15] The steward of this parable, like the one commended in Luke 12:42-48, could himself be a slave. He refers to the rich man as "my master." But this steward is not trustworthy. His predicament is caused by "squandering" his master's property, like the younger son of the preceding parable. Jesus insinuates that the master returns and finds things awry. Further, there are confirmed reports about this servant. As in the case of the parable of the use of talents in Matthew and the parable of the coins in Luke (19:11-27), it was customary for the returning master or landlord to expect a profit for his investment and, at the accounting, reward or punish servants depending on the extent of their return. If the master would not tolerate inactivity or loss, he would certainly punish squandering.

The manner of the servant's initial dishonest squandering is not really important to the story. Until the master's return, he has not been trustworthy. Once again Luke pictures a person in a quandary talking to himself. In this case the steward comes up with a clever plan. He will make friends with his master's debtors! The parable turns almost comical, with the troubled steward springing quickly into action and admonishing others to act quickly as well. The steward will make his master's debtors beholden to him by doing them a favor. Later they can be expected to reciprocate by welcoming him into their homes.

Luke reveals some dependence on Greek thinking here. The notion of friendship in Greek society implied that favors or loans were ways people could become indebted to others. Recently Luke had pictured Jesus teaching that "Blessed indeed will you be" when you invite the poor, the crippled, the lame, and the blind to a banquet, because of "their inability to repay you" (14:13-14). In the case of the dishonest steward, it is implied that he is making the debtors indebted to him, and they will be required to repay him. In his Sermon on the Plain, Jesus had asked, "If you love those who love you, what credit is that to you? Even sinners love those who love them. And if you do good to those who do good to you, what credit is that to you? Even sinners do the same" (6:32-33). Luke's presentation of the golden rule implies that reciprocity is self-serving and carries its own reward. Sinners have no "credit" owed since they are only "doing good" for the benefit they will receive. Participation in the reign of God involves a new way of thinking and acting based on a different set of standards.

That the servant of the parable is still acting the way a sinner would and setting himself up for an acceptable future is not what is commendable. His "cleverness" is praised when, seeing the handwriting on the wall, he prepares for his moment of accountability and makes it the priority of his calculations. He is still a "child of this age," but it is his single-mindedness that makes him a model for the disciples.

He does not protest that he has been wrongly judged nor does he beg his master to reconsider or to give him more time, as does the servant Matthew describes (see Matt 18:23-35). Rather, Luke's steward turns to others who are somehow indebted to his master. There are two debtors, as in the parable Jesus told to the Pharisee, Simon, while dining in his home (Luke 7:41-43). Again the significance of what the steward does next is debatable. When he tells one to cut his debt in half and the other to reduce it, it is not certain whether he is further scamming his master or simply eliminating his usual cut. Probably the latter, since the master praises him for acting prudently and cleverly. What is not debatable is the steward's change of perspective and behavior in preparation for facing the master's judgment. His new focus and priority is also what is praiseworthy.

The *kyrios* of verse 8a most likely refers to the rich man of the parable. He is not commenting on the legality of the servant's action, and he probably would not wish to have those actions publicized lest other servants follow suit. The master is commending his wayward servant for putting the best possible face on his expulsion from service. In view of the crisis facing him, the steward takes action to secure his life. Finally, Jesus, in verse 8b, adds his own judgment on the action of the manager, noting that the "children of this generation or world" are often more ambitious for its rewards than the "children of light" are for the reign of God.

We may also glean some insight by noting the links between this parable and the one of the prodigal father that immediately precedes it. Both parables are introduced in the same way, with the phrase, "A certain person" (15:11; 16:1, author's translation). In both, the main character is the head of the household; in the first a father of two sons, and in the second a "rich man" also called by the steward "my master." In both, a crisis caused by the "squandering" of one of the characters brings him to a decisive moment. Luke heightens the tension through use of literary devices: the son's homecoming and the steward's quick negotiations. Both stories are interrupted by the surprising, even extravagant reaction of the main character. Both parables are left open-ended, leaving listeners to wonder if the elder son accepts his brother or the steward is reinstated after his quick-thinking is praised.

Even the differences between these two stories may help us to gain insight into the meaning of this new, more puzzling parable. The previous story was directed to the scribes and Pharisees, while this one is specifically addressed to Jesus' disciples. In Luke's only other use of the term "steward" in 12:42, his role is described as someone put in charge of other servants to distribute their "food at the proper time." The steward of our parable shows himself ready to distribute mercy at the decisive moment by reducing the debts of the other servants accountable to him.

A common and essential link between the story of the prodigal father and the parable of the steward is the theme of forgiveness and mercy. The master may have forgiven and ultimately praised this enterprising steward because his actions resulted in a win-win situation for everyone. The steward reduced the amount owed, but perhaps only in the amounts equal to his own cut of the profits. In exchange for the lost revenue, he gained the respect and gratitude of his fellow servants. The master would still be repaid, but now he will be renowned for his mercy because the steward would be thought to have acted in his name. Now the master will be seen as a benefactor. And those who had their debts reduced will be grateful.

The steward represents the disciples who act as servants due to give an accounting of their tenure. They take their cue from Jesus who associated with sinners and offered them freedom, healing, mercy, forgiveness—in short, access to the kingdom of God. Critics notice only that Jesus appears to be too lenient with sinners and forgives them, claiming that he does not have the proper authority to do so. In contrast, the steward-disciples recognize Jesus as the prophet come to inaugurate the time of favor or grace and to bring God's salvation for all (Luke 4:18-19). The children of this age are enterprising when their self-interests are at stake. The disciples are called to be children of light, as single-minded, clever, prudent, and wise in executing their stewardship over the gifts of the kingdom, especially mercy and forgiveness.

The Parable of the Rich Man and Lazarus (Luke 16:19-31)

Still speaking about discipleship and still in the context of a shared meal, Jesus proposed yet another parable contrasting two people, one very rich and the other destitute. Since the poor man is named, classic commentaries have used a name for the rich man (i.e., Dives, derived from the Latin term "rich") as well. Lazarus is not only poor, but ill and hungry. Dives literally lives like a king, with costly garments and daily feasts. The differences between them, at least for the first part of the story, are described primarily in terms of their contrasting social conditions, with nothing said about any other moral qualities they might have possessed. One is extremely wealthy and the other extremely poor, and a chasm exists between the two. Yet Lazarus lies daily at Dives' "door" as if invisible to him. Here's how Luke tells the story:

> [19]"There was a rich man who dressed in purple garments and fine linen and dined sumptuously each day. [20]And lying at his door was a poor man named Lazarus, covered with sores, [21]who would gladly have eaten his fill of the scraps that fell from the rich man's table. Dogs even used to come and lick his sores. [22]When the poor man died, he was carried away by angels to the bosom of Abraham. The rich man also died and was buried, [23]and from the netherworld, where he was in torment, he raised his eyes and saw Abraham far off and Lazarus at his side. [24]And he cried out, 'Father Abraham, have pity on me. Send Lazarus to dip the tip of his finger in water and cool my tongue, for I am suffering torment in these flames.' [25]Abraham replied, 'My child, remember that you received what was good during your lifetime while Lazarus likewise received what was bad; but now he is comforted here, whereas you are tormented. [26]Moreover, between us and you a great chasm is established to prevent anyone from crossing who might wish to go from our side to yours or from your side to ours.' [27]He said, 'Then I beg you, father, send him to my father's house, [28]for I have five brothers, so that he may warn them, lest they too come to this place of torment.' [29]But Abraham replied, 'They have Moses and the prophets. Let them listen to them.' [30]He said, 'Oh no, father Abraham, but if someone from the dead goes to them, they will repent.' [31]Then Abraham said, 'If they will not listen to Moses and the prophets, neither will they be persuaded if someone should rise from the dead.'"

This parable has two parts. The first part, contrasting the experiences of the rich man and Lazarus, tells of the reversal of fortunes in this life compared with the afterlife (16:19-26). The reversal is illustrated by means of a dialogue between Abraham and the rich man. The second part asserts that even the testimony of one returned to life from the dead will not convince the stubborn rich to repent (16:27-31). The dialogue between Abraham and the rich man continues, but the rich man now shows more concern for his five brothers and would make Lazarus a passive figure sent to warn them to change their ways. It may be that Luke compounded a simple story of the reversal of fortunes of the rich and the poor with a warning to the rich about judgment and the need to share their material wealth with the poor among them.

This story functions as an example, like the story of the good Samaritan and the prodigal father. All three are found only in Luke. Listeners are challenged to identify with one or another of the characters as if asked, "Which one are you?" This parable serves Luke's concern about the proper use of material goods and the responsibilities of the rich toward the poor. It further emphasizes the requirement of faith for eternal life, not only as an act of intellectual assent but as bearing fruit in social action.

There are parallels, especially for the first part of the story, from ancient literature outside the Bible. There are Egyptian, Greek, and rabbinic tales of retribution in the afterlife for failure to use material resources to help the less fortunate. Some of these refer to a tour of the afterlife to review what happens to those hardened to the needs of people while on earth. Some even include the element of the deceased person's concern that someone alert their loved ones to the consequences of such neglect.

The parable of Dives and Lazarus as it appears in Luke carries a message typical of the gospel. The story further illustrates the teaching of the Lukan Jesus about the wise stewardship of material possessions and sheds new light on the meaning of being "welcomed into eternal dwellings" (16:9). The parable echoes the opposites of the "blessing" and "woe" in Luke: "Blessed are you who are poor, / for the kingdom of God is yours" (6:20); but "Woe to you who are rich, / for you have received your consolation" (6:24). It also illustrates the proverb at the end of 16:15, "What is of human esteem is an abomination in the sight of God."

The lifestyles of the rich man and Lazarus are reversed in the afterlife, according to the first part of the parable in 16:9-26. His fine garments and lavish feasts[16] evidence the extent of Dives' material comforts. Although we do not hear about his other virtues or vices, Dives' disregard for the poor and the ill is blatantly apparent. While Lazarus lies at his door, ill and hungry, Dives dines in sumptuous extravagance. The picture of neglect screams out in judgment, all the louder because Dives had to be continually amply supplying himself and his guests at his daily feasts while Lazarus was denied even scraps from the table. Dives' exclusivity is the opposite of the inclusiveness of dining in the kingdom of God.

The detail that dogs licked Lazarus' sores suggests a number of interpretations. Were dogs more solicitous than human beings? At least they notice Lazarus whereas Dives does not. Or are they a nonhuman, additional source of Lazarus' torment, an indication on how many different levels he suffers? Dogs are considered unclean animals, so their association with Lazarus contributes to his misery. Dogs could be allowed to feed on the scraps that fall from the table, as the story of the Syro-phoenician woman insinuates (Mark 7:24-30; Matt 15:21-28). Lazarus is like the younger son of the prodigal father story who longed to eat of the food available even to pigs and dogs, but was not given even that. The contrast between the rich, overindulgent man and the miserable Lazarus could hardly be expressed any more vividly, although Luke paints this contrast in three short verses.

Then Lazarus died and was "carried away by angels to the bosom of Abraham." Even in death he is neglected by human beings and left unburied. But after death his fortunes are reversed. Heavenly beings are dispatched to bring him to Abraham where he will enjoy honor and peace in the afterlife. "Bosom" may suggest either a place of honor for a guest near the host or even the association of intimacy. Listeners have the impression that Lazarus is fully compensated. He is in the company of angels and of Abraham. Dives will see him there and envy him.

The rich man also died and was given a suitable burial. Abruptly, though, we learn of his torment. He enters Hades, a name for the underworld. This is a place of the dead contrasted with heaven (see 10:15; also Matt 11:23; Isa 14:13-15) where the angels, Abraham, and Lazarus abide. Hades may have been considered a part of Sheol, a shadowy world where the spirits live. But whereas Sheol is not a place of either punishment or reward, Hell or Hades suggests a place of torment (Isa 66:24), symbolized here by the "flames" that afflict great pain on the rich man who cries out for some little comfort (Luke 16:24; see also Sir 21:9-10).

There is now a chasm between Dives and Lazarus, in contrast to their proximity in this life, when Lazarus laid at Dives' door. Dives can now "see" Lazarus, comforted at last, even though he could not see him when he was poor and needy. Dives calls out across the chasm, "Father Abraham," claiming kinship with the patriarch (vv. 24, 27, 30). The rich man prays to Abraham, "Have mercy on me" (see 17:13; 18:38-39), despite the fact that he himself had shown no mercy. Dives asks that Abraham "send" Lazarus, using the former beggar's name, an indication that he, in fact, knew him. But Dives wants Lazarus to "cool my tongue," as if he is still in the position of master and Lazarus still in his service.

Abraham addresses Dives as "my son," the same greeting used for the elder son in the story of the prodigal father. Abraham recognizes Dives as his son but not as having acted as his child. Abraham continues, "You received blessings in life and Lazarus only evil." The afterlife is true life that lasts; it corrects and, in this case as often in Luke, reverses the values and the experiences of the present life. Abraham further explains that now there is a great chasm between "us and you." Dives' request cannot be granted. He still thinks of Lazarus as some sort of servant or messenger who should do his bidding. The chasm has been "established" and cannot be crossed. The first part of the parable ends with an implied warning: take care for the values that guide your life. There are eternal consequences.

Luke's insistence on the danger of riches cannot be expressed more emphatically or clearly. Jesus' parable does not indict Dives for any other sin but the neglect of the poor. Jesus' own ministry to the outcast was announced in his inaugural sermon following his baptism and temptation (see Luke 4:16-30). By this ministry Jesus accepted his identity and his mission as God's son. Dives refused the invitation to grace that Lazarus represented. Lazarus' voiceless plea for food and care went unanswered by a merciless Dives who attended only to his own comforts. Not having prepared for any other reality by a life of service to the needy, Dives suffers a remorse without possibility of repentance, a misery without promise of reprieve.

The second part of the parable is probably a postresurrection reflection supplied by Luke. The dialogue between Dives and Abraham continues but now focuses on a second request from the former rich man. Lazarus is given only peripheral importance in this part of the story. Dives again calls Abraham "father" and begs him to send Lazarus to his five brothers to warn them to change their own lives lest they also come to this place of torment. Dives says that an eyewitness would be convincing to his brothers. Lazarus should tell them not only that there is an afterlife (remember, Luke pictures Jesus speaking to Pharisees (16:15) who believed in the resurrection from the dead), but that it was retribution for the life and values a person had exemplified on earth.

But Abraham replies in the negative for the second time. Your brothers have "Moses and the prophets," that is, the Scriptures. They should read and obey them.[17] If Dives and his brothers did not heed the Scriptures, they would not accept the testimony of one even if he returned from the dead. Luke's readers would make the obvious connection between these words and the resurrection of Jesus. Outsiders would continue in the disbelief by refusing to hear and believe the good news that Jesus is alive and present with the community.

Summary

The meal setting for all the parables of chapters 14–16 has not changed, although it is hard to envision Jesus at table and so many different listeners being within earshot. In chapter 14 Jesus is at table in the home of a noted Pharisee. Since 15:1-2, Jesus was eating with toll collectors and sinners, while scribes and Pharisees, observing this, were criticizing him. The meal continues in chapter 16 and so does the discourse in parables. Jesus appears alternately to address his critics (15:3; 16:14-15) as well as his disciples (16:1; 17:12). Luke, who often revels in details, studiously neglects a further clarification of the setting. All these parables are Jesus' table talk, shared in the context of a meal. Listeners are challenged to place themselves there and identify their own reaction to Jesus and his message. They have choices. They can attend to Jesus' teaching, accept it, ponder it, and bring it to fruition. Or they can distance themselves from Jesus and refuse to accept him as the prophet come to inaugurate the kingdom of God.

The signature themes of the Gospel of Luke are expressed and developed in the parables Jesus uses to instruct his disciples. Many of these parables are unique to the Gospel of Luke. There Jesus is often portrayed as the master or host who invites all to the messianic table. Disciples are those who hunger for mercy and forgiveness, who listen intently to Jesus' message. They are willing to abandon their former ideas and behavior and transform their lives in response to Jesus. Luke's Gospel presents a positive, realistic, practical call to live according to the values of the kingdom present already among them.

Conclusion

Parables are especially well suited to teaching and proclaiming the Good News of the kingdom of God. Parables engage the listener with details from ordinary life experiences. They surprise the listener and stir the imagination with new possibilities. Parables, on the lips of Jesus, become an invitation to a new way of being in the world.

The Synoptic writers emphasize that, in Jesus, God's rule has come and changed everything. Jesus uses parables as he calls, leads, and forms his followers to become tools of transformation. Discovering parables and hearing them with our hearts, we are empowered, just as the earliest disciples were, to teach and act as Jesus did.

Mark tells us that Jesus' teaching ministry began and ended with parables. These visual images challenge his disciples to hear and to penetrate their meaning. Matthew and Luke likewise show that parables characterize Jesus' way of teaching his disciples. Parables are magnets that attract attention, interpretation, and action. Parables are irresistible; we are led to wonder about their meaning. We are moved to accept or reject them. Some do reject Jesus' teaching and its implications, and even this rejection is explained by the use of parables. But many accept the Gospel, and to them the parables offer hope, encouragement, and promise.

The parables are Jesus' chosen way to speak about and spread the kingdom of God already present among us. The kingdom is not a place nor merely a hope for a better future. The kingdom of God is relational, describing a reality begun among us in faith. We are led by the parables to see as God sees and judge as God does. The kingdom of God promises us a better, truer way of relating to God and to one another. The kingdom of God offers an alternative possibility of a new and just society.

We cling to the images Jesus has shared with us, like so many windows into his kingdom. The prodigal landowner, the woman making bread for her family or lighting lamps, the sowings that scatter the word far and wide, the diligent scribe pondering things old and new—all become a lens that adjusts our vision and enables us to finally catch a glimpse of the kingdom. Through parables we draw back the veil and we can begin to understand. The reliable steward and the prudent attendants become symbols of hope and fidelity for us as we seek to recreate our broken world in the image of one where God reigns. The parables stir in us the desire to accept and to participate wholeheartedly in the kingdom of God.

Parables in the Synoptic Tradition

	Mark	Matt	Luke
The Sowings	4:1-9	13:1-9	8:4-8
Explanation	4:10-25	13:10-23	8:9-18
Lamp	4:21	5:15	18:16
Seed Growing secretly	4:26-29		
Wheat and Weeds		13:24-30	
Explanation		13:36-43	
Mustard Seed	4:30-32	13:31-32	13:18-19
Woman and the Leaven		13:33	13:20-21
Hidden Treasure		13:44	
Pearl		13:45-46	
Net		13:47-50	
Treasures Old and New		13:51-52	
Two Debtors			7:41-43
Shepherd Seeking Lost Sheep		18:10-14	15:1-7
Unforgiving King and Servant		18:23-35	(17:3-4)
Good Samaritan			10:29-37

	Mark	Matt	Luke
Rich Fool			12:16-21
Barren Fig Tree	(11:12-14)	(21:18-19)	13:6-9
Wedding or Great Banquet		22:1-14	14:15-24
Salt	9:49-50	5:13	14:34-35
Woman Seeking Lost Coin			15:8-10
Prodigal Father			15:11-32
Master Who Praises Ingenuity			16:1-8a
The Rich Man and Lazarus			16:19-31
Persistent Widow			18:1-8
Pharisee and the Tax Collector			18:9-14
Prodigal Landowner	(10:31)	20:1-16 (19:30)	(13:30)
Two Sons		21:28-3	27:29-30
Wicked Tenants	12:1-12	21:33-46	20:9-19
Flood and watchfulness	(13:35)	24:37-44 24:17-18; 25:13	17:26-36 12:39-40
Faithful or wicked servant		24:45-51	12:42-46
Fig Tree	13:28-29	24:32-35	21:29-33
Doorkeeper	13:34-37		
Ten Attendants		25:1-13	
Wise and Foolish Use of Talents (Pounds)	(13:34)	25:14-30	19:11-27
Sheep and Goats	(8:38)	25:31-46 (16:27)	(9:26)

Notes

Chapter 1 (pp. 1–15)

1. C. H. Dodd, *The Parables of the Kingdom* (rev. ed. London: Collins, 1961), 16.

2. George Martin makes a good analogy in this regard: "Some parables are like diamonds, revealing many facets of meaning when examined from different angles." See George Martin, *The Gospel According to Mark* (Chicago: Loyola, 2005), 79.

3. The term "eschatological" or "eschatology" comes from the Greek word *eschaton*, meaning "last." It is an anglicized theological term coined in nineteenth-century biblical studies to refer to the overall view of the afterlife that can be gleaned from Jesus' or the early church's descriptions, such as we find in Matthew 24–25. The Jewish notion of the "return to the beginning" refers to a correspondence between creation and the final destination of humanity. We are becoming what we were meant to be. We ought to distinguish between "eschatology" and "apocalyptic." Much of the early church's reflection on life after death or eschatology is apocalyptic, that is, envisioning an end, usually catastrophic, of the present world and a new beginning described as a new heaven, a new age, a re-creation of the world that signifies the destruction of evil and affirmation of all that is good. In a sense, apocalyptic is a subdivision of eschatology, a certain view of eschatology.

4. Cf. Daniel J. Harrington, *The Gospel of Matthew*, Sacra Pagina 1 (Collegeville, MN: Liturgical Press, 1991), 194.

5. Nevertheless, it is important to note that, although the Johannine *paroimia* ("figures") are usually left off lists of parables, many are similar to Synoptic-style parables—such as the extended metaphor of the shepherd, the thief, and the doorkeeper (John 10:1-18), the saying about the grain of wheat (12:24), Jesus' identification of himself as the "Vine" and the disciples as "vine-branches" (15:1-6), and John the Baptist's comparison of himself to the "friend of the bridegroom" (3:29-30).

6. For more information, see Harold W. Attridge, "Gospel of Thomas," in *Harper's Dictionary of the Bible* (San Francisco: Harper & Row, 1985), 355–56.

173

7. For a good summary of these criteria, see Keith F. Nickle, *The Synoptic Gospels: An Introduction* (Atlanta: John Knox Press, 1980), 157–64.

8. The term means "coming" and referred in common usage to the arrival of the emperor or an imperial ambassador. The occasion was often marked by displays of patriotism such as parades with the citizenry lining the streets and paying respect and tribute to their rulers who were called "Lord" or "Savior." Christians took over this imagery and referred to Jesus' return or "second coming," pictured as accompanied by angels to judge the world. In this regard he was referred to as the Son of Man, an image derived from Daniel 7:9-13.

Chapter 2 (pp. 16–48)

1. For this and a list of distinctive characteristics of Mark's Gospel, see Mark Allan Powell, *Fortress Introduction to the Gospels* (Minneapolis: Fortress, 1998), 40–45.

2. Barbara E. Reid, *Parables for Preachers, Year B* (Collegeville, MN: Liturgical Press, 1999), 93.

3. John R. Donahue and Daniel J. Harrington, *The Gospel of Mark*, Sacra Pagina 2 (Collegeville, MN: Liturgical Press, 2002), 143.

4. Ibid., 144.

5. Madeline I. Boucher, *The Parables*, New Testament Messages 7 (Wilmington, DE: Michael Glazier, 1983), 86.

6. Elliott Maloney, *Jesus' Urgent Message for Today: The Kingdom of God in Mark's Gospel*. (New York: Continuum, 2004), 57.

7. Donahue and Harrington, *Mark*, 144.

8. Ibid., 139–40.

9. Many commentators suggest that this explanation for why Jesus spoke in parables came not from Jesus himself but from the early church, which had to account for why so many of Jesus' own people rejected him.

10. Note that "mysteries" (plural) appears in the parallel versions of Matthew (13:11) and Luke (8:10). The term "mystery" occurs more frequently in Paul (see, for example, Rom 11:25; 16:25; 1 Cor 2:1, 7; 4:1; 13:2; 14:2; 15:51).

11. But note that all three of the Synoptics have this explanation between the parable of the sower and its interpretation by Jesus. This unanimity suggests that it was Jesus himself (rather than an addition of the later tradition) who answered the disciples' query about the meaning of the parables and who distinguished those who accepted the explanation and those who did not. See David Wenham, *The Parables of Jesus* (Downers Grove, IL: InterVarsity Press, 1989), 242.

12. The fate of the seed will stand for response to the word. In 1 Corinthians 3:5-9, Paul uses sowing as a metaphor for preaching. Sowing also suggests moral activity, as in Hosea 10:12, which says, "Sow for yourselves righteousness; reap steadfast love." See Donahue and Harrington, *Mark*, 141.

13. Maloney, *Jesus' Urgent Message*, 58.

14. See also Donahue and Harrington, *Mark*, 142.

15. See Matt 5:15; 6:33; 7:2; 10:26; 25:29; Luke 6:38; 11:33; 12:2, 31; 19:26; Luke joins these sayings in 8:16-18; see also *GTh* nos. 5, 6, and 33.

16. Donahue and Harrington, *Mark*, 152.

17. Boucher, *Parables*, 155.

18. Josephus, *Life*, 45.235. See Eric M. Myers, "Galilee," in *Harper's Bible Dictionary*, Paul J. Achtemeier and others, eds. (San Francisco: Harper & Row, 1985), 329–30.

19. Cf. Wenham, *Parables of Jesus*, 72.

Chapter 3 (pp. 49–76)

1. See Matt 13:3, 10, 13, 18, 24, 31, 33, 34, 35, 36, 53; 15:15; 21:33, 45; 22:1.

2. See John R. Donahue, "The Parables of Jesus," *NJBC* 81 (83–85): 1368; also see John R. Donahue, *The Gospel in Parable: Metaphor, Narrative, and Theology in the Synoptic Gospels* (Philadelphia: Fortress Press, 1988), esp. 63–70.

3. The parable of the sowings could have circulated independently, without interpretation, as it appears in the *GTh 9*. Almost all scholars agree that the explanation of Matthew 13:18-23 was not part of Jesus' original parable. Only in this case in all three Synoptics and in the added example of the wheat and the weeds unique to Matthew do we find an explanation of the parable. These explanations are allegorical, that is, attributing symbolic meaning to various elements of the parable. A parable is by nature open-ended and this quality is one of the reasons it is an effective teaching device preferred by Jesus. These two "explanations" are likely representative of the meaning that early Christian communities put on the parable, rather than reflecting the very words of Jesus himself. See Barbara Reid, *Parables for Preachers Year A* (Collegeville, MN: Liturgical Press, 2001), 80.

4. Matthew's five discourses all end with the phrase, "After Jesus finished saying (these things)," or a slight variation as here: see 7:28; 11:1; 13:53; 19:1; 26:1.

5. Daniel J. Harrington, *The Gospel of Matthew*, Sacra Pagina 1 (Collegeville, MN: Liturgical Press, 1991), 194–95.

6. Matthew (and Luke) omit the last part of Mark 4:12 that says, "that they may not be converted and be forgiven."

7. Luke has a different context for this saying in Luke 10:23-24 where it is part of Jesus' response to his disciples when they return from a mission reporting to him all that they were able to do in his name.

8. A similar idea is found in Paul who urges the Philippians to remain faithful "that you may be blameless and innocent, children of God without blemish in the midst of a crooked and perverse generation, among whom you shine like lights in the world as you hold on to the word of life" (Phil 2:15-16).

9. It is possible that these parables were paired also in Q. But the fact that they are not paired by Mark (who does not include the parable of the woman and the leaven) or in the Gospel of Thomas suggests that they originally circulated independently. *GTh 20* says: "The disciples said to Jesus, 'Tell us what the Kingdom of Heaven is like.' He said to them, 'It is like a mustard seed, smaller than all seeds. But when it falls on plowed ground, it puts forth a large branch and becomes a shelter for the birds of heaven.'" *GTh 96* says: "The Kingdom of the Father is like a woman, she took a bit of leaven, she hid it in dough; she made big loaves. He who has ears let him hear." It is interesting that this version of the leaven parable in the Gospel of Thomas stresses the action of the woman; although less often, women as well as men are used as an image for God.

10. It is debatable whether these are actually "parables" or similitudes, i.e., images that illustrate some aspect of Jesus' teaching. The final image of the scribe of the kingdom is hardly a parable at all, but it does complete the symmetry Matthew favors and adds a distinctly Matthean touch to the conclusion of the day of parables.

11. Benedict Viviano, "Matthew," *NJBC* 42:93, 657.

12. Ibid. In Matthew 23:34a Jesus says, "Therefore, behold I send you prophets and wise men and scribes."

13. Similarly, in the parable of the Two Sons that immediately precedes this parable, the leaders answer correctly and implicitly judge themselves (see Matt 24:28-32). Many contemporary interpreters alert readers to dangers of supersessionism that implies that all the claims of Israel have been taken over by the church. For example, Harrington, *Matthew*, 304–5; Reid, *Parables Year A*, 175–76. Such replacement views not only stifle the efforts and progress of ecumenism, but lead to a dangerous arrogance, pride, and complacency.

14. Matthew uses the phrase "kingdom of God" only here and in 12:28; 21:31. The phrase "kingdom of heaven" occurs in Matthew 35 times, especially in the parables of chapters 13, 18, and 19.

15. With Matthew's addition of other parables to this one of the fig tree, there is more emphasis on the idea of judgment that the parousia of Jesus will bring; we will examine these additions and shift in emphasis in our next chapter on Matthew. See below, chapter 4.

16. For the term parousia in reference to the return of Jesus in glory, see Matt 24:3, 27, 37, 39; 1 Cor 15:23; 1 Thess 2:19; 3:13; 4:15; 5:23; 2 Thess 2:1, 8; Jas 5:7; 2 Pet 1:16; 3:4, 12; 1 John 2:28.

Chapter 4 (pp. 77–112)

1. Other examples of Peter's special role in Matthew include Peter's walking on water (Matt 14:28-33), Jesus' blessing on Peter and entrusting him with the "keys to the kingdom" (16:17-20), and Peter's finding the coin in a fish's mouth to pay the temple tax for himself and for Jesus (17:24-27).

2. Warren Carter notes that "ironically 10,000 talents was the amount that the Roman general Pompey levied when Rome took control of the newly subjugated Judea in the 60s B.C., according to Josephus (Josephus, *Antiquities*, 14.78)." Warren Carter, "Resisting and Imitating the Empire: Imperial Paradigms in Two Matthean Parables," *Interpretation* 56 (July 2002): 260–72, 266.

3. Carter, "Resisting and Imitating," 268.

4. This title is suggested by Daniel Harrington who notes that if Luke's parable can be called the "Prodigal Father," Matthew's might be called the "Prodigal Employer." Daniel J. Harrington, *The Gospel of Matthew*, Sacra Pagina 1 (Collegeville, MN: Liturgical Press, 1991), 284.

5. The NAB translation is given here. But in this case, a more literal translation of Matt 20:15b ("Or is your eye evil because I am good?") is preferable because it reflects Matthew's tendency to state a clear opposition between good and evil.

6. The day was divided into hours beginning with dawn, around 6:00 A.M. The Greek refers to the owner's going out to hire workers around the third, the sixth, the ninth, and the eleventh hour, or at 9:00, noon, 3:00, and 5:00 P.M.

7. The previous parable dealt with "talents," an exorbitant amount of money (see Matt 18:24). The "denarius" of this parable means a single daily wage, not necessarily one that was just or even adequate for a worker and his family. It is almost impossible to give a contemporary equivalent for these sums. But it is noteworthy that both parables are given in answer to Peter's questions, one about forgiveness and the other about rewards. When Jesus talks about forgiveness, he tells the story about settling accounts with extravagant amounts. When Peter asks about compensation for the sacrifices the disciples make, Jesus uses the smaller amount of a denarius. Jesus' answer rejects the *quid pro quo* standard and refocuses the disciples' attention to the gracious gifts given to those to whom the vineyard owner shows mercy.

8. The NAB translation of Matt 20:15 ("Are you envious because I am generous?") is inadequate and, in the words of Barbara Reid, "misses the mark." Barbara E. Reid, *Parables for Preachers, Year A* (Collegeville, MN: Liturgical Press, 2001), 148. Matthew makes this contrast between good and evil clear in several places: e.g., 5:45; 7:11, 17-18; 12:34-35; 22:10. This contrast is also evident in the parable of the Wise and Foolish Servant in 24:45-51.

9. This parable ought to be seen as part of Jesus' response to Peter's interjection in Matthew 19:27 (see Mark 10:28), after Jesus' encounter with the Rich Young Man. Peter asks Jesus, "We have given up everything and followed you. What will there be for us?" Only in Matthew does Jesus' reply begin with an allusion to the "new age" and a promise that when the "Son of Man is seated on his throne of glory," the disciples will sit on thrones "judging the twelve tribes of Israel" (19:28). The reward has the same upside-down character as the kingdom. It is not given to the powerful or rich, but to the last, who have left behind everything in order to follow Jesus.

10. A similar rhetorical device appears in the following parable when Jesus interjects the question, "What will the owner of the vineyard do?" (v. 40). Only Matthew has Jesus' opponents answer. Their response is again a self-incrimination.

11. See Luke 14:15-24 and also *GTh64*. Matthew and Luke have such different details in their telling of this parable that it remains uncertain whether they share a common source or received this parable independently. Common to both versions is the refusal of the invited guests to come, substitution of others for the original guests, and the missionary significance of the command to go out and bring in all who may be found to join in the banquet.

12. There are several factors that influence this identification (e.g., Jesus is in Jerusalem, the king has unlimited authority) that were not true of the parable of the unforgiving servant in Matthew 18:23-35 when we argued that the king did not represent God.

13. Matthew follows Mark closely in the first part (see Mark 13:1-37). The second part is drawn from Q and incorporates some material unique to Matthew.

14. The NAB phrase that the master "will punish him severely" is overly tame. The Greek means dismemberment, cutting to pieces.

15. *Phronimos* is found in Matt 7:24; 10:16; 24:45; 25:2, 4, 8, 9; Luke 12:42; 16:8; Rom 11:25; 12:16; 1 Cor 4:10; 10:15; 2 Cor 11:19; the adverbial form appears also in Luke 16:8. The cognate verb *phroneo* means "think, keep in mind, care for, be concerned about."

16. The Greek word, *sophia*, appears in Matt 11:19; 12:42; 13:54; Mark 6:2; Luke 2:40, 52; 7:35; 11:31, 49; 21:15. Also see Matthew 11:25-30: "I give praise to you, Father,

Lord of heaven and earth, for although you have hidden these things from the wise and the learned you have revealed them to the childlike. Yes, Father, such has been your gracious will. All things have been handed over to me by my Father. No one knows the Son except the Father, and no one knows the Father except the Son and anyone to whom the Son wishes to reveal him. Come to me all you who labor and are burdened, and I will give you rest. Take my yoke upon you and learn from me, for I am meek and humble of heart; and you will find rest for yourselves. For my yoke is easy and my burden light."

17. The word "hypocrisy" was originally a stage word referring to actors who played a role, wearing masks to cover their real identity. It came to mean a pretense or outward show, with the insinuation that this was different from what was real. The word "hypocrite" appears once in Mark (7:6) and three times in Luke (6:42; 12:56; 13:15).

18. Although Matthew uses the term "virgin" (*parthenos*) here, the same word applied to Jesus' mother in Matthew 1:23, the virginity of these servants is not relevant to this parable, except that virginity was an eschatological symbol adopted early as such in Christian thinking. The function of these servants as wedding attendants is to await the arrival of the groom. It is unusual for Matthew to make the protagonists of the parable female. This is yet another indication that this parable calls for an allegorical interpretation.

Chapter 5 (pp. 113–135)

1. In the course of this journey, Jesus shares meals with the powerful as well as the outcast. Likewise, as he makes his way to Jerusalem, Jesus eats with his disciples. The meals are teaching moments describing some of the most significant aspects of the kingdom of God. Meals in Luke take on the tone of a Hellenistic Symposium, that is, a sharing of ideas by means of which the participants of the meal express their solidarity and friendship with one another. See Eugene LaVerdiere, *Dining in the Kingdom of God: The Origins of the Eucharist According to Luke* (Chicago: Liturgy Training Publications, 1994), 16–21. Many of the parables unique to Luke are found in this journey section. These meals provide a special occasion for instruction, often in parable form.

2. John R. Donahue, "The Parables of Jesus," *NJBC*, 81 (86–87): 1368. See also John R. Donahue, *The Gospel in Parable: Metaphor, Narrative, and Theology in the Synoptic Gospels* (Philadelphia: Fortress, 1988), 126–28.

3. In Acts, Luke refers to the young community of disciples as the "Way": see Acts 9:2; 19:9, 23; 22:4, 14, 22; see also 9:17; 16:17; 18:25-26.

4. See Luke 4:23; 5:36; 6:39; 8:4, 9, 10, 11; 12:16, 41; 13:6; 14:7; 15:3; 18:1, 9; 19:11; 20:9, 19; 21:29.

5. Luke 5:36 reads: "And he also told them a parable, 'No one tears a piece from a new cloak to patch an old one. Otherwise he will tear the new and the piece from it will not match the old cloak.'"

6. I am indebted to Barbara Reid for many of the following insights on this parable. See Barbara E. Reid, *Parables for Preachers, Year C* (Collegeville, MN: Liturgical Press, 2000), 36–37.

7. This is a characteristic idea in Luke, usually suggesting negative scheming (e.g., the rich fool in 12:16-21, the authorities in 21:5 or the wicked tenants of 21:14). Without explicitly saying that Jesus can read people's thoughts as John observes (John 2:24-45; 6:64; 16:19), Luke has Jesus respond as if he is very aware of what Simon and others are thinking. Jesus tells the parable to challenge Simon to perceive things differently.

8. Although Luke tells us nothing about a previous encounter with Jesus that transformed her, the woman clearly must have encountered Jesus before and experienced forgiveness. She appears as someone who has been touched by mercy and healing. The hospitality she extends to Jesus identifies her as one who loves extravagantly. That is the lesson of the parable Simon is challenged to see.

9. Reid, *Parables for Preachers, Year C*, 93.

10. Luke had already alluded to Jesus' speaking in parables, for example, the story of the two debtors in the preceding chapter (7:41-43). So Luke does not emphasize the idea that the sowings parable is the beginning of a new way of teaching, as Mark and Matthew do. Compared to his source, Mark, Luke's version of the sowings parable discourse is abbreviated and not given the prominence that Mark assigns it. Luke omits the image of the measure (Mark 4:24-25) that Mark had paired with the lamp (4:21-23). Luke also omits the parable of the seed growing secretly (Mark 4:26-29) and postpones the image of the mustard seed to another time and place (Mark 4:30-32; see Luke 13:18-19). Luke probably also borrows the image of the fig tree from Mark, but Luke makes it into a parable and combines it with the image of the mustard seed in chapter 13; cf. also Mark's use of the fig tree as a "parable" or "lesson" in Mark 13:28-31. This last "parable" (see Luke 21:29-33) is hardly a parable at all, but is a lesson to be taken from the recurrence of the annual budding of the fig tree; this is a sign that summer is near. "In the same way," disciples will read the signs that the kingdom of God is near, Jesus says (21:31).

11. Here Luke is closer to Matthew 13:11 with emphasis on "secrets and knowledge" than Mark who uses the singular, "mystery." See Luke Timothy Johnson, *The Gospel of Luke*, Sacra Pagina 3 (Collegeville, MN: Liturgical Press, 1991), 132.

12. Johnson, *Luke*, 134.

13. Luke substitutes the Greek term, "the devil" for the Semitic term, "Satan" of Mark 4:15.

14. Johnson, *Luke*, 132.

15. The NAB title "parable of the lamp" is misleading (see title for Mark 4:21-25; Luke 8:16-18). Mark presents three proverbial sayings as a unit, but they were probably independent originally. They are scattered in Matthew (see Matt 10:26; 7:2; 25:29). Luke also has all three repeated in separate places (see Luke 12:2; 6:38; 19:26). But Luke follows Mark here in placing all three sayings with the parable of the sowings and presenting them as part of Jesus' explanation for why he speaks in parables.

16. But see Luke 6:38 that says: "Give and gifts will be given to you; a good measure, packed together, shaken down, and overflowing, will be poured into your lap. For the measure with which you measure will in return be measured out to you."

17. The barren fig tree told as a parable, is unique to Luke. The image of the mustard seed is used in parable form by Mark (4:30-32). Mark does not join to the parable of

the mustard seed the image of the leaven as Luke and Matthew do (Mark 4:30-32). Matthew's wording (Matt 13:31-33), except for the introductory formulas, is almost identical to Luke's. The Gospel of Thomas also has both images, but they appear separately. *GTh20* says: "The disciples said to Jesus, 'Tell us what the kingdom of heaven is like.' He said to them: 'It is like a grain of mustard seed, smaller than all seeds. But when it falls on the earth which has been cultivated, it puts forth a great branch and becomes shelter for the birds of heaven.'" *GTh 96* says: "The Kingdom of the Father is like a woman; she took a bit of leaven, hid it in dough, (and) made it into big loaves. Whoever has ears take heed."

18. Since it is an important link between the parable of the fig tree and those of the mustard seed and the leaven or yeast, the story of the cure of the crippled woman is cited here. Luke tells us:

> [11]And a woman was there who for eighteen years had been crippled by a spirit; she was bent over, completely incapable of standing erect. [12]When Jesus saw her, he called to her and said, "Woman, you are set free of your infirmity." [13]He laid hands on her, and she at once stood up straight and glorified God. [14]But the leader of the synagogue, indignant that Jesus had cured on the Sabbath, said to the crowd in reply, "There are six days when work should be done. Come on those days to be cured, not on the Sabbath day."

19. The Gospel of Thomas 65 has the following: "A good man had a vineyard. He gave it to tenants that they might cultivate it and he might receive its fruit from them. He sent his servant so that the tenants might give him the fruit of the vineyard. They seized his servant and beat him; a little more and they would have killed him. The servant came and told it to his master. His master said, 'Perhaps he did not know them.' He sent another servant; and the tenants beat him as well. Then the owner sent his son. He said, 'Perhaps they will respect my son.' Since those tenants knew that he was the heir of the vineyard, they seized him and killed him. He who has ears, let him hear."

20. See the note on Psalm 118:22 in the NAB. The next verse goes on to attribute the selection to God: "By the Lord has this been done; it is wonderful in our eyes" (Ps 118:23). This verse appears in Mark 12:11. Although it is omitted by Luke, the idea that God's plan and actions are quite different from human projections is not. Indeed, the notion that God has a plan for universal salvation is central to Luke's vision.

21. See, for example, the use of the term in Matthew 13:41: "The Son of Man will send his angels and they will collect out of his kingdom all who cause others to sin and all evildoers."

Chapter 6 (pp. 136–170)

1. John notes in telling the episode of Jesus' encounter with the Samaritan woman, "Jews use nothing in common with Samaritans" (John 4:9). Jews and Samaritans had different legal traditions regarding the cleanliness of vessels and, in general, they avoided contact with one another (4:7-10). The negative attitude of the Jews toward the Samaritans is reflected in Jesus' statement in Matthew 10:5 that links Samaritans with Gentiles in contrast to "the house of Israel." A similar idea is expressed in John 8:48 where the adversaries of Jesus refer to him contemptuously as "a Samaritan"—

and demon-possessed as well. The itinerary of Jesus in Mark 10:1 (followed by Matthew 19:1), is altered somewhat by Luke. Mark and Matthew seem to reflect the Jewish practice of avoiding Samaria in pilgrimages to Jerusalem. Luke, who has the most references to Samaritans of the gospels, paints them in a relatively positive light; he and John picture Jesus and his disciples as passing through the heart of Samaritan country (Luke 9:51-56; John 4:4).

2. Samaria appears in Luke 17:11; John 4:4, 5, 7, 9; Acts 1:8; 8:1, 5, 9, 14; 9:31; 15:3. Samaritan appears in Matt 10:5; Luke 9:52; 10:33; 17:16; John 4:9 (2x), 39, 40; 8:48; Acts 8:25.

3. Luke had described two other meals in the course of Jesus' journey to Jerusalem, one in the home of Martha in 10:38-42, and a second in the home of a Pharisee in 11:37-54.

4. Only Luke contains this episode based on the wisdom saying of 14:11; but the saying itself, which has a parallel in Matthew 23:12, most probably came from Q. It is also found in Luke 18:14.

5. See Denis McBride, *The Parables of Jesus* (Liguori, MO: Liguori/Triumph, 1999), 123.

6. Ibid., 126.

7. Joseph Fitzmyer indicates that neither "publican" nor "tax collector" is an accurate translation of the Greek term which technically designates "toll collectors" i.e., those engaged in the collection of indirect taxes such as tolls, tariffs, imposts, and customs. Joseph. A. Fitzmyer, *The Gospel According to Luke* (AB28; Garden City, NY: Doubleday, 1981), 469–70. Although, the designation "toll collectors" is preferable, the more usual translation "tax collectors," found in the NAB, will be followed here. The combination "tax collectors and sinners" occurs in Mark 2:15-16; Matt 9:10, 11; 11:19; Luke 5:30; 7:34; 15:1 and implicitly also 19:7 referring to the tax collector Zacchaeus, who is also called a sinner. See McBride, *Parables*, 123–24; John R. Donahue, "Tax Collectors and Sinners," CBQ 33 (1971), 39–63; "Tax collector" in *Anchor Bible Dictionary*, vol. 6, 337–38. See Madeleine I. Boucher, *The Parables*, New Testament Message 7 (Wilmington, DE: Michael Glazier, 1983), 100–01.

8. Luke 3:12-13 says: "Even tax collectors came to be baptized and they said to him, 'Teacher, what should we do?' He answered them, 'Stop collecting more than what is prescribed.'"

9. Joachim Jeremias, *The Parables of Jesus*, 2nd rev. ed. (Upper Saddle River, NJ: Prentice-Hall, 1954), 132.

10. The fact that the parable of the shepherd is also found in Matthew tells us that Luke obtained this story from Q. Matthew 18:12-14 says: "[12]What is you opinion? If a man has a hundred sheep and one of them goes astray, will he not leave the ninety-nine in the hills and go in search of the stray? [13]And if he finds it, amen, I say to you, he rejoices more over it than over the ninety-nine that did not stray. [14]In just the same way, it is not the will of your heavenly Father that one of these little ones be lost." The *GTh 107* has: "Jesus said, 'The kingdom is like a shepherd who has a hundred sheep. One of them, which was the largest, went astray. He left the ninety-nine behind and looked for the one until he found it. Having tired himself out, he said to the sheep, 'I care for you more than the ninety-nine.'" Note that in Thomas, the sheep

that went astray is the "largest," which supplies a motivation for the search. And in Thomas, the shepherd addresses the sheep.

11. Fitzmyer notes that under Nero the drachma was replaced by the denarius, which had about the same worth. A denarius was about 1/100 of a pound (see Luke 19:11-27) and only 1/6000 of a talent (a term only used by Matthew, see 18:24; 25:14-30). Joseph A. Fitzmyer, *The Gospel According to Luke* (AB28A; Garden City, NY: Doubleday, 1985), 1081.

12. Luke uses a Greek term (*splangnizomai*) that means "moved with pity." It is used of Jesus in the story of the raising of the son of the widow of Nain (7:13) and of the Good Samaritan in 10:33. Luke conveys the idea that the restoration of the son was the result primarily of the father's compassion.

13. This accusation may imply a reproach for those who accuse Jesus of also consorting with the same type of people; see Luke 15:1-2; 7:34, 39.

14. The NAB and the Lectionary attach verses 8b-13 to this parable as if the sayings there represent Jesus' own allegorical application of this parable. But, as Joseph Fitzmyer points out, the puzzling aspects of this parable are only compounded by considering the sayings that follow it part of the parable proper. Fitzmyer, *Luke*, 1095. The sayings between the two parables of chapter 16 (the parable of the steward and the parable of the rich man and Lazarus), both of which deal with the proper attitude toward material possessions, were probably originally separate sayings that Luke simply inserts here as teachings on discipleship.

15. One of the debated issues is whether *kyrios* in verse 8a refers to the master of the parable or to Jesus, who is pictured as the speaker in verse 8b, comparing the dishonest servant with the "children of light." It is actually the master and his praise that provides the focus of this parable rather than the servant for whom the parable is often inaccurately named.

16. The color purple appears only two times in the New Testament, here and in reference to Lydia's business dealings in Acts 16:14. As a "dealer in purple," Lydia was a woman of means who invited Paul and his companions to stay with her in Philippi, a house church that would become especially strong and dear to Paul (see Acts 16:11-15, 40; Philippians). Once again Luke refers to food and, incidentally, the significance of hospitality (or lack thereof). Luke here uses a term also found in 12:19 of the rich fool and in 15:23, 29, 32 of the celebrations of the prodigal father and his sons. The extravagance of this man is expressed in that this is a daily occurrence.

17. This assertion suggests that the early Christian community held that the Old Testament was guidance for a good life and that belief in Jesus was in continuity with the teachings of the Law and the prophets.

Glossary of Basic Terms for Study of the Parables

Allegory refers to a developed metaphor or series of metaphors in which several details are symbolic, often with a hidden or mysterious meaning. Sometimes Jesus' parables are given allegorical meanings by the evangelists; for example, the parable of the sowings is interpreted allegorically so that the reception of the seed or word is represented by different types of "soil."

Apocalyptic and **apocalypticism** are terms used to describe a type of literature popular between 200 B.C. and A.D. 300. Based on the Greek word *apokalypsis*, or revelation, apocalyptic imagery originated in times of great suffering as an attempt to comfort the faithful. It prophesized God's ultimate victory over evil, especially reward for the just and punishment of those who oppress them. Apocalyptic literature uses symbolic language to interpret past and present events in the light of God's ultimate and imminent revelation in power.

Eschaton and **eschatological** are terms derived from the Greek word (*eschaton*) meaning "last." The term eschatological was coined in Germany in the nineteenth century and redefined in the twentieth century to describe those aspects of biblical and related writings that refer to such realities as afterlife, salvation, the ultimate victory of God over evil, and the individual and universal "judgment" of humankind.

The Gospel of Thomas is a nonbiblical collection of 114 sayings attributed to Jesus, originally in Greek and probably from the second century. Lacking a narrative setting, these sayings can only loosely be called a "gospel." A Coptic version of this collection was discovered in 1945 as part of the Nag Hammadi Library. The Gospel of Thomas contains variants of more than a dozen parables found in the Synoptic Gospels, making it valuable for studying the evolution of such sayings, sources, and traditions.

Quelle (or Q), named for the German word meaning "source," refers to a hypothetical group of sayings used by both Matthew and Luke, but unknown to Mark.

Synoptics (or **Synoptic Gospels**) include the Gospels of Matthew, Mark, and Luke. All three show some interdependence or share a similar (*syn*) view (*optic*).

Testimonia or **"Testimony Books"** are collections of references or passages from the Old Testament that might have been used by the early Christians, especially in discussions with Jews. These passages explain problematic elements of faith such as why the Messiah suffered, or why so many Jews were rejecting the Gospel whereas many Gentiles accepted it.

Two-Source Hypothesis helps to explain the common features found in the Synoptic Gospels. Most scholars believe that Mark was the first gospel to be written and that Matthew and Luke had access to and used Mark, along with the sayings source known as "Q," in the composition of their gospels.

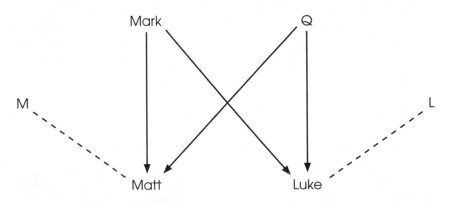

This graphic depicts the proposed relationship between the Synoptic Gospels, indicating that Matthew and Luke both used Mark and Q, although Matthew did not have access to Luke and vice versa. Some scholars suggest an additional independent source for Matthew and for Luke (known as "M" and "L" respectively).

A Three-Stage Gospel Transmission was described by the Pontifical Biblical Commission in 1964 and reiterated as part of formal church teaching by Vatican II. The general description of such stages was also approved by the World Council of Churches as an appropriate way of understanding the prehistory of the written gospels.

> Stage One: *Jesus and His Disciples* (early 30s): oral preaching and tradition passed on from the first generation of Jesus' followers.

> Stage Two: *The Disciples and the Early Christian Communities* (ca. 34–65): the preaching of the early disciples to the early communities of believers.

> Stage Three: *The Early Christian Communities and the Evangelists* (60s to 90s): based on the oral accounts of eyewitnesses, writers gathered traditions about Jesus and his preaching and passed them on to their communities. The evangelists each demonstrate their particular concerns, interests and circumstances in the unique features of their respective gospels.

Septuagint (LXX) refers to an early third-century B.C. Greek translation of Scripture (that later became the Old Testament) and was widely circulated in the Greek-speaking world. The text became a vehicle for the spread of the Gospel throughout the Gentile world and was generally used by New Testament authors to support, explain, and defend the Christian message. The name Septuagint (from the Latin for "70") reflects a popular Jewish legend about the composition of the Greek translation by seventy elders.

Abbreviations

AB	Anchor Bible
CBQ	*Catholic Biblical Quarterly*
CBQMS	CBQ Monograph Series
Int	*Interpretation*
LXX	Septuagint (Greek Translation of the Hebrew Old Testament)
NAB	*New American Bible*
NCBC	*New Collegeville Biblical Commentary*
NJBC	*New Jerome Biblical Commentary*
NTM	New Testament Message
SacPag	Sacra Pagina

Bibliography

Achtemeier, Paul J., and others, eds. *Harper's Bible Dictionary*. San Francisco: Harper & Row, 1985.

Attridge, Harold W. "Gospel of Thomas." In Paul J. Achtemeier, and others, eds. *Harper's Bible Dictionary*. San Francisco: Harper & Row, 1985, 355–56.

Beavis, Mary Ann, ed. *The Lost Coin. Parables of Women, Work and Wisdom*. London/New York: Sheffield Academic Press, 2002.

Boucher, Madeleine I. *The Mysterious Parable. A Literary Study*. CBQMS 6. Washington, DC: CBQ, 1977.

———. *The Parables*. NTM 7. Wilmington, DE: Michael Glazier, Inc., 1983.

Brown, Raymond E. *An Introduction to the New Testament*. New York/London: Doubleday, 1997.

Brown, Raymond E., Joseph A. Fitzmyer, and Roland E. Murphy, eds. *The New Jerome Biblical Commentary*. Englewood Cliffs, NJ: Prentice Hall, 1990.

Buttrick, David. *Speaking Parables*. Louisville, KY: Westminster John Knox, 2000.

Carter, Warren. "Resisting and Imitating the Empire: Imperial Paradigms in Two Matthean Parables." *Int* 56 (2002) 260–72.

Davies, Stevan L. *The Gospel of Thomas and Christian Wisdom*. New York: The Seabury Press, 1983.

Dodd, C. H. *The Parables of the Kingdom*. Rev. ed. London: Collins, 1961.

Donahue, John R. *The Gospel in Parable: Metaphor, Narrative and Theology in the Synoptic Gospels*. Philadelphia: Fortress Press, 1988.

———. "Jesus as the Parable of God in the Gospel of Mark." *Int* 32 (1978) 369–86.

————. "Tax Collectors and Sinners. An Attempt at Identification." *CBQ* 33 (1971) 39–61.

————. "The Parables of Jesus." In Raymond E. Brown and others, eds., *NJBC*. Englewood Cliffs, NJ: Prentice Hall, 1990, 81 (57–88): 1364–69.

Donahue, John R., and Daniel J. Harrington. *The Gospel of Mark*. SacPag 2. Collegeville, MN: Liturgical Press, 2002.

Ellis, Peter F. *Matthew: His Mind and His Message*. Collegeville, MN: Liturgical Press, 1974.

Fitzmyer, Joseph A. *The Gospel According to Luke I–IX*. Anchor Bible 28. New York/London: Doubleday, 1981.

————. *The Gospel According to Luke X–XXIV*. Anchor Bible 28A. New York/London: Doubleday, 1985.

Gowler, David B. *What Are They Saying About the Parables?* New York/Mahwah: Paulist, 2000.

Hare, Douglas R. A. *Matthew*. Louisville, KY: John Knox Press, 1993.

Harrington, Daniel J. *The Gospel of Matthew*. SacPag 1. Collegeville, MN: Liturgical Press, 1991.

Harrington, Wilfrid. *The Prodigal Father. Approaching the God of Love*. Wilmington, DE: Michael Glazier, 1982.

Hedrick, Charles W. *Many Things in Parables. Jesus and His Modern Critics*. Louisville, KY: Westminster John Knox Press, 2004.

Jeremias, Joachim. *The Parables of Jesus*. Rev. ed. Upper Saddle River, NJ: Prentice-Hall, 1954.

Johnson, Luke Timothy. *The Gospel of Luke*. SacPag 3. Collegeville, MN: Liturgical Press, 1991.

Lambrecht, Jan. *Once More Astonished. The Parables of Jesus*. New York: Crossroad, 1981.

LaVerdiere, Eugene. *Dining in the Kingdom of God. The Origins of the Eucharist According to Luke*. Chicago: Liturgy Training Publications, 1994.

Maloney, Elliott C. *Jesus' Urgent Message for Today. The Kingdom of God in Mark's Gospel*. New York: Continuum, 2004.

Martin, George. *The Gospel According to Mark*. Chicago: Loyola Press, 2005.

McBride, Denis. *The Parables of Jesus*. Liguori, MO: Liguori/Triumph, 1999.

Meier, John P. *Matthew*. NTM 3. Wilmington, DE: Michael Glazier, 1980.

Meyers, Eric M. "Galilee." In Paul J. Achtemeier, and others, eds. *Harper's Bible Dictionary*. San Francisco: Harper & Row, 1985, 329–30.

———. "Josephus." In Paul J. Achtemeier, and others, eds. *Harper's Bible Dictionary*. San Francisco: Harper & Row, 1985, 508.

Nickle, Keith F. *The Synoptic Gospels. An Introduction*. Atlanta, GA: John Knox Press, 1980.

Patella, Michael. *The Gospel According to Luke*. NCBC. Collegeville, MN: Liturgical Press, 2005.

Perkins, Pheme. *Hearing the Parables of Jesus*. New York/Ramsey: Paulist Press, 1981.

Powell, Mark Allan. *Fortress Introduction to the Gospels*. Minneapolis: Fortress Press, 1998.

Reid, Barbara E. *Parables for Preachers Year A*. Collegeville, MN: Liturgical Press, 2001.

———. *Parables for Preachers Year B*. Collegeville, MN: Liturgical Press, 1999.

———. *Parables for Preachers Year C*. Collegeville, MN: Liturgical Press, 2000.

———. *The Gospel According to Matthew*. NCBC. Collegeville, MN: Liturgical Press, 2005.

Scott, Bernard Brandon. *Hear Then the Parable. A Commentary on the Parables of Jesus*. Minneapolis: Fortress Press, 1989.

Viviano, Benedict. "The Gospel According to Matthew. " In Raymond E. Brown, and others, eds. *NJBC*. Englewood Cliffs, NJ: Prentice Hall, 1990, 42:630–74.

Wenham, David. *The Parables of Jesus*. Downers Grove, IL: InterVarsity Press, 1989.

Witherup, Ronald D. *Matthew*. New York: New City Press, 2000.

———. *The Bible Companion. A Handbook for Beginners*. New York: Crossroad, 1998.

Young, Brad H. *The Parables. Jewish Tradition and Christian Interpretation*. Peabody, MA: Hendrickson, 1998.